CAPTAINS OF INDUSTRY BUILDERS OF WEALTH

MIGUEL ANGEL FALLA
The Cuban Sugar Industry

Editor Oscar A. Echevarría

La versión en castellano comienza
después de la página 118

New House Publishers Inc.

CAPTAINS OF INDUSTRY
BUILDERS OF WEALTH

MIGUEL ANGEL FALLA
The Cuban Sugar Industry

Editor Oscar A. Echevarría
Prologue Carlos Alberto Montaner

New House Publisher Inc.

CAPTAINS OF INDUSTRY, BUILDERS OF WEALTH

First Published by New House Publishers Inc., 2002

For information, address New House Publishers Inc.
1901 Pennsylvania Ave. NW, Suite 407 Washington D.C. 20006,
newhouse@echevarria.us

SECOND EDITION
Printed in the United States by
Eagle Lithographers, Inc. 2727 N.W. 17th Ave.
Miami, Florida 33142

Cover and Layout Design: Luis García Fresquet
Translations: Monique Fernandez and Ileana Fuentes
English Editing: Lara J. Evans
Statistics and Charts: Santiago Moralejo del Arco

Library of Congress Cataloging-in-Publication Data (in progress)

Echevarría, Oscar A.

Captains of Industry, Builders of Wealth. Miguel Angel Falla. The Cuban Sugar Industry / Oscar A. Echevarría.-I[st] ed. p. cm.
Includes Index
ISBN 0-9725547-0-X
1. Cuba - Sugar Industry. 2. Cuba - Economy 3. Cuba - History
4. Biography

Index

To the builders of Cuba's wealth, with gratitude and admiration

To those that must rebuild Cuba, with encouragement and hope.

Inaugural Notes

As Publishers, we believe it is in the interest of all our readers to know the why and how this Series came into being. We hope these notes will also entice some of those readers to become co-publishers on subsequent books which cover their areas of interest. Ours intends to be an inclusive effort, open to all those who want to preserve Cuba's Economic and Entrepreneurial Heritage.

Why this Series

There are a plethora of books on Cuba's architecture, depicting residences that were once magnificent. These books preserve an image, albeit limited and in some ways distorted, of what the vibrant and splendid city of Havana was and could be. Besides the documentary evidence offered by the publications put out by such publishers, the United Nations has helped to preserve some of Havana's architectural Heritage. Similarly, the many travel guides on Cuba recently published, reflect a greater awareness of the Island, but as they are written on the basis of Government information, their historical references utterly distort the past.

By contrast, the genre about Cuba's outstanding socio-economic position in 1959 has been relegated to learned articles of limited distribution. To compensate for this lack of information on Cuba's Economic past, we cannot expect UNESCO to sponsor an effort, nor will Castro allow it, to preserve the innovative Cuban business DNA. Such imprints have taken the Cuban exile community to commanding positions in the United States business world and elsewhere. This state of affairs represents a dangerous vacuum, and threatens to wipe out our invaluable economic heritage.

Captains of Industry - Builders of Wealth, launched with this book, intends to avoid having the builders of Cuba's economy and their accomplishments relegated to an oblivion by Castro's mismanagement and propaganda in rewriting history. The profiles of those **innovators, entrepreneurs and managers** who took Cuba to its commanding positions by 1959, offer the human side of the Cuban businessmen of their times. Describing, as background to the characters, their corresponding economic sectors, will provide evidence of Cuba's economic success before all vestiges of Cuba's place in the world economy in 1959 disappear.

When Castro's reign of inefficiency, terror and hate is finally over, Cuba will be rebuilt. To facilitate the reconstruction of Cuba it will be invaluable to have the original blue prints, to expedite the process and help improve on the past, as is true with rebuilding any system or installation. For any such reconstruction, access to the original builder is the optimal situation, as he can forewarn against mistaken paths that appeared attractive but led to faults later on.

Unfortunately, most of those pioneering builders are gone and so are their evidence and records, except for their descendents' recollections. Only the memories of their ancestor's genius, toils, mistakes, perseverance, and triumphs, are left as a link to our economic past. Making such information available to the younger generation, that will eventually rebuild Cuba, is the best contribution that our generation can give to the entrepreneurs in waiting. This series is an insurance policy to preserve such Heritage.

How the Series was born

To validate; if my perception of the need was a valid and worthwhile effort, I sought the opinion of some friends. In the first round I talked to Panchito Blanco, Amadeo López Castro, Guillermo Fernández, Amada López Cantera, Silvia Odio, Carlos Quijano and his wife Maritza Solís, and Mariano Echevarría, all descendents of pioneering figures in various economic sectors. Encouraged by their favorable response, I turned to Carlos Alberto Montaner, champion of Cuba's cause, prolific author and experienced publisher.

Carlos Alberto responded with enthusiasm, proposing many candidates, selected not based on their wealth but on specific achievements, as our goal is not to create "Una Guía Social de Empresarios", or wealthy people, but to focus on those that excelled in their respective fields, regardless of their monetary achievements. He rejected my "on the cheap" business model, which relied on graduate students of journalism and economics. Instead he proposed a centralized approach, relying on professional historians and biographers. He then called Ena Curnow.

The next day Carlos Alberto described to Ena our vision to the last level of detail. The first book was to be ready within a year. Ena reacted with joy but also with concern about funding books of limited market, with great confidence he said, "Oscar will take care of the money".

Scrambling to devise an Investment Memorandum I saw the need for a prototype to show "the Names", borrowing a very appropriate denomination from The Lloyds of London, the famous London insurance market. So, I requested a sample chapter of some 30 pages. Ena suggested a woman, and asked if we agreed. As Montaner, so well versed in Cuba's History, remained silent, I, recalled, Elena's references to her aunt Isabel Falla Bonet de Suero, and suggested her. How a Chapter on Isabel Falla Bonet turned into a book on her cousin Miguel Angel Falla Alvarez we will leave for the book's Introduction.

What will be the format of the Series?

Carlos Alberto proposed that the size should be important but not a "coffee table book", 8.5" by 11". He will write the Prologue for each book. They will have 10 to 12 Chapters, one per subject, written by a professional historian or biographer, on the basis of testimonials, documents and interviews. Economists, not necessarily of Cuban origin, will write an overview of the Industry where the individuals covered toiled and triumphed.

We recognized that the market for these books is by nature limited, so we have considered a way to both finance the publication and assure sufficient distribution to the general public. We intend to make the series an economic proposition, not a sophisticated "Vanity Press" venture. As Publishers, we will adhere to the truth about the individuals to be covered and the Cuban economy. We believe the truth is powerful and will command the respect of the Academic World and the Media. But, we intend to make the reading attractive so as to obtain one important collateral benefit, or Externality as we economist will say. What is that benefit?

Despite the success of the Cuban business community in the United States and elsewhere, many well meant Americans and Europeans, have formed a distorted and derogatory opinion of Cuba circa 1959. The series will be in English, the *lingua franca* of business so that it will be accessible to a wider audience.

This first book departs from the prototype just described, as it has a chapter of "Memories of Miguel Angel Falla". It is fortunate, however that the Series is inaugurated with a key management figure in the Sugar Industry. Let me explain. First, Sugar production and exports had been the flagship of the Cuban economy for over a century. Second, the fact that Miguel Angel was a manager serves to stress that **this series is not about wealth ownership, but wealth creation**, done through innovation, entrepreneurship and management, all factors that contribute to economic and social development. Finally, being "The Cuban Atlantic Sugar", the World's largest sugar producer, when Miguel Angel took over its Presidency, gives us an outstanding perspective on the relationship of a Cuban Executive with a powerful American company and family, the Loeb's, dispelling Castro's utterly distorted description of Cuban - American relations prior to 1959.

So, with this book the Captains of Industry series is launched, before time takes its toll on everyone's memories. We hope that many of the heirs of similar figures will accompany Carlos Alberto and I in documenting, with a human twist, Cuba's economic structure prior to 1959 and, most importantly, the lessons that the Builders of Wealth can give to future generations. And now lets turn to the book

Oscar A. Echevarría
Washington D. C, September 18, 2002

Prologue

Shortly before writing these lines I put the finishing touches on a book entitled, *Cuba: a century of painful learning.* The book is an overview of the mistakes and attitudes, which led to the Island's situation. Naturally, the sad recount left an uncomfortable question unanswered: Isn't the negative view of our political mistakes unfair? Wasn't there anything exemplary and salvageable in the history of the country?

Of course there was. It is sufficient to look at Havana, once a beautiful city, today in ruins irresponsibly vandalized by Castroism. This fact proves that once upon a time in Cuba there was a notable group of builders of wealth. Without a doubt, one of the areas where excellence arose in the thrust of civil society could be seen in the drive and modernness of the business class. That is why it seemed so appropriate to me when Oscar A. Echevarría – an economist and businessman himself-proposed we edit a series of monographs dedicated to various personalities that helped to make it possible, by 1959, for Cuba to be in the most advanced group in Latin America and among the top 25 in the world (according to the Economic Atlas published in those years by Ginsberg).

It was also logical to begin with Miguel Angel Falla, a manager of several different sugar mills and, eventually, of the largest sugar production company in the World. He was also a member of the Falla Gutiérrez family, one of the most prominent families in the country's economy. While Miguel Angel was Elena's father and she is Oscar's wife, he is here due to his human quality and managerial achievements, as witnessed in the Remembrances found in Chapter II, in a complex agro industry that made up the spinal cord of the Cuban economy.

“Without sugar – said a pre-revolutionary slogan – there is no country.” “Sin azúcar – decía un lema prerrevolucionario – no hay país”. A very exaggerated statement that could be combined with another more truthful assertion: "without sugar Cuba would have been completely different". One of the differences would have been the type of business class that would have developed on the Island.

The production of Cuban sugar – well described by Echevarría in this book – timidly began around the XVI century and flourished around the end of the XVIII century. It constituted a complex industrial, technological and labor intensive an economic process that required the highest level of administrative management. It was not simply planting and harvesting. The sugar industry relied on 60,000 “colonos” (independent cane growers) for planting and cultivating the sugar cane. In turn, each mill, especially the large ones, built "bateyes" which were in reality, small communities with a certain sense of urbanism where one could obtain a higher quality of life than in the rural hamlets not associated with reputable sugar mills. In general, the “bateyes” were fairly clean, peaceful and organized.

The mills required large industrial equipment, technical know how, responsible record keeping and strong logistical and negotiation skills in order to participate in an economic based activity, predominantly for exportation. Exportation dictated another fundamental element: the stock market. Simply put, the Cubans interested in sugar could not ignore fluctuations of the market from London to New York. Before anyone spoke of “globalization” the Cuban business class, due to its sugar production, was completely “globalized”. It had trading houses such as, Julio Lobo and Czarnikow – Rionda, with seats on the New York and London Sugar and Coffee Exchange, that ruled the market.

The production and commercialization of sugar, in which hundreds of thousands of people participated, gave Cuba a world profile in terms of economic transactions and raised the general technical level and quality of management. This included areas of the economy that seemed to have no connection with the sugar industry.

When Cubans, with good reason, boast that they had the first train ever to run in the Hispanic world, they usually don’t realize that this advancement was made possible only to serve “her majesty”, the sugar. The same can be said about the administration of the ports and the early development of the first telegraph and, later, telephone.

What I am trying to say is the level of development or underdevelopment of a society is dictated by the complexity of its principle production factors. When the sugar press or "cachimbo" – two rocks which grind sugar cane – prevalent in the Middle Ages, gave way, slowly but surely, to actual mills, the century long path dragged all of society in the direction of modernization. What does that mean? It is not a coincidence that during the XXth century, businessmen such as, Goar Mestre – actually all three brothers – arose, capable of running television stations before anyone else in Latin America. It was a consequence of a level of excellency previously established by the sugar industry. It was also not a coincidence that cheap, fast food chains started in Cuba by Domingo Moreira (Pollos el Caporal) appeared in Cuba at the same time as they did in the United States. Other examples are abundant, such as Mariano Guastela in advertising, Crusellas y Cubas who succeeded in competing with Procter y Colgate, Solís, whose associates, after separating from El Encanto, started Department stores in Spain. The history of these and other pioneers and businesses that were created and developed, will be covered in subsequent editions.

Sugar set the bar very high and created a business class, surely without even noticing, simply responding to a standard, as if it were a secret tradition. And without a doubt, one of the best examples of this important socioeconomic phenomenon is, Miguel Angel Falla. Let's take an up close look at him.

Carlos Alberto Montaner

Introduction

In its original conception this was to be an unedited collection of memories of Miguel Angel Falla, a tribute to him and a birthday present to my wife, Elena, available only to his extended family. This would have really been an easy endeavor had it been done immediately upon his death on February 8th, 1973, but it wasn't. Thirty years later, time has thinned the ranks of first hand witnesses and Diaspora has made it more difficult to reach those that remain. In June I asked our friend Rita Moreno de Blain, unbeknownst to Elena, for help and, after her best efforts, we had received only five testimonials to print. Needless to say, neither those who wrote the notes, nor I, claim to have the sole source of memories of Miguel Angel, and certainly we all welcome contributions for a third edition.

Printing those five testimonials would have resulted in a book, modest in size, but important in content thanks to the quality of the remembrances and the subject they cover. However, those heartfelt testimonials shed new light on the outstanding managerial and human stature of Miguel Angel Falla, whom I remember simply as a neighbor and, at that time, the father of my girlfriend. His is a story worth telling.

To understand how a private printing of Memories turned into a book available to the public at large, I would like to take the reader to where I left him during my last meeting with Carlos Alberto and Ena, about the series of books we are working on. I had requested a sample Chapter and Ena suggested a possible woman to profile and asked for names of candidates. Montaner, so well versed in Cuban History, remained silent, while I, recalled Elena's references to Isabel Falla

Bonet de Suero, and suggested her. The following day, when Ena asked me for material on Isabelita Suero, I remembered the difficulties just encountered in the case of Miguel Angel and decided to change the person to be profiled, recruiting Ena to work on my project.

Chapter I, written by Ena, in her poetic prose, can be considered a foreshadowing of the amenable short biographies that will provide 10 to 12 Chapters, on as many subjects, in each book in the Series. I believe Ena has done a wonderful job of lacing together great material. Ena's prose, at times funny and at times melodramatic, converts a dry chronology into an entertaining storytelling, and that is the art of a biographer.

Chapter II, entitled, Remembrances, is unique to this book. It is here that I keep the implicit promise I made in requesting such testimonials. While each of them contributed their material with graceful notes authorizing me to select what I needed, their quality persuaded me to keep them intact and the reader will appreciate that. In the series, the testimonials will be blended into the body in the same way as Ena did in Chapter I, including, if available, direct quotes of letters from the subjects.

Before a reference to Chapter III, and in keeping with the objective of the Series, a note on what the testimonies tell us, without saying it, is in order. First, the four men went to work at entry-level clerical jobs and without a college education. All of them left the Industry, with one or more University Degrees, by the time Fidel took it over destroying it. They went to School, while working, with the encouragement of Management and taking advantage of Cuba's free and highly respected Universities. Paraphrasing Medardo's statement they entered the mill as "guagiro cerrao" and left the company with University degrees. Is that the Capitalist exploitation that Castro claims for Cuba's past?

The fact that de la Cruz and Rocío kept Miguel Angel's letters, and their anecdotes about him, tells volumes in dispelling the lies about a social division in Cuba that the communist propaganda had lead us to believe existed. Certainly, not every one was like Miguel Angel, taking personal care of his employees during their illness, talking and laughing with them after dinner, and drinking goat's milk at every farmer's house, as he inspected the fields, and opening his house and his heart to his employees. The Captains of Industry series will probe that there were more Miguel Angels than the likes of "robber barons" of Castro's propaganda.

Finally, as evident from the references to Miguel Angel's father, his brother Laureano, other members of the Falla Gutierrez family and Miguel Angel himself, this was not a group of rich absentee owners. As those that know the industry will attest, most were hands on managers-owners. Their families may have moved to nearby towns or eventually to Havana, but they followed where business dictated and circumstances permitted. Obviously, in a regulated industry that exported more than ninety percent of its production and imported equipment and key industrial chemicals, offices in the Capital were a must. It was in Havana where the mill owners could manage their relations with the Government and Trading Houses and best handle their foreign purchases, however they kept their presence in the Mills during the repair and milling seasons.

As Editor, I have no particular recommendation on whether to start the book with Chapter I or to go straight to Chapter II, the Memories, first. Reading the wonderful story weaved by Ena Curnow from the available material provides an orderly overview and interpretation of the "virtual" Miguel Angel who comes out of such diverse sources. Going to the testimonials directly will wet the reader's appetite with their spontaneity and warmth.

Chapter III, presents the mills under Miguel Angel's command. Chapter IV, "Cuba and the International Sugar Market", I certainly recommend reading last. It was difficult to do justice to such a complex industry in so few pages. Sugar experts might find my chapter wanting, while the general public might reel at so much detail. I hope I kept an adequate balance but recognize that both audiences might be right.

Equally important could be the omissions, inaccuracies and errors of interpretation in the chapter. I am not a sugar economist, as my Professor José Antonio Guerra was, nor am I a man of the "Industry". My hands on experience with the industry relate to the end of the process, the "Trading," which is more a financial and mathematical endeavor than the tangible and romantic part of production, the scenario of Miguel Angel's success. Obviously, four years as Chairman and CEO of Czarnikow-Rionda, at the beginning of its Second Century, does not make me an "Expert" on the Industry. To compensate I have profusely quoted my sources. I welcome all and any comment or criticism from "real sugar people", and from my fellow economists, the latter, of course, "comes with the territory". All will be given acknowledgement and consideration in future editions.

Before parting, let me make three statements on my vision of the Cuban sugar industry. First, I came to the conclusion that Cuba, prior to 1959, was the premier sugar producer of the World. The fact that neither my family nor I were mill owners or "colonos" lends special credibility to this professional judgment. I challenge any one to dispute this affirmation. This does not mean that Cuba's sugar industry was perfect. Certainly not, as witnessed by the continued efforts of most sugar mill owners and large plantation owners. Finally I will venture that today Cuba would not have not retained a premier role in the World Sugar market. However, given the genius of Cubans, that, without spare parts, still keep forty year and older American cars running, the country would have certainly evolved, in an orderly way, to other industrial and service activities, including tourism and information technology, as Mexico has done in changing the composition of its exports.

Publishing this book has been very rewarding for its objective and content, and because it got me back to my father's trade, after forty two years of not being a publisher, let alone a printer. This last item is of great sentimental value, albeit without the sensual pleasure of smelling the ink, and listening to the presses roar, and seeing the beauty of white cover stock coming alive with full color covers at 10,000 sheets per hour in huge four-color presses, and even faster for the text. Holding in one's hands, with their smell, look and texture, newly finished books, through a highly automatic process, is by far a more pleasurable experience than staring at a computer screen. This time we did not print what we were publishing, as was the case in Cuba. Mitigating this is the fact that for the seventeen years my father published in Miami, always waiting, as Miguel Angel, to return, thus reluctant to build a printing plant. Oscar Vidal was his printer of choice, from 1965 until my father's death in 1979. As he is also the printer of this book, it will be published under my father's corporation name, still registered, New House Publishers.

On the side of the challenges were the time constraints and the secrecy of the project. The first one put a burden on Ena, and the translators, Monique Fernandez and Ileana Fuentes. Lara J. Evans devoted her free time, while in Spain, to review my English. This burden was alleviated by the understanding and efficiency of Oscar Vidal. The dateline also conflicted with the content of my chapter, as I struggled to include many interesting aspects discovered in the process. I hope I included enough but more will be added as we publish the updated Chapter in individual or combined volumes covering outstanding sugar personalities such as Julio Lobo, Manuel Rionda, Francisco Blanco, and others.

The secrecy of the project deprived me of the valuable support of my "Chief Editor," who does to my English texts what Rita did with her father's. When time permits, Elena reviews my important documents providing, most of the time, excellent contributions in substance and, all the time, in style. The other hazard of the secrecy was the inability to explain being on my laptop at 5 am. Two weeks of such routine provoked a serious threat. "In January I am going back to work so I can have some one to talk to, as my husband is married to his computer." I hope that the book will warrant reconsidering the thought.

On that light note, I leave the acknowledgements to another section and invite the reader to embark on a journey into Miguel Angel's character and his sugar world, so nicely mapped out by Ena Curnow and the five "testigos" speaking from their hearts.

Oscar A. Echevarría
September 20, 2002

Acknowledgements

Both a finished book and a 350-pound bag of sugar hide an extremely complex production processes. No one element of the process or factor of production is more important than the other, as the absence of any of them could impede reaching the final product. So, to avoid any connotation of rank I will acknowledge my contributors as in a Play Bill, in the order they made their appearance.

First of all, was the enthusiastic response of Rita Moreno de Blain. Not only did she write her testimonial, but she provided two pictures and recruited Saturio Rocío, who besides his testimonial and pictures, invited Juan de la Cruz, a source of numerous letters, and Angel Naveiras. José Medardo Pino also sent his contribution through Rocío.

Dolores Carrillo provided the book "Recuerdos de mi Pasado" of Miguel Cervera Falla and facilitated access to Viriato Gutiérrez, residing in Honduras. Cristina de Cardenas, besides her own recollections, opened the door to Javier Cervera and pointed to the book on Laureano Falla Gutiérrez she had given to her daughter Tina, who in turn provided two photo copies for us to work with.

From the Inaugural Notes, the reader knows that by September 4, when Ena accepted the challenge to write the short biography, we could provide her only the five testimonials, fortunately translated. My sister in-law Cristina Falla Drebbin, provided valuable information and some pictures. Under a disguise of Ena writing a story for a paper, as consequence of Cuba dismantling the sugar industry, Elena gave her a telephone interview and reviewed some of the material. In order to meet the deadline of October 12th, we had to rush to gather all the previously mentioned material. Ena got to work, stealing time from her rest, finishing her chapter by Friday September 20 at 2.30 AM, but then continuing to devote time to reviewing her's and other manuscripts.

Carlos Alberto wrote his Prologue while finishing his latest book that went to the printers that same day. And I wrote the Sugar Chapter expanding, by more than five fold, and updating a paper I wrote in 1995.

Our friend of many years, Si Friedman, gave me some direction on the cover and format. Luis García Fresquet interpreted the concept and motive of the book to produce the beautiful and telling cover; and struggled with my piece meal delivery of the final copy.

My Teaching Assistant Santiago Moralejo del Arco, helped in producing all the tables and graphs, completing the research, and reviewing all the chapters in Spanish.

Last but not least, my gratitude to Oscar Vidal, who as I said in the Introduction bore the brunt of the time crunch, created by the delay in providing the final copy.

Contributors

Carlos Alberto Montaner. Born in Havana in 1949, moved to Madrid where he is both a prolific author and recognized Publisher. He has penned some twenty books. His most recent ones include "Las Raíces Torcidas de América Latina", (The Twisted Roots of Latin America) "Viaje al Corazón de Cuba" (Travel to the Heart of Cuba) and "No Perdamos También el Siglo XXI". (Lets Don't Lose the XXI Century). In collaboration with Alvaro Vargas Llosa and Plinio Apuleyo Mendoza, he is the author of the "Manual of the Perfect Latinamerican Idiot" and "Makers of Misery." Amongst his nonfiction are novels, "Perro Mundo" y "1898: la Trama". He has been a university professor at several different colleges in Latin America and the United States. In 1990 he founded the Cuban Liberal Union with the objective of trying to spread liberty and democracy in Cuba. In 1992 he was elected the vice president of the International Liberal.

Ena Curnow. Born in Havana, Cuba, where she obtained a degree in History from Universidad de La Habana. She is author of "Manana: detrás del Generalísimo," a biography of Bernarda Toro de Gómez, wife of Cuban independence hero General Máximo Gómez; and co-author of "La Mujer Cubana: Historia e Infrahistoria." Ediciones Universal, Miami, Florida, published both titles. She is presently completing a biography of Emilia Casanova de Villaverde, a 19th century Cuban exile to the U.S. who dedicated her entire life to the cause of Cuban independence. The Recovering the U.S Hispanic Literary Heritage Project of the University of Houston, Texas awarded Ms. Curnow two seed research grants for this book project, in 1999 and again in 2001. She has been scriptwriter and historical and literary consultant to film and television projects, and has served on the editorial staff of several publications. Ms. Curnow resides in Miami, where she is a reporter for Diario Las Américas.

Rita Moreno de Blain. The daughter of Dr. Eduardo Moreno, Dean of The School of Business Administration at the University of Villanueva and President of Dun & Bradstreet, Havana, Cuba. Rita who was called to attend to Miguel Angel from the Engineering Department at Cuban Atlantic Sugar Co. worked with him until Castro confiscated the Company. She started working in New York at Wertheim and Co. from 1961 to 1971, except for two years when she followed her husband to Puerto Rico. Upon returning to New York she worked at the European American Bank until 1973 when she began working at Abitibi Price, one of the largest producers of paper products in the world. After retiring in 1987 she worked in Real Estate and after 1993 she earned an insurance license in 23 states. From there she retired with her husband to Miami in 1996, where they have been starring in many TV commercials.

Saturio Rocío Chávez. While working with Miguel Angel Falla, he developed a large Academic curricula in Journalism and a Doctorate in Philosophy and Letters from the University of Habana, Accountant and Doctor of Commercial Sciences in Cuba. After arriving in Miami, and at Miguel Angel's suggestion Rocío left for New York and found a job as an accountant for the Refined Sugar Department of Olavarria and Company. After that he worked as Accountant and Treasury Secretary for Hogan & Company Inc. They were the exclusive sellers of Costa Rican sugar. As the Sugar Houses dwindled, Rocío decided to teach Spanish and High School Equivalency at Bryant High School in Queens, New York, from where he retired to enjoy more time with his children and grandchildren in Stamford, Connecticut.

Juan M. de la Cruz. Valedictorian of the San Juan de Bosco Commerce school of Güines, Province of Havana, he landed his first job as Deputy Head of the General Store of the Central Adelaida. He then made a lateral transfer to Central Lugareño, where he was promoted to head of the office and then Manager, until the time Castro took over and then he fled to the United States. He began working as an accountant in a Department store and in a mail order house. Juan then became the Administrator of a private company. Collaborating with the four owners he helped to raise the capital from $500 thousand to $60 million in 1990 when he retired.

Dr. Angel P. Naveiras. Naveiras initiated his work life at the Central Adelaida and stayed there until its confiscation. He left the mill as the head of the Payroll Department. The Revolution ruined his aspirations of practicing law. When he immigrated to the United States he obtained his Masters from Mount Saint Mary College in California and dedicated himself to teaching until retirement, moving then to Miami.

José Medardo Pino. Shortly after finishing Business School in La Escuela Profesional de Comercio, in Santa Clara, Las Villas, in 1942, Medardo went to work in Central Patria. A year later he was offered a position at the larger sister mill, Central Adelaida, where in a few years he went on to become Head of the Accounting Department of the Commercial Department. After the mill was confiscated in 1960, he was transferred to the Ministry of Commerce in Habana until 1966 when he was fired upon requesting an exit visa to the United States. Shortly after arriving in 1968 he went to work at the Remington Arms Company where he stayed until his retirement in 1985. At his farewell a poem was delivered by one of his co-workers and highlighted, "An empty spot will soon appear – no one can take your place – you have no peer."

Chapter I

The Life and Times of Miguel Angel Falla

The Life and Times of Miguel Angel Falla

"Here, man, take the reins:
and he loosened up the bridle
and let them through."

(From Cirilo Villaverde's Cecilia Valdés)

Miguel Angel Falla stood still, listening undisturbed to the proposal being presented to him: that he be, from that day forward, the administrator of the sweet family jewel, the Adelaida sugar mill. The Adelaida had been his Uncle Laureano's pride and joy. He had toiled with great care and love to make it the grand enterprise that it now was. Miguel Angel's emotions were not easily detected in his tiny eyes. Those eyes might have been small, but their gaze was wider than the horizon. His closest associates remember well how, when spoken to, he would look piercingly into the person's eyes, especially if the discussion dealt with an important matter. His handsome and elegant figure made every occasion a solemn affair. His nose pointed slightly upward, proud and aristocratic, in the tradition of the Falla family, according to his daughter Elena. One had to know him very well to notice the slight flutter around the nostrils when something on his mind was worrying him.

Even if Miguel Angel regarded his selection as an honor and appreciated it, it certainly could not have taken him by surprise. He had worked tenaciously during many, many years at the Patria sugar mill. Patria belonged to the Sucesión Falla Gutiérrez; his father, Don Miguel, had been a Patria shareholder all the while developing his own plantation. He certainly deserved the recognition, for he was a seasoned administrator. He was not being offered the job because he was next in the hierarchy. When it came to business, the family enforced a strict policy: just because one was a direct descendant of the Falla Gutiérrez clan did not mean automatic ascent up the familial corporate ladder. Miguel Angel's promotions had been gradual, from the lowest rung, all the way to the top. Under his father's mentorship, he had learnt everything there was to know about the workings of sugar mills. His tenure at the Patria mill had been a step-by-step, hands-on experience, from planting sugar cane to the intricacies of grinding it at the mill. Sugar, the bitter-sweet taste of Cuba.

**** ** ****

Laureano Falla Gutiérrez was born on Christmas Day, 1859 in the town of Hoz de Anero, a poor community in the mountain region of Santander, in the northern Spanish province of Asturias. His brother Miguel was born a few years after. Cuba was still a Spanish colony when young Laureano journeyed to the island at the behest of his maternal uncle, Don Laureano Gutiérrez Diego. The year was 1874; he was 15 years old. In Cienfuegos he attended school for two years, and went on to work as salesman at his uncle's grocery store. The store was located in a neighborhood called El Salto within the municipal boundaries of Santa Isabel de las Lajas. He saved every penny he earned, as did typically all Spanish immigrants.

Miguel stayed behind in Spain, and took over the care of his widowed mother and two younger siblings, Juan José and María. He was a timber man in the Llúa forest. So long and exhausting were his work shifts that on one occasion, he lost his balance and fractured a leg. He never quite forgot the terrified look on his mother's face when they carried him into the house. By the time he joined his brother in Cuba he was 20 years old. Moving to Lajas was the start of a new life. He worked in several grocery stores until he was able to buy his own. He also bought a sugar cane plantation; at harvest time, he used the San Agustín mill facilities to grind the sugar cane. His brother Laureano was in charge of San Agustín. Laureano became a planter in 1894 when he purchased the Villarreal farm, and rose to the level of landowner in 1901 with the acquisition of the Santísima Trinidad mill. He was elected president of the Spanish Society in Cienfuegos – where he lived most of his life – and Casino Español in Havana.

According to their nephew Miguel Cervera Falla, Laureano and Miguel made up a formidable duo, whether they worked as a team or on their own. Each brother brought to the relationship a specific talent: Laureano, his instinct for business; Miguel, his incomparable resilience for hard work. The first investment they made together was the purchase of the Patria mill near Morón, in Camagüey province. Patria was a small mill, but it would yield enough profit to build the two brothers a small fortune. Miguel agreed to his brother's suggestion that he contribute twenty percent of the purchase price. As part of the arrangement, Miguel was named administrator, freeing Laureano to pursue other business deals in Havana.

Don Laureano moved to Havana in 1915. By then, both he and his brother were married and had families. Don Laureano married Dolores Bonet Mora and had four children: Isabel, Adelaida, María Teresa and Eutimio. Don Miguel married

María de los Angeles Alvarez. As the story goes, on his wedding day, Miguel rose at four o'clock in the morning and traveled some four kilometers from Lajas to inspect his sugar cane fields. He wanted to make sure that his foreman did not take advantage of the distractions created by the wedding and the festivities. Miguel and María de los Angeles had five children: Miguel Angel, Laureano, Cristina,

Don Miguel's children – Carlos, Laureano, Cristina, Isabel and Miguel Angel, dressed up for a costume party.

Carlos and Isabel.

Miguel Angel was still a teenager when he started working as hired hand at the Patria mill. Born on February 9, 1903 in Santa Isabel de las Lajas, Miguel Angel graduated from the Jesuit school Colegio Montserrat in Cienfuegos, as did his brothers Laureano and Carlos. But where Laureano and Carlos were sent to medical and law school respectively, Don Miguel sent his first born to business school in Philadephia. In the 18th and 19th centuries, wealthy Cuban families sent their children – mostly their male children – to school in Spain and France. In the 20th century, that destination changed to a closer and more familiar place: the

[1]Falla Cervera, Miguel. Recuerdo de mi pasado (Memories). Unpublished manuscript, circa 1979. The author wishes to thank Javier Cervera Falla, Miguel's son, for allowing her to consult this manuscript. It provided very valuable material about the lives of Miguel Angel and his father, Don Miguel.

United States. "You know already all you need to know," said Don Miguel to his son when he finished school. There was no time to waste: business was the business at hand. He was, after all, the oldest son in a Spanish family.

In the United States he developed an eye for modernity and a sense of the growing business world. He learnt English, and he spoke it fluently and correctly, but with a Cuban accent. He wrote it adequately. His Spanish was also impeccable. I have read some of the letters Don Miguel Angel wrote to such colleagues as Juan Manuel de la Cruz y Saturio Rocío, who cherish the documents like family treasures. They reveal a distinguished penmanship: his handwriting was strong and elongated, with the upward motion typical of far-reaching and resolute personalities.

Blessed with a keen intelligence and the discipline and willpower that enabled him to learn quickly on his own, young Miguel Angel learnt even the most insignificant aspects of a sugar mill's operation. Daughters Cristina and Elena remember the stories of how their grandfather had made sure Miguel Angel rotated from one detail to another at the mill. By the time this hands-on training had come full circle, Miguel Angel had done everything at Patria, from sweeping the office floors, to making rounds as messenger, to weighing sugar cane at harvest time.

It didn't take long for Miguel Angel to obtain his first promotion to office assistant. In that position, he learnt to type, process invoices, put files in order, do payroll, and record keeping on actual production. His father, who had been Patria's administrator since 1917, bestowed on him no special favors or treatment. Miguel Angel surely must have wondered what purpose it served for his father to treat him so. But life taught him later on that it was essential to know the hardships every step of the way in order to be a good boss.

Endowed with a bright mind, graced with a good disposition, and a relentless will to get ahead, Miguel Angel listened to his father's every advice. He listened to the mill's elders as well, for he knew their years of experience made them wise. He knew how to listen. Aided by a sharp memory and a sixth sense for identifying the real important issues, he kept a close watch on the mill's daily output of 2,500 metric tons. This was a sacred number: the goal for the annual harvest was set at 225,000 arrobas, equivalent to 5,626,000 pounds.

Patria sugar mill, located in the vicinity of Morón, was listed in the corporate registry as *Azucarera Central Patria, S.A. Compañía*. It became a forge, a veritable training ground to all the heirs of Laureano Falla, the stern brains behind the Falla fortune.

Miguel Angel looked up to his uncle. Good observer that he was, he didn't miss even the slightest thing about his uncle. Don Laureano was a quick thinker, and had great entrepreneurial acumen. To his uncle and his father, young Falla was like biblical molding clay, a breath of life unto his elders' ventures. From each he took the very best.

At harvest time, his keen eye became even sharper. He watched over the inspectors as they took inventory in the warehouse, and kept track of how many bags of sugar were being transported to the docks for export. He had a great imagination, and enjoyed taking risks. Miguel Angel constantly asked questions of the technicians and stewards. He wanted to know the level of sucrose in the sugar cane juice and how many pounds of sugar cane were weighed on a daily basis. He would go out to the fields to talk to the foremen and workers, and ask them questions as well.

The son of Don Miguel was intent in absorbing every aspect of the sugar mill's operations. Folks at Patria admired his spirit, and liked him a lot. They saw the tall and slender young man learning to be a man the hard way in the green fields. "Will you look at this lad? … Isn't this boy something!" the older field hands often exclaimed as they shook their heads side to side. In turn, he treated them affably, exercising great care not to trespass the threshold of authority. His own demeanor ensured that others regarded him as just another worker, not as a privileged society boy. He trained his men to call him by his baptismal name: Miguel Angel.

He also tended to the sugar cane plantation La Granja. At a rate of 6% annual interest, his uncle Laureano had financed the purchase of La Granja for him and his cousins Ricardo, Manolo, Eutimio and Miguel Cervera, another pillar of sugar mill administration in the Falla family. In his memoirs, Miguel Cervera narrates many details about his work at the Andreíta sugar mill; his uncle, Agustín Batista, had sent him there to get things in shape.

Those fields were needed to guarantee the volume of sugar cane that was required to meet target production goals. They proved to be a major headache. During the first year, the fields were plagued with the Mossaic virus, which attacked the Cristalina variety of sugar cane that had been recently planted. They would soon develop a superior stock, P.O.J. 2878, which proved more resistant to the disease.

**** ** ****

On August 13, 1915, Don Laureano launched a strategy to consolidate the planters and their land holdings into what would become the Adelaida sugar mill, named after his daughter Adelaida, married to Mr. Viriato Gutiérrez. The Adelaida was located in the Nauyú Estate some fifteen kilometers from the Patria mill. Construction of the Adelaida started in 1916; the town of Falla gradually emerged around the Adelaida. Between 1910 and 1929, Don Laureano opened several factories, including a paper mill and an electric utility company in Cienfuegos and Cárdenas. In association with other concerns, he was shareholder and manager of the Andreíta, the Manuelita and the Cieneguita sugar mills. He owned real estate in Havana and Cienfuegos, as well as numerous farms and saisal plantations in Cárdenas. Don Laureano was on the board and was stockholder of several insurance companies, as well as Polar ice manufacturers. He was president of the Cuban Fishing and Navigation Company and the Agricultural and Industrial Union Insurance Co. Together with H. Upmann and Armando Godoy, Laureano Falla became a partner of Jose Marimón Juliach in the Spanish Bank of Cuba project. Marimón Juliach had already joined with José López Rodríguez, principal owner of National Bank, to form an alliance of Cuban and Spanish sugar venture capital to offset foreign investment.

In June 1922, Miguel Angel was promoted to office manager at Patria. Changes were precipitated by the untimely death of José Planas, administrator of the Adelaida sugar mill, who was killed by an unhappy and vengeful planter. Raúl Román, the number-two man at Patria, was named administrator, and cousin Manolo [Cervera] to the same post at Adelaida. Both sugar mills remained under Don Miguel's supervision.

The Falla brothers were particularly affected by the death of their long time friend. Born in Catalonia, José Planas was very much loved by the Falla clan. He and his older brother Manolo had been pivotal in bringing the planters into the fold of the more modern Adelaida sugar mill. They were the ones who convinced the planters to sell their land and remain shareholders of the Adelaida in proportion to the value of the land they had sold. The Planas also became shareholders.

Miguel Angel acquired three additional sugar plantations in partnership with his cousins Manolo, Ricardo and Miguel Cervera. They named the new parcel Concha, in honor of the Cerveras' mother. Miguel Cervera worked tirelessly to forge ahead. Soon those fields became the best of Adelaida's plantations, and netted great profits for its owners.

From the moment Miguel Angel took over the administration of the offices, his father decided it was time to take it easier. The signs of old age were beginning to show. He was feeling tired after so many years of hard work, and began to space his visits to the plantations, traveling by shuttle engine rather than on horseback.

Miguel Angel followed his father's advice to the letter. "Don't let anyone fool you. When you feel that something is not right, find a solution and give it all the time and effort that it requires." He made it a practice to corroborate things with his own two eyes, and never to rely on the information of others alone. He surveyed the ground like his father before him, combing the plantations on horseback, sometimes for as long as ten and twelve hours in one day. "Seeing is believing" – *Vista hace fe* – was the old proverb that guided him as he navigated the ins and outs of the agro-industrial sugar world.

Miguel Angel was an innovator when it came to managing. He established modern accounting methods; eliminated some of the red tape; and perfected control systems in all aspects of planting, cutting, transportation, storage and sugar production. The administration of a sugar mill is as complex as the equipment that makes it work. It's not just about sowing, harvesting and processing sugar cane; it's also about dealing with the very difficult human dimension of life on a sugar plantation. Behind his stern and steady walk, behind the high leather boots, the white shirt, and his riding trousers, hid a big and noble soul.

Saturio Rocío, who was for many years his personal secretary, assures us that what appeared to be an arrogant demeanor was only that: an appearance. By all accounts, Miguel Angel was graced with a compassionate and sensitive heart. "Many people blessed the generous hand of Miguel Angel," says Rocío, who is full of anecdotes. Like the time Miguel Angel sent an ailing newborn baby to a hospital in Havana; the infant had been hurt during delivery. And then there was the daughter of one of his employees from the Alarcón farm. The girl had been left blind by an illness; Miguel Angel paid for the girl's medical care and special education.

Various accounts confirm that he sent teas and adequate food to one of his accountants, José Medardo Pino, who was very ill and without a soul to nurse him back to health. Pino never forgot his boss' gesture. Dr. Angel P. Naveiras writes about Miguel Angel's kindness when he tells the story of how young Falla hired a most eminent physician to treat his terminally ill brother. Miguel Angel granted Naveiras a leave of absence from work so he could be with his brother in those terrible final days.

The development of the sugar industry changed the rural landscape of Cuba. A sugar mill was a town microcosm where entire families lived generation after generation. During harvest, seasonal workers – the *jornaleros* –, joined the work force. In the areas around the factories, farmers often found better living conditions.

The workforce at Patria numbered over 3,000 workers. Miguel Angel knew all of them, some even by name. He made it a practice to stay in direct contact with all his employees, the farm hands as well as the sugar mill staff.

As for the production aspects of the business, he continued implementing the kind of technological reforms his uncle Laureano had introduced before him. Miguel Angel increased the extension of land used for farming, and utilized better quality fertilizers. He was always searching for a better, more resilient and more productive variety of sugar cane. At the same time, he saw to it that all industrial equipment was repaired and kept in top form. Which explains how he kept production levels at 150,000 bags of sugar, a high output for a mill the size of Patria. In 1917, the year that Don Laureano purchased it, Patria yielded only 60,000 bags of sugar.

**** ** ****

Sucesión L. Falla Gutierrez, incorporated on May 27th, 1929, was founded in order to continue the business operations of Laureano Falla Gutiérrez, who died in Cuba on March 25th of that year. The new corporate office was located at 110 Oficios Street, Second Floor; a bank account was opened in its name at The Trust Company of Cuba. The Sucesión's capital was estimated at between $65 and $75 million. It was the legal owner of seven sugar mills, to wit: the Adelaida, the Andreíta, the Manuelita, Azucarera Fidelidad, Azucarera Buenavista, Central Patria and Central Violeta. At the time it was considered the second most important coalition of sugar barons in Cuba. It owned shares of other companies: Cuban Electric Refrigeration Company, a home appliances dealership; Nauyú Distilling Company, the second largest alcohol producer in the country, located in the Adelaida mill proper; Inmobiliaria Payret, S.A.; the National Paper Company, the Cuban Fishing and Navigation Company, the Cuban Fibre and Tackle Company, and Henequenera Estrella.

Sucesión's beneficiaries were Laureano's three children: Eutimio, Isabel and Maria Teresa Falla Bonet, as well as Viriato Gutiérrez, his daughter Adelaida's widower, and Agustín Batista, president of Trust Company S.A. Falla Bonet. The Board of Trustees was composed of Alejandro Suero, Eutimio Falla, Agustín Batista, Carlos and Miguel Falla, and Miguel Cervera. Alejandro and Eutimio were president and treasurer respectively; the others were Board advisors.

He felt very grieved about his uncle Laureano's passing. Everyone in the family mourned his death. He had last seen him during Christmas in 1927. His health was

Julia Bulle-Merry, Mrs. Miguel Angel Falla

frail already, and had wanted to gather the whole family at the Adelaida family mansion, which had been ready for occupancy since the previous summer.

Miguel Angel decided to marry Julia Bulle-Merry, a young woman of French and British heritage. He was formally engaged to her for three years. Julia was extremely attractive; she came from a good family and was of sound moral character. They corresponded regularly and had come to know each other quite well even though she lived in Havana. Miguel and Julia made an enviable couple. It wasn't long before their daughters Cristina and Julia came into the world, one after the other.

The oldest was born in El Vedado, in Havana; the second daughter was born at Patria. Then, just when they thought no more children were forthcoming, they had Elena, who was born on Almendares Street in Kohly, also in Havana. Everyone thought this third child might be a boy who would be named after his father.

Don Miguel greatly enjoyed the company of his oldest granddaughter Cristina, who grew up at the sugar mill just like her dad. The old patriarch no longer went to Patria to make rounds, but instead to play with the little one, who would take him by the hand, shower him with kisses, and ask him endless questions. "Why this, grandpa... why that, *abuelito*?... It was a plethora of questions, one after another, after another.

**** ** ****

After the 1935-36 harvest ended, Miguel Angel took over the reigns of the Adelaida sugar mill. He replaced his cousin Miguel Cervera whom the Sucesion's Board of Directors had transferred to the Andreíta. Things at the Andreíta were going from bad to worse, and the mill needed a strict hand. Cervera was the ideal person for the job.

Nothing surprised Miguel Angel at his new post. He knew the sugar mill inside out, not only because his own plantation, La Granja, was located inside the Adelaida proper, and he came around quite frequently, but also because he had been at the Adelaida countless times with his father when Don Miguel was administrator and supervisor. He, better than anyone else in the family, knew the workings of that marvel of a sugar mill.

He was quite confident of his managerial style of relying on a team of capable professionals, and motivated workers who wanted to get ahead to get the job done. He would meet the new challenge head on. Miguel Angel's vision was that of a great entrepreneur. He encouraged workers who showed potential to get a university education. He even helped pay for their studies. He was right in thinking that the men he helped this way would make up a pool of in-house talent. Such was the case of Saturio Rocío, who dedicated his doctoral thesis to Miguel Angel in a gesture of gratitude.

A group dynamic thus developed. Those men also had to take lessons from him. "As the fine mentor that he was, he would train the men in the tricks of the trade," Rocío reminisces. "And when he named someone to any position, he demanded total commitment and delivery." Dr. Naveiras recalls that "he always expressed his opinion outright" but he was as generous with criticism as he was with sincere praise, always acknowledging people for their good work. He didn't hesitate to give credit were credit was due.

Central "Adelaida"

Juan M. de la Cruz had a clever way of describing his boss' habit of educating and encouraging his staff. Whenever he was asked what university he graduated from, Juan answered, "From UCA... from the University "Central Adelaida" (from Adelaida Sugar Mill University).

The Adelaida was capable of yielding 330,000 *arrobas* - 8,250,000 pounds - of sugar; it boasted 21,000 hectares of land, and employed 2,970 workers. It had been Don Laureano's favorite endeavor, one whose development he watched from start to finish. Three years after the Adelaida started its operations, it became number one in profits yielded per bag of sugar.

After the 1934-35 harvest, the Adelaida started shipping its sugar from Chicola to Caibarién, and no longer through the port of Tarafa. That translated into savings of $200,000 per shipment.

The sugar mill was situated in the middle of the Nauyú Estate. Nauyú spanned some 1,300 *caballerías* - 43,290 acres - of land. The rest of the land was part of *Realengo Sabana la Mar*, which lay between the estate and the coast. The planning for this area served to establish new construction guidelines for the surrounding landowners. It boasted running water, electricity and telephone service, and great means of communication thanks to 130 kilometers of private railroad divided into five rail lines that connected the sugar plantations to the mill.

In other words, the sugar mill was located at the very center of the *batey*[2], and nearby, but in separate buildings, were the various workshops: one for servicing and repairing engines, another for carpentry, and yet another for the upkeep of railroad cars. There was even an emergency clinic. In order to reach this intricate compound, one had to pass through the main gate. Once inside the sugar mill proper one could see Don Laureano Falla's bust on the right, and the chapel on the left. Monsignor Pérez Serantes, then Bishop of Camagüey, celebrated Mass in that chapel many times. He was a personal friend of Miguel Angel's. In keeping with the family's philanthropic tradition, Miguel Angel gave both money and community service time to Catholic organizations. The monsignor admired his friend's generosity, for Miguel Angel was always ready to contribute to worthy causes, especially the treatment of contagious diseases, and cancer.

The setting as you entered the Adelaida led the visitor through a wide avenue surrounded by laurel trees that formed a natural green tunnel. Twenty-four houses had been built on both sides, to house the main bosses. In addition, there were 20 individual dwellings for staff members with families; five halls for single men and two restaurants where they ate. Close to the *batey*, but outside its boundaries, were the rural police station and between 30 and 40 additional houses. A modest urban area was developing half a kilometer from the sugar mill; it had paved streets and other amenities of modern life. Individuals could purchase property there, either to dwell in it, or to set up food shops for the benefit of plantation workers. That place, first known as *Reparto Falla* - the Falla development - later would become the town of Falla.

**** ** ****

Dr. David Suero Rodríguez, Isabel Falla's husband and Alejandro Suero Falla's father, was Sucesión's original administrator until his death in June 1938. He had been named General Administrator of the family business assets in 1923. In 1943, Rafael Jiménez-Rojo Saladrigas, a long time employee of Falla Gutiérrez as far back as 1918, became its attorney and remained so until his death April 18, 1953. Alejandro Suero Falla, Isabel's son, rose to the leadership of the sugar consortium in 1945, and by 1958 was president of every one of the consortium's companies. Julio Prado Rodríguez, who had replaced Eutimio Falla Bonet, was vice president of all the companies with the exception of the Manuelita sugar mill. Urbano Monasterio Díaz held that position. Suero also owned stock in "Petrolera

[2] The batey was the industrial-residential compound where life and work took place. The *batey* is located at the center of the sugar mill, surrounded by the cane fields.

Julia Bulle, Mrs. Miguel Angel Falla, with her daughters Julia, Elena and Cristina

Transcuba, S.A." and "Corporación Intercontinental de Hoteles de Cuba S.A." He had been the later's president until November 21, 1957.

At the top of the hierarchy of the Falla Gutiérrez clan, Miguel Angel was regarded as a champion of the sugar mills. Alejandro "Alín" Suero, who had been at the helm of their emerging empire since 1945, felt deep admiration for him. By chance, and not by design, he enjoyed his cousin's affection and good will, which did not stop them from disagreeing every once in a while. With "Alín", another side of his personality revealed itself: a sense of humor. Whenever they were alone, they teased each other and exchanged jokes all the time. Miguel Angel also enjoyed teasing his nieces, Cristina de Cárdenas among them. Today, years later, she still remembers his wit and personal charm.

Juan M. de la Cruz, who worked beside him for over thirty years, remembers two such anecdotes that speak of Miguel Angel's good temper. There was the time he sent the office messenger for a "*botella de agua con gas*", literally, a bottle of water with gas, meaning a soda pop or club soda. The boy returned with a bottle of kerosene. Miguel Angel thought the mistake was very funny. On another occasion, he sent the same young man to read the rain gauge; the boy returned with a

Cristina Falla, today Mrs. Drebbin, with her mare Peggy.

reading that was simply not possible. Miguel Angel sent him back, this time with instructions to check to make sure the rain gauge was clean. Sure enough, there was a toad inside the rain gauge, whose body volume had elevated the reading. When told of the hidden amphibian, Miguel Angel laughed and made endless jokes out of the incident.

He took pleasure in laughing. His oldest daughter Cristina remembers her father sitting on the porch of the office every night, some 150 meters from the main house, and calling the workers to join him so he could talk with them. She could hear her father laughing endlessly during the course of the conversations.

Life at the sugar mill was different from life in Havana, a major consideration when it came to his daughters, who had to attend school. They could not stay at the Adelaida all the time as they had when they were little. Although their mother had attended the French Dominican Academy, the three girls attended the School of the Sacred Heart. This meant that Julia had to travel frequently between the sugar mill and Havana to be with the girls.

Things were different during vacation. The whole family came together, and his daughter Cristina loved to go with him during his habitual rounds of the plantations. She had her own horse, a mare named Peggy. Miguel Angel had a fine specimen of a horse named Candela, a feisty animal that tested Miguel Angel's riding ability every time. The only problem with Candela was that he went wild around mares. Miguel Angel made it a habit of stopping here and there to talk to people, always with the excuse of drinking fresh goat's milk, his favorite sardines, and a good cup of coffee. He always took the time to listen to their worries and inquire about the sick. He even granted favors and requests during those visits. Cristina loathed fresh milk. On those field visits, she never got off her mare.

It was the same during Christmas. The whole family gathered, and they went to Mass at 10 o'clock in the morning at the Church of Our Lady of Candelaria, in Morón. Miguel Angel was a devout Christian. He carried his rosary beads in his pocket everywhere he went, and would pray the rosary in a whisper during trying moments, like when his father died, on July 13, 1938.

Losing his father left a terrible void in Miguel Angel's life. During the days immediately following his passing, he could still hear him giving orders. Nothing could have been further from reality: for the longest time it was Miguel Angel, not his father, who had been giving the orders at the Adelaida. Miguel Angel had let his ailing father retain the illusion of power, not a difficult thing to do, for he always regarded his father as the highest authority.

Miguel Angel worked tirelessly during the rest of the year. He possessed great vitality and was not the type to be content with putting in an eight-hour day at the office. His closest associates attest to that. There are anecdotes told by evening shift workers that have him walking in during late evening or early morning hours and taking roll call. He certainly never slept enough, but that did not affect his tight work schedule. Come hell or high water, he always walked into the office at eight o'clock in the morning sharp.

During World War II, the family built a distillery in the Adelaida mill proper, to make fuel from molasses. Due to fuel shortages, the government had ordered the production of fuel from the alcohol byproducts of sugar cane. The Falla Gutiérrez hierarchy set out to meet demand, and although Miguel Angel knew very little about the industrial aspects of ethylic fuel production, he met the challenge and exceeded all forecasts and expectations.

Nauyú Distilling Company was one of the largest of its kind in Cuba. It produced 80,000 liters of alcohol daily. The competition, however, refused to be outmaneuvered. It was upset at the calm and level-headedness behind the construction of the Nauyú facilities, which included several floors and met all technical state-of-the-industry requirements. In their eagerness to be first, Nauyú's competitors wasted no time, and entered the market before completing proper testing of the experimental product.

In spite of all his precautions, a veritable invasion of flies was set off. The flies bred in the discarded must. The news spread like wildfire from railcar to railcar, as travelers raised their windows to prevent the flies from storming the cars. Regardless, the fly infestation spread from town to town.

Miguel Angel did not panic, on the contrary. With his usual patience and wisdom, he got the crisis under control, but not before it hit Havana's newspapers and received national publicity. Serenity and caution were at least two of his virtues. He gave proof of this in the way he handled crisis. Rocío tells of a disgruntled worker who, after being fired, prepared to take revenge by joining the rural police. Several months later, the vengeful man returned to the mill, stepped into the office, and held Miguel Angel at gunpoint. Without batting an eyelash, he continued doing the paperwork he was doing, and called his assistant under pretext of checking some figures, thus enabling him to go out and get help. In no time, the police sergeant showed up and arrested the intruder.

Miguel Angel was a man of principles, and never gave in to blackmail or extortion. One time the local press published an article titled "The naked truth" attacking the sugar mill's administration. According to the article, the Fallas had promised to provide gowns to all the local children for their first communion, but had failed to make good on the promise. The paper claimed that some of the children had no gowns to wear for the ceremony. People were upset. A few days later, the author of the piece paid him a visit, and offered to correct the story as a favor, for a price. Miguel Angel responded quickly: "Are you now planning to dress up the truth?"

There were many such incidents. The local radio station berated him one time for the cutting down of forests to make way for planting more sugar cane. Rocío was asked to give a public explanation. That is how the press was handled. The unions also learnt of his negotiation skills first hand. Miguel Angel had cordial relations with the unions and he listened always to their demands. However, he only granted those he felt were fair and necessary. He never harassed his workers, but nonetheless he was relentless in his mission to protect the financial interests of the company he represented. In general, he always managed to forge friendly agreements with the unions.

The success of the Adelaida sugar mill crowned all his efforts. According to Rocío, Miguel Angel foresaw that cutting down adjacent forest areas would translate into greater harvests, and he managed to do this with the cooperation of the planters. He introduced mechanized methods for cutting sugar cane and for lifting the bundles off the ground, and introduced higher yield varieties that were also more resistant to plagues. On the industrial end, he introduced innovations across the board: new and modern scales, cane shredders, roller mills, centrifugal machines, juice clarifiers, ovens, boilers, a generator, sewing machines for the production of the sugar bags. The results were soon forthcoming: in 1952, the Adelaida yielded 421,783 bags of sugar, at 325 pounds per bag. The harvest itself yielded 43 million arrobas – 1,08 billion pounds – of sugar cane.

"Alín" Suero, president of *Sucesión L. Falla Gutiérrez,* proposed a new challenge to Miguel Angel: harvesting rice. He put his mind to this new endeavor, a physical and logistic challenge in and of itself, due to the nature of the crop, which requires the availability of deep wells, for it needs inordinate amounts of water, and leveling the fields into scaled terrazas. Miguel Angel's administrative talents rose to the challenge once more," recalls Rocío. "The rice farms prospered and yielded great profit."

**** ** ****

Don Laureano's heirs multiplied manifold the inheritance they received. In 1946, they purchased the San Germán sugar mill, and in 1951, the Punta Alegre. In 1958, they bought the Violeta sugar mill, and in 1943 a bank, The Trust Company of Cuba.

Miguel Angel had decided to take a much-deserved break with his family in their beautiful Havana home. The house was located in the recently inaugurated Kohly district, at Number 33 Almendares Street. He lived in that house until he abandoned the island. Cristina and Julia were old enough already to have marriage and children on their minds. He wanted to be abreast of every development. But "Alín" Suero came looking for him: he was urgently needed. *Sucesión Falla Gutiérrez* had just purchased the Punta Alegre sugar mill, and they wanted Miguel Angel to take charge. The sugar mill urgently needed restructuring so it could operate under the same system as the rest of the mills and be placed under Falla control. It was too great a temptation. All that rest was making him restless! Body and soul, Miguel Angel Falla was always ready for work. Now, at fifty, he agreed to become Punta Alegre's administrator, and return to the countryside. The year was 1953.

The sugar mill's previous administration was American. They had granted too many privileges and employed more workers than were actually needed. Those standards were much higher than Cuban managerial practice would allow. Rocío summarizes the challenges succinctly: "It was a matter of rebuilding and modern-

Miguel Angel and his brother Carlos

izing the sugar mill, and to organize it in a way that unnecessary costs and manpower were eliminated." True to his managerial style, Miguel Angel brought with him a team of trusted experts, and set out to evaluate staff position by staff position, a delicate and complicated task indeed. He had to determine which of those were truly essential.

He started with the industrial sector, and worked his way to the agricultural aspects. At the factory, he soon realized that there were too many workers, and that some costs could not be justified. Out in the fields he detected endless irregularities, the most important among them: that sugar cane was planted only along plantation perimeters, thus creating an inadequate supply of sugar cane which in turn affected the sugar yield of the mill. With not a moment to waste, he asked the plantation inspector to survey the fields with him. Forced to admit his own incompetence, the inspector quit right then and there.

Many workers panicked, thinking they would loose their jobs. But Miguel Angel soon restored their confidence. At the same time that he dismissed the incompetent, he motivated those who proved themselves efficient, and promoted them. Radical improvement soon followed.

With the larger house in order, he took time now to make some changes in his daily routine. The Punta Alegre was located amidst a tropical paradise. The main house was right next to the ocean. Elena remembers that, "it had its own private dock where our cook went fishing for *majúas*, and he fried them for us to eat." Media Luna and Guillermo Keys were close by, and he could visit them often aboard his yacht "The Ailicec".

**** ** ****

Sucesión Falla Gutiérrez remained interested in expanding its production capabilities. A posible expansion strategy could have been the purchase of some of Cuban Atlantic Sugar Company's sugar mills. At the time, Cuban Atlantic owned ten sugar mills: the Violeta; three mills that belonged to the Hershey Corporation – Hershey, Rosario and San Antonio; another three in Matanzas province – Alava, Conchita and Mercedes; and three more in Camagüey province – Lugareño, Morón and Stewart. Cuban Atlantic was regarded as the most important sugar consortium in the world, a reputation it enjoyed since the 1930's. Alejandro Suero Falla, head of the Sucesión consortium, had been a member of Cuban Atlantic's Board of Directors since before 1930.

Miguel Angel was in Havana when his cousin "Alín" Suero came looking for him. "Alín" had been talking to John L. Loeb, who had recently taken over control of Cuban Atlantic by buying a majority of stock in the New York Stock Exchange. In their conversations, Loeb had brought up the subject of Cuban Atlantic, and expressed a sense of urgency in finding the right man who could reorganize and manage that venture.

"Alín" and Loeb were friends since Loeb's first trip to Cuba in 1928. He had an answer for everything, and did not hesitate a second to make recommendations. "My cousin Miguel Angel is the best sugar mill administrator that I know."

It's not easy to discern the degree of motivation that prompted "Alín" to make such a recommendation. He certainly was convinced that his cousin Miguel Angel was indeed the best man for the job, and he surely wanted to assist his American friend. But we also can speculate that as head of the second most powerful group of sugar barons in Cuba, "Alín" knew the advantage of having his cousin Miguel Angel head the sugar giant that was Cuban Atlantic. Who could be better than Miguel Angel? He knew first hand the sugar interests of the Sucesión after heading its three Camagüey sugar mills for years. If his cousin were to be appointed to the position, "Alín" thought, he would be given first option in any sale of Cuban Atlantic assets.

No offer could have been more tempting, thought Miguel Angel. It wasn't just about being the administrator of yet another sugar mill while still running the Punta Alegre and supervising the affairs of the Patria and the Adelaida. This opportunity was about crossing the threshold. It was a career leap. Cuban Atlantic owned ten sugar mills. Destiny was handing him this opportunity on a silver platter. Destiny's name was "Alín". This could be the crowning glory of his career as Captain of Industry.

The Wall Street financier set up a meeting with Miguel Angel at Hotel Nacional, in Vedado. With its colonial style and its majestic presence, there was no better place in all Havana to discuss important matters.

There are no direct references about this meeting. Surely Miguel Angel must have arrived at the exact time, and impeccably dressed for the occasion. And when he and John Loeb sat down to talk, Miguel Angel must have demonstrated his mastery of the sugar business, from planting to production, and revealed himself as the eminent businessman that he was.

They also must have discussed the need to improve the living conditions of the cane cutters across the board. Loeb was familiar with the Fallas' progressive stance on those issues, and especially Miguel Angel's track record and he wanted to apply those same policies to his corporate giant.

And so a strategy was laid out. To start out, Miguel Angel would have Power of Attorney with full authority. Two or three months down the pike, he would be named President of Cuban Atlantic.

**** ** ****

Cuban Atlantic, which in 1952 had produced close to 900,000 metric tons of sugar; was the largest sugar concern in the world in 1956. It owned 550 miles of railways and a distillery in central Morón that was inaugurated on March 1, 1944.

Miguel Angel and his brother Laureano at the engagement of their nephew Celso Miguel González, in Angelica, their mother's home.

Its nominal capital was registered in Cuba, and in 1957 it amounted to more than 10 million dollars. Its value on the New York Stock Exchange was much higher. Loeb & Rhoades and Company, John Loeb's brokerage firm, owned the majority of the company's stock. The Rionda family and Sucesión Falla Gutiérrez also owned Cuban Atlantic stock.

John L. Loeb[3] was Chairman of the Board of Directors and Lawrence A. Crosby president of the firm and its subsidiaries. Cuban Atlantic was founded in 1915 together with Cuban Cane Sugar Corporation, headed by Manuel Rionda Polledo. Cuban Cane went bankrupt in 1921. After several attempts at recovery under the name Cuban Cane Products Company Inc, Rionda demolished half of the sugar mills. The Rockefeller and Sullivan & Cronwel group took over the company. It is from Rockefeller-Sullivan that Loeb takes control through stock acquisitions in the New York stock market.

Felix drove down 23rd Street and turned right at Infanta. He parked the car in front of the Ambar Motors building. He was an excellent chauffeur, the type to speed cautiously so as not to incur any traffic violation. Such skill was important in

[3] Loeb, John L. All in a Lifetime: John L. Loeb. New York, 1990. Page 168

Havana, a veritable urban jungle of cars and buses back in the good old days. Miguel Angel got off the vehicle and instinctively looked up to the top floors. There, overlooking the ocean, were the headquarters of Cuban Atlantic.

In her memoirs, Rita Blain speaks of Miguel Angel during that period. "I was asked to help him become familiar with the different departments and company personnel. At first I was going to remain temporarily, until his transition into the presidency was completed."

To Rita, all the good things that have come her way in life have been touched by magic. Her meeting Miguel Angel was no exception. They liked each other from the moment they met, and a spirit of comradeship and mutual respect soon followed. All the years they worked together, they held each other in that same spirit. In fact, their bond extended to their respective families. Rita and Miguel Angel's youngest daughter, Elena, would become best of friends, so much so that they love each other like sisters.

Miguel Angel was extremely diplomatic during this initial period. He did not want to hurt Lawrence A. Crosby's feelings, the man he would soon replace. "He showed utmost discretion and respect for Crosby while he remained in his position. Slowly he took over control of the company," recalls Rocío, who Miguel Angel had brought with him. He did what he had done with every corporate move: bring along his team of competent experts to help him get the job done.

He was so busy with the myriad details that he was surprised when his first paycheck arrived. When he returned to his Kohly home that night, he kissed Julia, his wife, and handed her the check as a gift. There was a triumphant smile on his face.

Once in full exercise of the company presidency, Miguel Angel set out to undertake the necessary transformations, both with respect to staff as well as departmental infrastructure. As for finances, he reviewed all the books, the level and justification of expenses, and rounded off the numbers to make the pertinent adjustments to the budget. To Rita, these changes seemed overwhelming, while to Rocío they did not appear as radical as the changes he had witnessed at the Punta Alegre sugar mill, for instance. As he puts it: "The sugar mills had to be reorganized and modernized," referring to the system of administrative control.

In any event, Loeb's plan was under way. His dream was to model Cuban Atlantic's sugar mills after those owned by Sucesión. To achieve that, he had found the key man and placed him at the helm of Cuban Atlantic.

When Rita's temporary assignment was over, he made every attempt to retain Lawrence's secretary, whom he had inherited. But he did not work comfortably with her, and asked Rita to come back and take that position. Lawrence's secretary was very gracious, as she herself agreed that she and Miguel Angel really did not work well together. She assured Rita that the situation was fine with her, and she stepped aside.

Miguel Angel loved his office. He could see the ocean from every angle, as the building was situated at the very corner of a forked intersection. The ocean reminded him of Punta Alegre. Rita helped him with the decoration. "There was nothing extraordinary about the décor. His style was austere with a very masculine touch." She contributed a soft touch of her own: a fresh rose bud on his desk every morning.

Miguel Angel Falla set out to strengthen and renovate the production infrastructure of the sugar mills. Where he could, he promoted the existing staff; in other instances, he called on former colleagues to join the company. This generated tensions with his cousin "Alín", who felt that Miguel Angel was strengthening Cuban Atlantic at the expense of Sucesión's sugar mills. Miguel Angel gave his cousin an acceptable explanation about the recruitment of Rocío and Juan M. de la Cruz. Those two transfers angered "Alín" more than any other. The move from the Punta Adelaida to Cuban Atlantic's Lugareño as office manager meant a promotion for de la Cruz, who in two years would be promoted to administrator. As for Rocío, he reminded "Alín" that he had left the Punta Alegre for reasons that were strictly personal.

The Hershey concerns particularly worried Miguel Angel. According to Rocío, Hershey was a complex company. In addition to owning three sugar mills, Hershey "owned a combination of parallel industries: a raw sugar plant; a refinery; a peanut oil factory; saisal and tackle factories; electric railroads; an electric power company; and several others." Hershey became the prime target of his reform strategy. Along with his right-hand man, he sent a team of accountants and engineers to conduct a full inspection; he even brought experts from New York.

He was sure of what the Hershey review would reveal, and couldn't get it off his mind. One evening he got home and in passing asked Julia what she had done with his paycheck. "Well, I gave the home care nuns money to buy a van so they can travel back and forth from the convent." That sounded fine to Miguel Angel. "And what else?" "Well, I also paid for their driving lessons because if they can't drive, how can they take advantage of the van?" Miguel Angel wasn't really taking inventory of Julia's expenses. He was playing a game with his wife. "And, what else?" "Well, finally I asked our servants to ask me for something they really wanted, and I went out and bought it for them." Miguel Angel shook his head gently as he thought to himself: "This wife of mine will never change!"

His entrepreneurial instinct never failed him: the situation at Hershey was as serious as he had foreseen. He immediately advised the Board of Directors in New York "to get rid of the white elephant, and to keep only the raw sugar enterprise," according to Rocío, who adds: "Julio Lobo signed an option to buy."

In the course of the Hershey deal, Miguel Angel traveled to New York several times, and often took his daughter Elena with him. Elena could come and go freely, for unlike her sisters, she was still single. Elena handled those social circles with great charm, and related very well to the wives of the Board members. She befriended Mrs. John Loeb, whom the family had nicknamed Peter due to her resemblance to the fairytale character, Peter Pan.

The youngest daughter of Cuban Atlantic's president recalls that her father said the rosary on the airplane each time he traveled. She remembers one time he had not finished saying the last set of Hail Mary's by the time the plane landed. He had to rush through the prayers so as not to be left all alone inside the plane.

Elena remembers the time she could not accompany her father, and she was miserable for having been left behind. To make up for it, her father bought her the most fancy and expensive dress he could find. As she opened the present, she thought to herself: "this gown cost daddy more than the trip and his stay at the Waldorf Astoria." She didn't know what to do with the dress. It was typical of her father: generous beyond belief, but like all men, an impractical shopper."

**** ** ****

"I was eager to sell Hershey for three reasons. First, I was worried about Castro's activities in the hills; second, the Falla organization were experts at growing cane and running raw sugar mills, but had no experience in refining sugar or marketing it; and third, in 1956 and 1957, the combination of the Hungarian uprising and the Suez crisis, a poor European beet harvest, and drought conditions in the Caribbean touched off a speculative boom that doubled the world price of sugar. Conditions could not have been better for selling. Julio [Lobo] was willing to pay a premium, and as [according to Miguel Angel's analysis] the refinery was not only very expensive to run but also needed new equipment, it all fit together".

Miguel Angel's recommendation was heeded. But as Loeb himself indicates, it wasn't just the administrative reasons and the state of the company that led to the negotiating table. Political unrest in Cuba, Fidel Castro's uprising in the mountains, and other reasons of an international nature, all conspired to hasten the final decision.

Julio Lobo was given an ultimatum: if he wanted to buy, the closing had to take place before midnight, December 31, 1957, or the deal was off. Lobo showed up on that day in the company of his lawyers.

As president of the Board, Miguel Angel chaired the board of shareholders at the negotiations. Miguel Angel's account of the meeting as told to Rocío indicates that the agreement would not be ready before midnight, the time the purchase option was due to expire. The transaction was so important, however, that everyone in the room agreed to pay no mind when one of the lawyers, seeing that it was only minutes before the clock struck midnight, stood up and stopped the hands of the clock that presided over the room. When the agreement was finally signed, he stood up again, and turned it back on. A few minutes later, the clock struck Midnight and rang twelve times. Everyone raised their glasses to cheer in the New Year and to celebrate the end of the negotiations. It was 4 o'clock in the morning, January 1st, 1958.

**** ** ****

Miguel Angel exercised utmost tact when dealing with his employees. He knew their personal problems and tried to help them in times of need. Juan M. de la Cruz is a witness to this. He was at the Ministry of Labor one afternoon discussing a new contract with the union, when all of a sudden the attorney interrupted the meeting. He informed the group that at the behest of Mr. Falla the meeting would be postponed until Mr. Cruz returned from Morón where his mother was to undergo an emergency operation. To this day, Cruz does not know how Miguel Angel learned of this, for since learning the troubling news, he had not shared it with anyone.

Rita Blain had a similar predicament regarding her father, Dr. Eduardo Moreno, who had undergone surgery. Miguel Angel went to the hospital to see him, and to offer his assistance in whatever was needed. She conveys an edifying and humane picture of her boss: "When he entered the room, my father was still woozy from the anesthesia. He greeted Mr. Falla saying 'How are you, doctor?' to which Miguel Angel answered 'I am not a doctor'. My father, realizing he had mistaken Miguel Angel for a physician, said to him, 'Good. Anyone can become a doctor, but gentlemen are born that way." That was a most ingenious out, which flattered his daughter's boss.

Rita, who knew him so very well, and who, as his secretary, shared endless hours of work with him, remembers many anecdotes that portray him at his best with regard to his staff. Perhaps the story that best illustrates his will to motivate his employees, and his sense of humility, is the one she tells about a dinner he organized for the personnel of Cuban Atlantic. She suggested that the comptroller and other department heads sit at his table. He had another idea: to make a seating arrangement that was more democratic so everyone felt equally important. "And, please, make sure Mr. Gener sits next to me," he added. Mr. Gener "was a mail-room employee."

Cuba's internal affairs were troubling indeed. It was the daily topic of conversation at the Falla residence. Julia was shocked by the televised summary trials and executions, and kept asking her husband how it was all going to end. Everyone asked the same question within financial and business circles: What would be the outcome of all this? No one knew for sure, but the worst was feared. In anticipation of a grim future, every industrialist, including the heads of Cuban Atlantic, halted implementation of new plans. It seemed best to wait and see.

Miguel Angel's experience with the Sierra Maestra rebels was only second-hand. He knew only what he was hearing. Rocío recalls his reaction when a friend [the administrator of a sugar mill in Oriente province] told him about what the rebels encamped around his area were up to. "Miguel Angel was speechless after hearing the accounts of the rebels' demands for money and revolutionary taxes, and the instances of extortion, theft, and execution by firing squad."

And their worst fears came true, a veritable Armageddon. Fidel Castro usurped power on January 1st, 1959, and launched his demented program of arbitrary measures. He not only drowned Cuba in an ocean of blood, but also made Cubans equal in collective poverty.

The first attacks felt at Cuban Atlantic were related to the Law of Agrarian Reform, promulgated on May 17, 1959. The objective of this law was to put an end to large private land holdings, or *latifundios*. It mattered little that the State would turn the land into public *latifundios* in the form of farm cooperatives doomed to failure from the onset. The sugar mill plantations were confiscated. The first incidents of friction between the United States and Castro took place. It was the dawn of chaos. "I went to see the recently appointed American ambassador, Philip Bonzal, and expressed my opinion that Castro was an out-and-out Communist and that there was no way of doing business with him," narrates John L. Loeb in his memoirs.

Now Miguel Angel had to submit his reports directly to the National Institute of Agrarian Reform, which now was in charge of all confiscated lands. Castro himself oversaw the Institute's operations. Rocío remembers the bitter and difficult moments experienced during that initial period of the Communist takeover. Miguel Angel described as "baffling and depressing" the news he received daily about the administrative collapse of the sugar mills as the supporters of the new regime ransacked and took them over.

"The news he received from the sugar mills were troubling," says his friend and associate. Rocío recalls a road trip they took to the Alarcón farm in Camagüey. There, Miguel Angel corroborated with his own eyes the state of total anarchy generated by Castro's new policies whereby people felt empowered to appropriate for themselves the product of someone else's hard work.

There was nothing anyone could do. Miguel Angel decided to move his family to safety and arranged to bring them to the United States.

**** ** ****

On a wonderful sunny August day 1960, Miguel Angel boarded the ferry docked at Havana harbor. With him were his wife Julia, daughter Elena, two of his grandchildren (Cristina's son and one daughter), the children's nanny, the nanny's daughter, Julia's pet dog *Huesito*, and her 57 canaries. He wanted to call as little attention to himself as possible, and so delegated to Elena all the arrangements for the trip. Fifty-seven canaries notwithstanding, there was nothing unusual about them: they looked like just another family going to Miami on a pleasure trip.

No sooner had she boarded the ferry that Elena, Miguel Angel's youngest daughter, ran into Ben. He was taking his pregnant wife Jan to Florida to give birth to the couple's youngest daughter, Louise. She was happy to see him, but was very discrete about it. Just knowing that he was on board the ferry gave her goose pimples. All the events of recent months flashed before her eyes. She thought she was leaving all that behind.

Benjamin C. Evans was the young political attaché at the U.S. Embassy in Havana. He and Oscar Echevarría were very close friends, and both collaborated in anti-Communist underground activities. Working underground requires contacts that can serve as couriers and enable meetings at a third party's house without raising suspicion. Such links are effective only if all persons involved are friends.

Elena had returned to Cuba after five years of boarding school at the Sacred Heart near Philadelphia. Upon her return, her strict mother made her attend secretarial school. At the same time, at the behest of Father Spiralli, she volunteered at the "Dispensario San Lorenzo" caring for the sick. She was so devoted to this work that she thought of becoming a nurse, but Julia didn't like the idea one bit. At the onset of the revolution, and perhaps anticipating the future, Elena's parents encouraged her to get some work experience. She found herself a job at the American Embassy.

There she met Ben, the newly arrived CIA undercover agent assigned to the post of political attaché. Ben thought that Elena would be the perfect link between him and Oscar, who she was going out with at the time, and would eventually marry. Not only did Elena work at the embassy, but she also lived across the street from Oscar. Ben felt that this arrangement would not put Elena at risk.

Suddenly Elena remembered all the details, the times she had to put aside propriety when she had to see Oscar for an emergency, and she would call him up to arrange that they meet for a "snack" at the Carmelo Restaurant on Calzada Street. Her imagination got the best of her when she ran into Ben. "What if they discover my connection with Ben and Oscar precisely now, when I am leaving Cuba?" she thought.

A few steps away, her mother had stopped to talk to a member of the crew. Elena went by her cabin, and then went to see her mother in hers. She only stayed a few seconds, for she was too emotional, had too many things on her mind to put up with Julia's traveling zoo: in addition to the dog, her mother's 57 canaries were all inside the cabin. At least their cages were covered and they weren't singing. Neither could she and the birds make each other more nervous than they already were.

The ferry sailed off. A few knots into ocean, she heard her name being called over the loudspeakers. "Report to the bridge," the voice commanded. Her legs began to shake: Castro's secret police, the G-2, must have come for her. But Ben was standing close by. "Smile. Relax," he said taking her firmly by her elbow to give her confidence. He, too, was worried about Elena. He thought about Oscar, who was like a brother to him. Ben stood by the young woman, thinking that perhaps his diplomatic immunity would come in handy. Cuba and the U.S. had not severed diplomatic relations yet. Ben was the type who never lost his cool, no matter what. At that moment he was conscious of the role he had asked Elena to play. Ben thought of how she had lent Oscar her Riley[4] so Oscar could use the car to visit him in the evening when needed, and to transport people, who were being chased by the secret police, to a safe place.

The ship's captain was waiting for them on the bridge. He said: "May I inform you, Miss, that of the four cabins you requested, I can only assign you one extra cabin so that you don't have to share yours with the canaries. I will gladly show it to you if you follow me."

The rest of the journey went smoothly. They arrived in Miami and registered at the University Inn, located on U.S.1, a main highway, in Coral Gables. Everyone gathered at the lobby while Julia filled out the registration forms. The clerk at the front desk looked up and pointed to the nanny and her young daughter. "Hotel policy does not allow Blacks as guests." Elena tells best her mother's reaction. She stared at the clerk with one of her "if looks could kill" glance, and spoke to him in her excellent English: "Young man, I am renting three rooms in this hotel for a period of three months, and I don't care if they are green or black. They are staying with us." That is the story of how Julia, with her quick answers, her humanity and her wit, advanced the cause against racism in the summer of 1960.

**** ** ****

Now that his family was safe, Miguel Angel returned to Cuba. As the captain at the helm of the business, he had to fight for his ship and most especially, for his crew. Back in July, before the family journey to Miami, he had gotten a head start by calling a meeting of all sugar mill administrators at company headquarters in Havana. There, they were apprised of the situation. Juan de la Cruz tells how Miguel Angel handed each one of them a check for $5,000. "Consider it a loan: if nothing happens here, you are bound to return the money when the time comes." He didn't want his best men to be left jobless and penniless if and when Castro confiscated the sugar mills. And confiscate them Castro did. As Juan de la

[4] Compact but elegant British car of which there were only two in Havana.

Elena possing at her mother's request when Castro's tanks went through Kholy on January 1959.

Cruz, administrator of the Lugareño sugar mill, narrates, the Lugareño was confiscated in August.

In October 1960, smack in the middle of hurricane season, Castro dealt the last blow to free enterprise and private industry in the island, when he ordered the expropriation of all domestic and foreign-owned companies. Most of the foreign-owned were American.

There was nowhere to turn, and only one way out. That afternoon, Miguel Angel gave Rita a briefcase with instructions to have the chauffeur deliver it to his home. That evening, Miguel Angel phoned his secretary. "Rita, I need that briefcase to take with me. Tomorrow morning I leave."

Rocío met him at the house. He stayed with Miguel Angel all night, and accompanied him to the airport. He waited until the plane took off. This time, there was no return date on Miguel Angel's ticket. The flight had not departed yet when the phone rang at the Kohly house. The cook answered: it was Julia calling her husband. The wise woman answered her calmly: "Mr. Falla went to Mass, and said he wasn't coming back for breakfast." Miguel Angel always came home for breakfast! Julia got the message.

* *** ** ****

"I haven't had any news from Cuba, and sometimes it's better not to receive any. It's useless to get upset. Fidel will be toppled. But, what will be left after everything is destroyed? I understand that sugar industry salaries will be lowered by 40 percent."

"He has destroyed Cuba selling sugar at 3 cents or less, there's an incredible surplus in the world, and all inventory has been depleted, and cash assets have been stolen. Who can rebuild the sugar industry? I feel very pessimistic."

(Excerpts from Miguel Angel Falla's personal correspondence)

What would be Miguel Angel's last trip must have been a terrible, desolate and infinitely saddening journey. He was leaving behind a legacy of years of hard work and sacrifice, generation after generation. Shoulder to shoulder, his father and uncle, his brothers and cousins, and he, not the least of them, had worked very hard to build an empire that was no more. He could not understand such travesty of destiny.

He must have said the rosary several times during the journey, as he did every time he traveled. He was a different type of immigrant, not the kind that came to the United States in search of wealth. On the contrary, he was leaving his fortune behind, his patrimony shattered and in the hands of strangers. His elders' luck had been quite different. They had come across the oceans and were able to build a dream. They emigrated at a young enough age to be able to start anew. Their bones didn't hurt like his hurt now. They had endless energy, where he was very tired. There would be no second chance for him, he thought. He had come full circle.

The feel of his rosary beads between his fingers as he recited the litany of Our Fathers and Hail Mary's, restored his serenity and gave him peace of mind. The

Postcard sent by Miguel Angel to de la Cruz, in 1964. It is a souvenir from Julia's successful attempt at integration.

beads had been blessed. Perhaps exile was not irreversible. Maybe in a few months things would return to normalcy. "We'll return, you'll see," he pondered to himself. God would not allow this murderous, arbitrary Communist system to last a lifetime, he thought. He gathered strength from the depths of his heart. "Yes, we'll return to Cuba."

**** ** ****

Once reunited, the family decided to move from Miami to Darien, Connecticut, a few months later. They wanted to be closer to Julia, their second daughter, and the grandchildren. Elena got a job in New York and visited her parents on the weekends. They also saw Rita, who met up with them as soon as she arrived from Cuba.

Miguel Angel worried quite a lot about the associates he had left behind in Cuba. He kept abreast of their individual circumstances, and they wrote to each other regularly. Juan M. de la Cruz and Saturio Rocío bear witness to his concern. "I don't want you to take any personal risks, under any circumstances. Nothing can be done about what's happened," he advised Juan, while he would write to Rocío counseling him on how to preserve the few assets he had left in Cuba. Rocío would report back, and also thanked him for the Riley that Elena had given him before she left, and which was a great help to him now. It was the same Riley Oscar used in the underground.

Rocío managed to obtain a tourist visa and left Cuba with his wife and children. Miguel Angel picked him up at the airport, and brought him to live in his house. Later he accompanied him to file for political asylum. Things did not go well for Rocío in Miami, and he moved to New York.

Getting Juan M. de la Cruz and his family out of Cuba was a saga. Miguel Angel paid John Loeb a visit to ask him for help, and he recruited his daughter Elena who had access to people with influence. Miguel Angel also showered Cruz with favors, especially when it came to learning English and finding a decent job.

Rocío and de la Cruz were not the exception, but the rule. From Miguel Angel's letters we know he reached out and helped those he found deserving of his help, like he did in Cuba. Juan de la Cruz states: "I have saved with great care several of his letters; from them one can see how he always worried about his friends. I am honored to have been one of them… I trust they will serve to tell his daughters about an aspect of their father's life that perhaps they did not get to appreciate."

Miguel Angel knew that Rocío and de la Cruz had arrived empty-handed, and he asked Loeb himself to grant them a remuneration for their services. He argued, successfully, that both men had been executives of Cuban Atlantic. He got Loeb to agree: Rocío and de la Cruz were rewarded.

Reading Miguel Angel's letters allows the reader to enter the more intimate, inner world of exile. They reveal him to be optimistic at times, depressed at others. On October 27, 1960 he wrote: "I haven't been feeling well, and I am so unhappy and annoyed with everything, that I do only what I must. It's partly indolence, and lack of interest, apathy, or else the blows have been too many… The government has stolen all the buildings. It has stolen whatever was left, our income… And still, we must thank God that we are in this country."

Like all Cuban exiles, he did his own countdown of how many months Castro had left in power. He had his hopes set on returning shortly to Cuba.

While he waited for that to happen, he was active in the anti-Castro movement in exile. As can be surmised from his correspondence, he joined the Sertoma Cuban

Club, and was on its Board of Directors. The organization did a great job in helping the refugees; Julia worked as a volunteer in the organization. In a letter dated December 25th 1965, he wrote how his wife distributed clothes to the new refugees, talked to them, and gave them hope.

That same letter reveals his political stance: "All of us have to do our part in some anti-Castro and anti-Communist organization."

Exile never made him bitter and never ruined his endless sense of humor. His niece Cristina de Cárdenas still laughs when she remembers the day she and her uncle went for their driver's license test. Miguel Angel never drove when he was in Havana, and at the sugar mill he was never too good at it. Elena used to make fun of him: "Daddy, did the tree move and get in your way?" To obtain that driver's license was one of his goals since arriving in Miami. After they finished taking the test, they met outside. Cristina de Cárdenas beat him to it, and showing him her license, said bragging: "I got it!" He surprised her when he humored her back: "Well, I didn't...but don't worry, I will try again!" They kept talking and he joked all along about all the mistakes he had made. "That was Uncle Miguel Angel for you!" adds Cristina.

His correspondence also reveals his incursions in the stock market. "I think the market will continue downward, but it will recover," he wrote to Juan de la Cruz on June 7th, 1967. His goal was to remain active investing his money, while passing the time trying his luck. In another letter he confesses: "After all, this is what gambling is all about!"

It is around that time that Miguel Angel returns to Miami. He was tired of living up north. He also wanted to be in a more Cuban environment. Or perhaps he was beginning to worry about his health. In a letter dated "Saturday the 14th, 1970" – no specific month mentioned – he wrote: "My heart condition must have improved, for I have been taken off medication."

In early February, Elena stopped in Miami on her way to Long Island. Her daughters Patty and Maggie came with her. She spent a few days with her parents. Before she left, Miguel Angel gave her his pocket watch. "I know you would prefer your mother's, but you can have mine." Around that time Miguel Angel had felt severe chest pain. A concerned Maggie asked her grandmother Julia to look after him. "Take good care of abuelito, grandma. I don't want him to die."

The following week, on February 8th, 1973, he, his wife and daughter Cristina were sitting in their Coral Gables apartment, located in the building Miguel Angel owned at number 240 Valencia. Other members of the family lived in the same building. While Julia and Cristina were getting ready to take Susana, the dog, to the vet, Miguel Angel felt a burning sensation in his throat. He remembered there was a special sale at Woolworth, and so he announced: "I am off to Miracle Mile to buy some Listerine."

He went into the store and walked up and down the aisles. Medicines and Listerine were toward the back. He took the largest bottle. "Julia will say sarcastically that I bought Listerine for all of Coral Gables," he thought. Miguel Angel was in no hurry. He walked up to the cash register. No sooner had he paid the cashier, he felt a terrible pain in his chest. He keeled over, holding his chest with his right hand while instinctively putting his left hand inside his pocket where he kept his rosary beads. He couldn't stand it, and collapsed on the floor.

People all around him started screaming for help. But he only heard his own voice, talking from afar, like a distant echo: "Juan, when we return to Cuba, I will buy a small sugar mill, and you will manage it."

**** ** ****

Author's Note

I wish to thank Carlos Alberto Montaner and Oscar A. Echevarría for the opportunity to write this biographical essay about Miguel Angel Falla, a most prominent figure in Cuba's sugar industry. It is difficult to escape the bewitching story that was his life. For that reason and for others that were stated earlier, I was not able to undertake a more extensive study of his environment, nor research the political and social aspects of Cuban reality during his lifetime, including the battles fought by the sugar sector labor unions. Such study, which would include the lifetime of the ancestors that lay the foundations of the Falla Gutiérrez patrimony, would be a requirement sine qua non of a more scholarly text.

Neither was that history the aim of this book. Cuba's "other face" has been very much discussed and intentionally distorted by Fidel Castro, inside Cuba, and by his supporters abroad. Also, it has become a habit of the academic left to blow out of proportion pre-1959 events. They forget that in those days, the bosses sat down with the workers to discuss their claims, and in the ultimate analysis, the workers could go on strike. Those were the advantages of democracy; they are the workers' rights that totalitarian regimes deny their people.

The goal of this project was to narrate a different story that revolved around a specific person and to highlight in the process the achievements of Cuba's pre-1959 entrepreneurial class that empowered the nation to compete on par with the most advanced economies in the world market. Cuba had one of the highest perspectives of development in the entire American continent. In the words of American economist, Byron White, Cuba "compared with Denmark." The U.S. Commerce Department also reported that Cuba was not an underdeveloped country in the strict sense of the word.

The sugar mills owned by Sucesión Falla Gutiérrez did not fit the mold of other sugar mills where workers were exploited. The Falla Gutiérrez organization did not subscribe to working conditions of marked inequality. In his book, John L. Loeb himself states: "The Fallas were progressive people and they supported our wish to improve the living conditions of our own workers." Had it not been for the national tragedy sparked by the 1959 revolution, many of those improvements would have been implemented, like so many other laws on a national level whose enforcement would have been made possible by Cuba's own sustainable economic growth, and the positive influence from our neighbor up north.

Ena Curnow
September 2002
Translated by *Ileana Fuentes.*

Chapter II

Remembrances of Miguel Angel Falla

Remembrances of Miguel Angel Falla

If I had to title these introductory words I would have chosen "In Their Own Words", since a formal introduction might have run the risk of unveiling the content of the chapter when highlighting or contrasting some points. Having done that would have deprived the reader of first-hand expressions by our five interlocutors in their own very personal style.

Consequently with the above, my purpose is only to emphasize the existence of these testimonials, the way in which they came into being, and the message they offer on their subject.

I have deduced three important elements from the reading of these testimonials.

The first thing is the spontaneity and enthusiasm in the reaction of my initial source: Rita Moreno de Blain; and later, the eagerness of Saturio Rocío, who quickly garnered the contribution of Juan de la Cruz, Angel Naveiras and José Medardo Pino who, spontaneously added their testimonials.

The reader will also relate to my appreciation of the clarity of the recollections even after more than forty years. Likewise of importance is the evidence that for these individuals their unique motivation is sincere devotion to Miguel Angel. Obviously they do not need, nor expect, material benefits by virtue of their participation in this homage.

Finally, I want to highlight how the five witnesses coincide on the managerial and human personality of Miguel Angel. This has permitted the biographer, Ena Curnow, to intertwine a concise biographical sketch of Miguel Angel, incorporating the other sources listed in the Introduction All provide proof of the loyalty and devotion that this strong but kind "colono" and Manager inspired. I have purpusely avoided using the term Hacendado, as it traditionally applied only to sugar mill owners.

Without other preambles, the Testimonials in their own words.

Some memories about Miguel Angel Falla

Rita Moreno de Blain

When our friend Oscar Echevarría told us about his project to start a collection on pre-Castro businessmen and his plan to include a biographical sketch of Miguel Angel Falla woven from the recollections of relatives and friends, we thought it was a terrific idea. Oscar plans to give the book to his wife Elena Falla, youngest daughter of Miguel Angel, for her birthday.

Oscar asked me to contribute to this document since I worked with Miguel Angel at the Atlántica del Golfo Sugar Company from 1954 to 1960. In 1960 Miguel Angel and his family left Cuba; my family and I left a few months later.

How I came to meet Mr. Falla

In 1954, after an exhaustive search to fill the post of Chairman of the Company, the Atlantic decided that Miguel Angel fulfilled the requirements for such an important position.

In those days I had already been working at the Atlantic for six years. I was entrusted with the responsibility of helping Miguel Angel become familiar with the various departments and with the staff of the Atlantic. Initially it was meant to be a temporary assignment for me, only for the duration of his transition to the Chairmanship/Presidency, which was estimated to take three or four months. Due to circumstances that arose later, those three months turned into more than five years of working together, which gave me a chance to get to know him in depth.

From the start I was happy to accept the assignment; it would give me a chance to work for a man of Miguel Angel's accomplishments, prestige and experience, from whom I would surely have much to learn. I was not disappointed.

Our first meeting was even more significant than we both expected, since a collaborative business relationship developed between us almost from the beginning. It was based on respect and lasted until the end of our business collaboration – and then continued later in the United States on a personal level.

Both exiled in New York, we stayed in touch. The friendship extended to his family, in particular his daughter Elena Falla, who is like a sister to me and who, I am sure, would make Miguel Angel proud as she does all of us who love her.

The noble sentiments of Mr. Falla

I remember how Miguel Angel Falla contributed on a large scale to significant changes in the administrative part of the Atlantic, as well as in staff relations. On the occasion of a dinner with the staff of the Atlantic, I helped Miguel Angel arrange the tables. I suggested we seat the Treasurer, department heads, etc., at his table, but he said, "No, Rita, it would be better to distribute the people in a more democratic way, so all of us will feel like equals, and please seat Gener by my side." Gener was an employee from the Mail Department. On that occasion and many others, Miguel Angel would demonstrate how caring he could be. (I have attached photos of that event.)

At the luncheon in the Hotel Havana Hilton: June 30, 1958 From left to right: Mr. Miguel Gener, Mr. Miguel A. Falla Alvarez, Miss Hortensia del Pino, Mr. Bienvenido Rodríguez, Dr. Pedro Pablo de la Cámara and Mr. Leonardo Fandiño.

From left to right Eng. Michelena, Mr. Rodríguez, Mrs. Rita Moreno de Blain, Mr. Naya, Mr. Miguel Badia, Mrs. Noemí Valero, Mr. Campanería, Mrs. Kiki de la Vega, Mr. Charmont, unknown.

The concept in which he was held

I remember another incident that showed, in a brief exchange, the high regard in which many other people held Mr. Falla, including my father, Dr. Eduardo Moreno. When my father had to undergo surgery, Miguel Angel went to visit him the same day of the operation to offer his support and assistance. He arrived just when my father was beginning to recover from the anesthesia. When he entered the room, my father, who was still groggy from the drug, greeted him by saying, "How are you, doctor?" – evidently thinking he was one of the doctors. Miguel Angel answered, "I am not a doctor." To this my father responded, "Well, even better. Anyone can become a doctor, but you have to be born a gentleman." I think that says it all.

I definitely agree with Oscar on his perception, among others, that Miguel Angel was one of the key pillars of the Cuban economy. He was a man who, despite his vast knowledge of the Sugar Industry, gained first in the Falla family's sugar mills, then as President of the Cuban Atlantic, always remained a down-to earth, gentlemanly, classy person. I feel honored to have known him.

My Tribute to Miguel Angel

Juan M. de la Cruz

I am one of those people who consider themselves privileged to have known Miguel Angel Falla for over thirty years.

It is not my intention to highlight my own personal history through this account; should I bring it up, it is only because these are experiences I shared with him. I trust these will be of value to his daughters in allowing them to know a facet of their father that they perhaps did not have a chance to appreciate.

I have zealously preserved several of his letters, which bear witness to his constant concern for his friends, among which I have the honor of including myself.

The Central Adelaida, my University

I had the pleasure of working with Miguel Angel first in the *Adelaida* sugar mill and then at *Lugareño*. I learned much from him by observing what he did and by listening to his advice. Someone asked me once which school I graduated from, and I replied, "I graduated from UCA." The expression on the speaker's face showed no recognition at all, so I explained the joke by spelling out the acronym: "Universidad del Central Adelaida" – "Adelaida Sugar Mill University."

At both sugar mills I have mentioned, I had the opportunity to observe how Mr. Falla made improvements not only in sugar production, but also in the fields, where he experimented with different sugarcane varieties, more adequate fertilizers, etc.

Miguel Angel's sense of humor

If I had to describe Mr. Falla in just a few words, I would say he was a man with a strong personality and a decisive, but kind way of thinking, who enjoyed doing favors for others and was concerned about the well-being of all those who worked with him. Many times I saw him ask humble mill workers about a sick relative and do countless favors for sugar mill families.

I remember two or three humorous anecdotes from the *Adelaida* sugar mill, which reveals his genial nature:

Carbonated mineral water or kerosene?

There was a new guy filling in for the office messenger, and Miguel Angel asked him to bring a “botella de agua con gas”, or soda pop. Without missing a beat, the young man ran to the commercial department and returned with a bottle of kerosene, the kind that served as fuel for the torches used to light up the fields. As soon as Miguel Angel took the bag, he recognized the peculiar smell and reproached the fellow, “What did I ask you for, carbonated soda or carbon oil?”

Too much rain or eight inches of toad?

That same young man, a temporary employee unfamiliar with the office routine, had forgotten to write down the reading from the rain gauge. When Miguel Angel noticed that he had not received that report, he asked the young man to go measure the rain that had fallen that day. A while later the fellow came back with the information: according to him, precipitation had been approximately eight inches. Knowing that so much rainfall was not possible, Mr. Falla asked him to go back and take the measurement again; making sure the rain gauge was clean. You can imagine the laughter inspired by the novice office worker when he explained he had found a toad inside the instrument.

Félix’s small gun

Another anecdote: The man in charge of maintaining the wooded areas around Chicola (the port used for Adelaida’s outbound sugar production) was a very responsible man. As a reward for his work and loyalty, Miguel Angel wanted to help him acquire a small sugarcane *colonia*, or farm. The man arrived at the office one day in a very cheerful mood with a small gun holstered at his waist. Miguel Angel took one look at it and said mockingly, “Félix, you’re so small – if you shoot at a man with that little revolver, he might kick you to death. If you want to use a revolver, buy a real one, so if someone’s going to attack you, you can actually shoot him.”

Small mistake, no! Major blunder!

I was still new in the sugar mill office; I had been transferred there from the commercial department office. One day Mr. Falla called me into his office to check his calculations of per-cubic-meter cost of dredging a canal. He had all the necessary information: width, average depth and length, as well as hours of labor, fuel consumption, etc. I took all the data he had compiled and went to my office. As soon as I started checking the first calculations, I realized there was an error that was affecting the successive calculations. I looked at my numbers several times to make sure they were correct, and I was satisfied. The next day, as soon as he arrived in the office, Mr. Falla inquired about the accuracy of his calculations. Since I was young and it was the first time I was dealing with him directly, I did not know how to tell him about his mistake. After several attempts with different approaches to the truth, finally I just informed him, "I think there has been a small mistake…" and pointed to the error I had discovered. He went over my figures carefully and after comparing them to his, he exclaimed, "It's not a small mistake… It's a major blunder…" And he thanked me.

A manager that trusted and stood up for his team

Calculating the milling quotas

When the law regulating the sugar harvest was first passed, I came up with my own estimate for the quotas that would apply to each mill, though certainly there were factors that could not be calculated based on the published statistics. Mr. Falla, who was aware of the work I had done, called the manager of the *Narcisa* sugar mill – which milled sugarcane from two farms under his ownership, *La Loma* and *Blanquizal*. He inquired about the quotas for these farms, but the figures he was given struck him as inadequate. He protested the quota assigned to him and informed his colleague in less than gracious terms that he was sending someone over who was familiar with the procedure, to teach him how to calculate the quotas. After the heated exchange on the telephone, he asked me to visit the *Narcisa* sugar mill with my calculations and point out their error to them. Once again, Mr. Falla was showing his trust in me.

My move to the Atlántica

Miguel Angel had already been made president of the Cuban Atlantic Sugar Company when he visited the *Adelaida* mill and asked me if I would be willing to go work with him should there be a vacancy. I replied without hesitation that it would be a pleasure for me to work under him again. He told me there was a vacancy for an office manager at the *Rosario* sugar mill at that time, but he would not suggest that I take it because the mill would very likely be sold, and I would no longer be under his protection. A short time later, through his assistant, I was summoned to Havana to receive an offer for the position of office manager of the *Lugareño* sugar mill. Two years later he appointed me manager of the sugar mill.

My mother's surgery

I was in Havana discussing a new contract with the Union at the Ministry of Labor, when my mother required emergency surgery. Although I did not tell anyone about my troubles and continued with the worker-employer talks, to my surprise, when the day's session was about to begin, the lawyer who was advising me asked that at the request of Mr. Falla the debates be suspended until my return from Morón, where my presence was required immediately due to my mother's failing health. The workers' delegation of the *Lugareño* sugar mill, the provincial officials and C.T.C. [Confederation of Cuban Workers] representatives all agreed to his request. That was Miguel Angel; he did not worry about the reaction of those workers' organizations or how much it would cost to delay the labor talks; he just wanted me, as a son, to be at my ill mother's side. Such a gesture is not easily forgotten.

$5,000 loan for our tranquility

At the first signs that U.S. sugar companies were to be confiscated by Fidel Castro's government, Mr. Falla called the managers of all the sugar mills to the Havana offices and personally gave us each a check for $5,000. He advised us, "Look at this money as a loan; if nothing happens, you are under the obligation to pay it back when the time comes." He was clearly attempting to provide anticipated relief from our precarious financial situation when we lost our jobs.

Nationalization and Exile, Miguel Angel always up to date

"Don't take any chances, there is no remedy for this"

The difficult political situation in the country resulted in my arrest and transfer to Nuevitas. Fortunately, I was able to ride out the storm without major complications. When Mr. Falla learned of my arrest, he sent me a message asking me to call him as soon as I got back to the sugar mill. "I don't want you to take any personal risks under any circumstances," he said, "this situation is beyond repair…"

There are more opportunities in New York, come with me

The mill was confiscated in August of 1960, and I immediately made the decision to come to the United States. I had all my documents in order. Mr. Falla, who was already living in Miami, left a message for me to call him as soon as I arrived in this country. And so I did. One piece of advice he gave me was not to stay in Miami but rather to work my way up to New York where I would have a better chance of finding opportunities to move forward. He happened to be traveling to New York around those days too, so we took the trip together. He even invited me to stay at his hotel, which I gladly accepted.

Board of Directors, we have to help our exiled Executives

At a company executives' meeting, Mr. Falla requested Mr. John Loeb to compensate those members of the Atlántica del Golfo's senior management team who had come to the United States. Days later he handed me a check that was very useful to me because I had only been able to bring $150 with me when I left Cuba.

Illusions of return

On later trips to New York, Mr. Falla would either call me on the phone or we would get together in person. He was always interested in knowing how I was doing at work. He gave me lots of advice. The last time we had lunch together he confided, "When we go back to Cuba I plan to buy a small sugar mill for you to manage." He never accepted the idea that we would never return.

My Memories of Miguel Angel Falla

Saturio Rocío Chávez

To properly respond to the request for a contribution to a book, which would weave together an image of Miguel Angel Falla, represents for me a rewarding but difficult feat. Rewarding because, as we will soon see, he was part of my personal and professional life from my very first job at Central Adelaida until I moved to New York. Difficult not because it stirs up very deep personal feelings, but because to cover the life of such a key player in the Cuban Sugar Industry, which at that time was the World's leader, in so few lines, is hard. I will attempt to present my memories covering the different facets of his personality, as a man and as a manager, through personal anecdotes to which I was witness and participant.

A royal entrance at the Adelaida

My first encounter with Miguel Angel Falla took place a few days before Christmas Eve in 1941. I had seen him on a few occasions before at 10:00 a.m. Mass at the Morón parish church, in the company of his wife and three daughters. I had never exchanged a single word with him, not even a look.

I was looking for a job and learned there was a vacancy in the offices of the Adelaida Sugar Mill[1]. On the train on my way to the interview, I happened to run into the bishop of Camagüey, who was involved in mission work in the areas around the mill. I had been a seminarist for five years and, although I had dropped out of priest school, I was on good terms with Monsignor Pérez Serantes.

During my interview with the head of the agricultural department, my lack of experience as an office clerk did not go unnoticed; however, he left the decision of whether to hire me or not up to Mr. Falla. That afternoon, upon his return from his tour of the colonias, or farms, Miguel Angel gave me the job without any ado. Evidently the Monsignor, who had also shared a ride with him, had put in a good word for me.

I was a high school student then, and my plan was to work during that sugar harvest and then go onto college. I started out as an assistant in the fields department,

[1] The Adelaida Sugar Mill, built brand new by Laureano Falla Gutiérrez, Miguel Angels' uncle, for its capacity to mill more than 4,200 TM was, at that time, the flagship of the Falla Gutiérrez Estate.

where I learned quite a bit about office tasks – though not enough. My job was supposed to disappear when the so-called dead season came. However, to my surprise, Mr. Falla took me in as his secretary when the milling was done.

Tell me, Rocío: where's that letter?

I had a lot of maturing to do, but working with him was a great learning experience. The following anecdote will give the reader an idea of how "green" I was. Mr. Falla was trying to locate a copy of a certain important letter and asked me whether I had seen it. I answered I had not.

"Are you sure you didn't file it?"

"Well, I can tell you that yesterday's letters have all been filed, but I didn't read them…"

A smile from him dissipated the tension of the moment.

"Let me see the letters you filed."

Sure enough, the document in question was in the portfolio. With fatherly affection he admonished me, "You need to read all the mail – incoming as well as outgoing – maintaining confidentiality, of course."

Although I was not a stenographer, I would take dictation from him at the same speed as trained secretaries. I invented my own system of symbols and half words, which, aided by my memory, allowed me to transcribe his letters verbatim. Of course I had to make a clean copy immediately. Most of the time, though, he would just give me the key points he wanted to express. The bond of trust that developed between us was such, that he would sign my letters without the slightest misgiving. Little by little we got to know each other, and he began entrusting me with private matters, such as certain personal bank accounts and the accounting for his farm Alarcón, which I visited often with him.

This administrator ain't no fool!

Dealing with him on a daily basis, I could personally appreciate his integrity, his capacity for work and his comprehensive knowledge of the entire sugar production process and industry. Never one to sit in his office for eight hours a day, he was the kind of manager who liked to be out in the sugarcane fields, chatting with the overseers and colonos, or farmers. He would visit the various departments of the sugar mill, talking to the workers and listening to their recommendations and comments for improving operations. Sometimes he would surprise the midnight shift by showing up unexpectedly just around the time that the Chinese house cook would sell baked meat pies after completing his daily chores.

As God rules heaven above, I rule below

Mr. Falla was a handsome man with an imposing presence, always neatly dressed. He walked with his head held high, as two small, almond-shaped eyes twinkled in his friendly face. His majestic voice inspired respect. Another characteristic of his appearance was his slightly upturned nose. Intuitively, he used to guess the intention of the person with whom he was speaking; which explains why he sometimes would make direct eye contact with that person and other times would direct his gaze vaguely to the surroundings. The awareness he possessed of his own capacity meant he never doubted his success when working toward a new goal.

I, who knew him well, can attest to the fact that the apparent arrogance some might attribute to him was actually a protective shield behind which he would hide his true human sentiments that filled his heart; just a bit of digging was enough to uncover them. Wisely, he would draw a line between the cold austerity of a businessman and the sensitivity of his inner conscience.

There were plenty of times when the tender fibers of his soul were exposed. Many people blessed the generous hand of Miguel Angel, as we respectfully addressed him at the sugar mill. We have a saying in Cuba about a button sufficing as an example, but I will give you a large sampling, if you will, of examples to highlight his humaneness:

» Moved by the sad situation facing the family of a suicidal worker, he allowed the widow to continue living in the house and promoted the younger son to a better job so he could support his many younger siblings who had lost a father's protection.
» He took to heart the case of an employee whose newborn child was hurt by the incompetence or neglect of the doctor who attended its birth. The newborn was rushed to Havana for treatment, which saved its life.
» When the daughter of the man in charge of his farm Alarcón was struck by an illness that left her blind, he pulled all the necessary strings to ensure the little one was given admittance to, and proper care in institutions devoted to the education and welfare of the blind.
» He took the time to send infusions and adequate foods from his house to the office employee who was sick and had no family in the area.
» The Catholic Federations always received all kinds of help whenever they needed it, both financial as well as in the form of services.
» A worker who wanted to migrate to the United States with his family, but whose visa request was denied for lack of the required guarantee, was able to obtain the necessary funds thanks to Mr. Falla.

»For an employee with a case of infectious disease in his family, he arranged for the patient to be admitted into the Las Animas Hospital of Havana. He granted the employee a long leave of absence while he dealt with the family crisis.
»When the labor contract for one of the sugar mills was being discussed, he personally requested that the workers associations and the C.T.C. [Confederation of Cuban Workers] put their "give-and-take" on hold so the manager could be with his sick mother.

All these anecdotes show who he was – a kind man who was always willing to lend a generous helping hand to anyone in need who knocked on his door, especially in cases of cancer or infectious diseases. He was always there to bring solace to the distressed.

Who are you calling old?

Talking one day with a department head, the latter hurt his feelings when he said; "I am older than you, yet I do not drag my feet." "Do I drag my feet, Rocío?" he asked me later.

The best are not far behind.

He was a very secure person who never felt his ego threatened by university graduates who might overshadow him. On the contrary, he would surround himself with all the bright professionals he could need, even giving his support to recent graduates when the ink on their diplomas was not dry yet. Similarly, he kept a sharp watch for those employees who sought intellectual self-improvement through higher education. For them he spared no effort in giving any support they might need in order to move ahead along their career paths. He saw them as reserve potential.

I dedicated my doctoral thesis in Commercial Sciences to the man who had helped me so much. When I brought him a copy of it, his daughter Elena remarked, "Daddy, now you can say your name appears in the files of the University."

He also never ignored the aptitudes of those office employees he felt had the makings of good executives. Several were anointed by him and taken under his wing; to receive the lessons that would help them develop latent abilities. As a good mentor, he would teach his protégés the ins and outs of the industry until they had achieved a complete education. He did demand one thing in return, though; when he assigned someone to a certain position, he expected the best that person could give, no vague half-commitments.

Elbow room at the negotiating table

Employer-Union relations are undoubtedly one of the keys to successful management of a sugar mill. The manager, as a representative of the company, must be fair and at the same time have his wits about him to know when to grant or deny labor demands. Miguel Angel's relations with the union leaders were cordial, which does not mean that he gave them everything they asked for. After listening carefully to the demands of the workers, he would agree to them – or reject them, depending on the case – always taking the time to clarify points and fight honestly for the company's interests without oppressing the workers. And, if on any matter they locked horns – as one might say of deer – he would be inflexible in defending his position while trying to reach a friendly compromise.

Threats won't get you anywhere!

It would not be accurate to state that his decisions were always well received. There was a case of a worker who, resentful at having been fired, decided to plan his revenge. He enlisted in the rural guard and some time later appeared at the mill offices to "settle the score". Taking advantage of his uniform, he slipped into the manager's office, where he gave vent to his anger and threatened to use his standard issue revolver. Serenely – I would even say coolly – Miguel Angel called his assistant with the excuse of asking him to check some calculations he wrote down on a piece of paper. A while later, the guard's sergeant arrived at the office and arrested his subordinate. The "calculation" was actually a discreet order to notify the sergeant and have him disarm the presumed murderer. My desk was just outside his office.

I admit he was not very fond of journalists; some of them had tried to blackmail him. On one occasion a reporter published an erroneous story about a religious act, implicating the management of the sugar mill. He entitled his article "The Naked Truth". Later he proposed a deal to Miguel Angel; he would retract what he had published in exchange for money. "Are you going to dress up the truth now?" was his witty response. Another reporter got all worked up on the radio denouncing the clearing of forest areas. I was sent to bring the vociferant reporter back to his senses.

Miguel Angel, the innovator

Miguel Angel started out as a manager for the *Patria* Sugar Mill, where he proved himself through his ability and discipline. On these merits he was transferred to *Adelaida*, which was considered superior in category. Miguel Angel, who understood the importance of having quality raw materials for the production of sugar, decided to ensure the highest level of success in the business he was going to run by taking some of his trusted men with him – those who truly believed in his agronomic policy. Full of enthusiasm and envisioning a reliable, adequate sugarcane supply, he mechanized the fields and ordered the clearing of new lands. The idea was to promote large sugarcane farms using different POJ varieties, which allow for greater yields. He summoned the farmers and asked for their cooperation toward his goal of increasing their processing rate. Then he focused his attention on the industrial aspect of the operation, with a view to achieving an increase in sugar production. This would require modifying the whole system: dumpers, leveler blades, grinders, centrifuges, clarifiers, furnaces, boilers, electric sub-station, sack-sewing equipment, etc. The result was a plant in such ideal condition that for the 1952 harvest, it produced 421,783 bags of 325 lb. sugar[2], from over 43,000,000 *arrobas* (each one equivalent to 25 lbs) of sugar cane processed.

Bag number 400,000 of "Adelaida" Sugar Mill. In the picture, workers and employees.

[2] Equivalent to 62.200 TM of sugar

Victory at the distillery

During World War II many sugar mills began to produce alcohol fuels[3] from sugar-cane molasses, in accordance with a government ordinance. The Falla-Gutiérrez hierarchy also prepared to experiment with this new industry, and Miguel Angel was entrusted with the project. He did not hesitate to accept the challenge, though he was not conversant with the details of this industry. He was a true manager at his core and knew he could achieve the goal as long as he had qualified staff around him.

Following the guidelines set by the central offices, he put all his efforts into setting up a splendid new distillery. At several stories high, it was one of the largest in Cuba and boasted an 80,000 liter per day alcohol production capacity. This turned out to be a much-criticized decision. While other companies simply jumped into this "ethylic experiment" using rudimentary "*cachimbos*" or "smoking pipes", taking advantage of the high demand for the product during the war and thrived, the Nauyú Distilling Co. was hard at work erecting concrete walls.

I had finished my studies in Philosophy and Humanities and was attending the third year of Commercial Sciences. Miguel Angel entrusted me with the accounting of the distillery so I could apply my skills. My abilities as an accountant had been put to the test already when I served as Head of Payroll and Cashier while the heads of those departments were on vacation.

Lack of experience in the production of alcohol resulted in a fly infestation of extreme proportions in the whole "batey" (hamlet) and surrounding areas. The pests proliferated in discarded musts. On trains going through the town of Falla, passengers would rush to close the windows because the swarms would invade the railroad cars; even so, the bothersome insects spread to other towns. With good sense and wisdom, Miguel Angel succeeded in overcoming a crisis that had received nation-wide attention through the Havana media.

---

[3] Used as a method to save gasoline, which had to be imported in large volumes. The government determined that gasoline fueled engines would still be able to perform adequately substituting 20% alcohol fuel for regular gasoline. This method is still used in Brazil to date.

Nauyú Distilling Co. "Building of Nauyú Distillery. To the left, the hospital of "Adelaida" Sugar Mill.

First it was sugar... and now there's rice, too!

The energetic president of the company, Alín Suero – always on the lookout for a new business – came up with another innovation. This one was not related to the production of raw sugar. It was experimental, even speculative – but he did not hesitate to entrust it to Miguel Angel. He knew his cousin (who never let him down) would drive the project forward. And he did; he got to work promoting rice cultivation, which is managed very differently than sugarcane production. Due to the fact that a lot of water is required for these crops, it was necessary to dig several deep wells and shape the land into perfectly level terraces so the plants could grow with irrigation. Once again, Miguel Angel's skill as a manager rose to the occasion, and the rice paddies flourished profitably.

Nostalgia takes its toll

During that time Miguel Angel was considering retiring in Havana. Of course in those days nobody talked about "stress", but it was obvious that everyday tensions from managing the company and being separated from his family were having an impact on his vigorous frame. Although he emanated vitality, he felt it was time to take his leave of the work scene. He was bothered by bursitis and gout attacks, which he took as a sign that the time had come to retire. Besides, his daughters had finished their schooling and were of marrying age. His brothers and other family members were also in Havana. He had already lived a productive work life.

The Punta Alegre comes full circle

But his respite in Havana was short-lived. Always a man of action, he could not be idle. The enterprising Alín, for whom he felt a profound affection, succeeded in bringing him out of his self-imposed retreat. The Falla-Gutiérrez group was purchasing the *Punta Alegre* Sugar Mill, so Alín put him in charge of restructuring the mill. Miguel Angel, in turn, invited me to join him. It was an attractive salary, undoubtedly, and a more pleasant location – and he even promised me a pretty house by the sea, yet I declined his offer. My reasons, which I expressed to him, were the following: I did not want to be far from my family, which lived in Morón and above all, on the verge of finishing my career as a public accountant, I had my sights set on a teaching post, either in the Institute of Higher Learning or at the School of Commerce. Additionally, the North Circuit highway, which went through Falla, was almost finished, which would afford me great mobility. In other words, all factors weighed against the invitation he was presenting to me on a silver tray. Determined to take me with him, he resorted to the good offices of the assistant manager to bring me around. The assistant manager painted a beautiful picture, making references to my aspirations and relating them to the economic advantages provided by the job. It would give me the opportunity to get close to Havana executives and perhaps secure a transfer to the Havana offices. I accepted the challenge.

The administrator's top men

Along with me he took the Head of the Fields Department, who would be responsible for restructuring the agricultural component of the new company. Miguel Angel's task was to adapt the *Punta Alegre* Sugar Mill to the "modus operandi" of the mills of the Falla-Gutiérrez block. The mill's payroll had been accepted as it was; however he soon realized there was a lot of fat to trim, and he began the cleanup. For this reason his arrival made some people uneasy. His upstandingness and solid values were taken as signs of roughness and arrogance. The reality was that he, like any savvy player, had decided to move some of the chips off the board after careful observation of the work and performance of each position.

When he focused his attention on the agricultural aspect of the business, he discovered that not everything was running smoothly. Certain sugarcane fields had intentionally and dishonestly been planted only along the perimeters. He had the deceitful inspector accompany him on an inspection, and when he tried to walk into the field, the man realized he had been caught in a flagrant crime and quit right then and there.

He found some other issues that were not so clear; however, he rewarded even those who had not shown integrity in the performance of their duties. This gave rise to speculation that a purge would be set off, which caused people to regard him with fear. Nothing could be farther from the truth; those who were innocent of any wrongdoing had nothing to fear – on the contrary: those who showed competence and loyalty and were being held back were given a chance to be promoted.

When I showed Miguel Angel my Public Accountant's diploma, he urged me to approach Julio Prado, vicepresident and general comptroller of the company, to request a transfer to the main offices. My request was not granted "because that would set a precedent for other sugar mill employees who would to expect to be relocated to Oficios 110[4] as well." Frustrated by this denial, I decided to burn my bridges and go to Havana to try my luck there, but Miguel Angel stopped me. "Don't rush into this; perhaps I can take you with if some plans are successful.

After all the hard work of setting Punta Alegre on the right track in accordance with the parameters set by the Falla-Gutiérrez block, his life at the mill was more peaceful and pleasant. Although the residence house was by the sea, and he had the yacht "Ailicec" at his disposal for recreation or even to go the keys (Media Luna or Guillermo), he decided to retire once and for all. It was the time to do it; he was over 50 years old and still full of life and energy. In Havana he would be able to fully enjoy home life; his two elder daughters, already married, had made him a grandfather. It was time to enjoy the small pleasures that he had denied himself until then and which he truly deserved.

At the farewell tribute offered to him by the employees and workers of the Punta Alegre Sugar Mill, it fell upon me to express his thanks in his name.

[4] The main address for the family estate offices in Havana

The Board of Directors of the Punta Alegre Club at the farewell tribute to Miguel Angel Falla, at the center in a white "Dril 100", the standard linen business suit of well dressed Cubans.

A little known fact is that during his time as manager, the unspoken rule of racial burials was eliminated. Until then, burials at that sugar mill took place in cemetery plots assigned according to the skin color of the deceased.

As soon as I finished my education, I decided to get married, and I asked him to be my best man, which he graciously accepted. Although he was living in Havana, he would still visit the three Camagüey sugar mills sporadically as a supervisor.

Photograph of Saturio Rocío extending on behalf of Miguel Angel Falla his thanks for the tribute

Follow me!

He had not forgotten his promise and sent for me. He made me his assistant as an adjunct to the Hershey Corporation payroll. At the same time he put me in charge of supervising the apartment building he owned, located at N and 21, as well as looking after his bank accounts. I was also overseeing his farm Alarcón (as I had been doing), where he was growing rice and sugarcane and raising cattle, though on a modest scale. I should point out that my public accountant's thesis "Establishing an Accounting System at a Rice Plantation" was based on my experience at that farm.

The rental Apartment Building which Miguel Angel Falla built in N and 21 in El Vedado, the prime residential location of Havana prior to the end of World Ward II. The building was situated across The Capri Hotel, which along with The Riviera, were the two best hotels built in the fifties in Havana In the Corner, the well-known Willie's Bar.

Cuba blames 'enemies' for bombs at 2 hotels

Photos by JOSE GOITIA / Canadian Press

The N and 21 building in the background of a recent first page news from Cuba

Miguel Angel Falla, best man (Padrino) at the wedding of Saturio Rocío and Gloria Molina in the parochial church of Morón - Our Lady of La Candelaria.

At the height of his career: The Atlantic

Mr. John L. Loeb, the financial magnate from Wall Street, set up an appointment with him at the Hotel Nacional of Havana and offered him a job (by recommendation of Alín Suero)[5] reorganizing the Cuban Atlantic Sugar Company. That company controlled the three sugar mills of the Hershey Corporation, plus three other colossi within Atlántica del Golfo. It was an overwhelming task, but not for a man as energetic as he was, with such in-depth knowledge of every aspect of the sugar production process. He accepted the challenge, secure and confident in his own capacity. For him it was ego flattery.

[5]John Loeb was the President of a prestigious brokerhouse in New York who, in addition to being in love with Cuba, saw a big opportunity in its sugar industry. Having met Alín Suero socially on trip, he asked him for a referral for a General Manager that could run his new company and Alín, without any hesitation said, "my cousin, Miguel Angel is the best General Manager I know."

My resignation from my post at Punta Alegre was not well received by Alín Suero, who reproached Miguel Angel for taking mill personnel with him. It was at that point that the story came out about my request to Julio Prado and his refusal to reward me for having bettered myself. "Not all the employees at the mill try to excel, and since Prado dashed Rocío's aspirations and he was determined to leave, I took him in." And so he appeased his complaining cousin.

A few months later Alín Suero became upset again when a competent office assistant at Adelaida accepted an appointment as office manager at the Lugareño sugar mill – a job I had offered him upon Mr. Falla's request. Suero reproached him for his recidivism in hiring away valuable personnel from the Falla-Gutiérrez sugar mills and forbade him to coax more employees away. But with the excuse that the offer had actually come from me, not him, Miguel Angel was able to allay his cousin's protests.

A businessman and a gentleman

In the short time during which the outgoing executive's presidency was still in effect, Miguel Angel, vice-president plenipotentiary, respected his rank and kept a low profile so as not to overshadow him, although he was gradually taking control of the companies. Once in full possession of the presidency, he inherited the former president's secretary; he did not wish to fire her, though he soon realized their working styles were not compatible. He was also unwilling to demote a male secretary - a relic of a previous management - who was far from qualified for his post (his English was described as "Pidgin" by a New York executive). In the end he decided to bring in a competent and active secretary from the Engineering Department.

Since the plan was to restructure the company completely, a good accountant was needed – someone to develop a system, someone who not only had the skill but also was willing to roll up his sleeves, get in the trenches with the team and reform the financial component of the company. An auditor was sent from a big firm in New York. He had a good contract; however, he did not turn out to be the man Miguel Angel needed so, very reluctantly, he terminated his contract.

It should be noted that the changes at the Atlántica del Golfo were less dramatic than at the *Punta Alegre* mill in terms of financial restructuring. An American management team had run this mill, and it enjoyed certain privileges and a much superior staff than those under Cuban management. It was simply to be adapted to

Falla procedures. In the case of the Atlántica, however, it was a matter of rebuilding and modernizing the sugar mills, implementing a management system aimed at cutting superfluous costs and substandard performance.

Unraveling Hershey

The Hershey corporation was complex: three sugar mills (*Hershey, Rosario* and *San Antonio*) and a jumble of parallel industries tagged on to the first: production of raw sugar, refining, peanut oil production, production of henequen rigging, electric railroads, electricity generation, golf clubs and gardens. The Atlántica del Golfo had the sugar mills *Alava, Conchita* and *Mercedes* under its control in the province of Matanzas, plus three colossi in Camagüey: *Lugareño, Morón* and *Stewart.* Upon the request of Miguel Angel, I visited each one of these sugar mills on administrative missions.

A white elephant up for grabs

Mr. Falla's intuition told him that some of the businesses within the Hershey sugar mill were not productive. He sent a group of accountants and engineers (myself among them) to try to break down the costs and disentangle their very complex accounting. We were unable to sort it out to our satisfaction. At that point he recommended to the Board of Directors in New York that they get rid of that "white elephant" and focus only on raw sugar production. Julio Lobo signed a call option.

He used to tell the story that, as President, it was his job to preside over the shareholders' meeting in New York, convened to finalize certain minor issues about the sale before the option date expired at midnight on December 31. At just fifteen minutes before the deadline, one of the lawyers got up from the table and stopped the clock that dominated the room: there still were a few points to work out and there would not be sufficient time to do it. The discussion continued until both sides were in agreement on all the details. Only then did the same lawyer stand up again and set the clock in motion. The record that was drawn up began something like this: "At 15 minutes before midnight…" (Actually, it was close to 4:00 a.m. on January 1.) When the clock belatedly struck twelve, everyone raised their champagne glasses to toast to the conclusion of the negotiations and celebrate the arrival of the New Year.

No hard feelings

Due to management policy reasons within the Hershey group, certain frictions had developed between the executive vice-president and Mr. Falla. Yet once the deal was closed, Mr. Falla – aware of the man's capacity for work and talent as a lawyer – requested that he be added to the payroll of the Atlántica del Golfo, along with me. This turned out to be a felicitous move; they eventually developed a liking for each other, which turned into an excellent collaborative business relationship and then a pleasant friendship. The new owners abided by the "status quo", except for the two transfers noted.

He who studies will get ahead

Miguel Angel wanted to transform the *Alava* into a model sugar mill that would be an example and incentive for other management teams, not only in terms of its agricultural component but also on industrial matters. His first step toward this goal was to purchase the *Pintó* farm under my name. Sugarcane was not being grown under unified management in the area, and Miguel Angel was convinced that he could not rely on the sugarcane supplied by the *colonos* to accomplish his goal. The Pintó came to achieve the best performance and production.

I cannot claim to have been the only one deserving of Miguel Angel's mentorship; any employee with the aspiration to better themselves would receive his blessing. Wisely, he had developed the habit of exploring and evaluating the various positions. When someone was nominated for a post, he would make sure the person actually had the capacity to fill it. His policy was to seek the right man for the job and not the other way around. Since the same company managed several operations, he could transfer professionals who were working as subordinates to better positions at other sugar mills – assuming they accepted the promotion, of course.

Regularly, once or twice a week, I would accompany him after business hours to "Willie's", a restaurant and bar located at the corner of his building. There he would socialize with friends and share impressions with them. Once in a while he would inspect his property. Then he would drop me off at home or close to it, on Línea Street.

A bunch of rebels in the Sierra Maestra hills

The period when revolutionary activities began was filled with anxiety, and many plans had to be put off. First the ensuing unrest and uncertainty took the wind out of the sails of many company executives. There was speculation about the rebels' political leanings, and the U.S. embassy muddled the issue even further with an irresponsible statement indicating that Raúl and Ché Guevara were communists, but not Fidel. A visiting friend confirmed to Miguel Angel the abuses being committed in the Oriente region, where the sugar mill under his management was located and where a large number of insurgents had converged. Miguel Angel was shocked by these first-hand accounts: the demands for money, revolutionary taxes, robberies, blackmail, executions, etc… beneath the façade of romanticism and democracy portrayed by the revolution were in truth something very different.

After the victory of the revolution, his faith in a return of those turbulent waters to a peaceful, normal course slowly waned. The much-touted agrarian reform required certain reports to be filled out and submitted to the INRA (Institute of Agrarian Reform). As president of the Atlántica del Golfo, Miguel Angel appeared at the government offices accompanied by his legal counsel and myself. After a five-hour wait, a low-ranking militiaman took the documents we had brought with us, which we had prepared with so much care and accuracy, and he threw them on the floor, in a corner. Miguel Angel thought he would be received by someone with authority and would have a chance to discuss certain aspects of the revolutionary legislation. With great disappointment he realized there could be no hope of changing anything anymore; that nothing mattered – not how competent, industrious or honest a person or business was; the whole thing was nothing but a farce. They had been going after the large estates, and now they were going to create a state-run estate. Evidently there was no sincerity in the plans introduced by the new government. That same day Monsignor Enrique Pérez Serantes had been kept waiting for eight hours to meet with Castro, without even being given an audience in the end.

Miguel Angel was receiving alarming reports from the sugar mills. Some of the managers were favoring and following all the measures dictated by the rebel cabinet. The whole situation was demoralizing. He decided to go to his farm Alarcón in the province of Camagüey and asked me to come with him. We traveled in his private car, with his driver. He could feel the current of popular sentiment and support for Castroism. Every so often we would get pulled over by groups raising funds for some revolutionary cause. I lost track of how many times we were forced to stop. Miguel Angel was beginning to get upset, when I took the matter into my own hands. Everytime we were pulled over, I would smile and state that we had already contributed a block earlier. When we got to his farm, the person in charge informed him that the INRA had purchased a drove of cattle from him, but instead of cash or a check, they had given him a roughly handwritten debit note. He remarked to me sadly, "You don't know how glad I am that my mother did not live to see this disconcerting and depressing situation…"

There is nothing left to do

Although he could sense disaster brewing over Cuba, in his heart he harbored the faint hope that this abnormal situation would be overcome. Yet those latent projects still stirring in his mind, awaiting better times, were dealt a cunning deathblow when the American sugar mills were nationalized. It happened one night in July (if memory serves), when a telephone call alerted me to the ill-fated resolution just bellowed out on television by Castro himself. I talked to my boss and went to his house. There I was met with a somber scene: long, drained faces and a cheerless mood that echoed dark foreshadowings. I stayed with him and his family until early in the morning, when I accompanied him to the airport to take the first flight to Miami.

A short time later his wife and the whole family joined him. His daughter Elena gave me her Riley car, which was very useful to me in completing her father's many assignments. My children named the car "Little Black Figurine", for the plastic ornament that hung from the rearview mirror – a little black figure in a tux and top hat.

Executor of his estate

As his representative through power of attorney, I was in charge of sending remittances of his cash to Miami, most of the time with total strangers – a risky endeavor. I was also looking after his wife's mother, paying wages to the servants and making sure everything was in good condition at their house. I was even considering moving to his residence in the hopes of preventing it from being confiscated, but in the end I dropped that plan, thinking it might turn out to be counterproductive.

Not theirs to take

A report by a jeweler who lived in the neighborhood caused their house to be searched. A trusted servant called me by order of the G2 agents (Cuba's political police), who wanted me to open the safe for them. It was well camouflaged in a cabinet in a bedroom. Finally they resorted to a locksmith's services, since they refused to let me return to my house to get the combination. The only thing they found in the safe was a porcelain trinket that rattled when shaken. No doubt they thought there were diamonds inside, but they were in for a big disappointment when they broke it. What rattled were small pieces of the same porcelain, which had come loose inside the figure.

That night I was taken to the G2, and agents went from there to my apartment. They wanted to see the accounting books of the Alarcon farm, which would contain a record of the "sale" of cattle to the INRA for more than $30,000. Luckily they didn't search my home where I kept a respectable sum of money ready for a fund transfer. They did not even bother to look at the books. I would communicate regularly with Miami, all in code. Miguel Angel would call me on the telephone without using his name. I would usually write to him, addressing the letters to ficticious persons at the correct address.

Reuniting with Miguel Angel

Finally, when I could no longer bear to stay in Cuba, I took what little money was left and distributed it among the people who had been receiving monthly payments. Then I left for Miami. I had no money to make a telephone call and let Miguel Angel know of my unexpected arrival, but someone was kind enough to make the call for me. He picked me up at the airport and lodged me in his house for three days with my wife and children. Later he put us up for two weeks at a motel, insisting that I should not worry, that everything would work out in the end.

I had entered the country on a tourist visa, so he went with me to apply for asylum and then obtain refugee status. I tried in vain to find a job in Miami. I also volunteered for some time at the Refugee Center in the hopes that a vacancy would come up and it would be offered to me in recognition of my disinterested help. Finally I decided to move to New York and try my luck there. He saw me off at the airport and again insisted that I should not worry about my family, which I was leaving behind. At least once a week he would pay a fatherly visit to my wife and children – just to check whether they needed anything. He would always bring candy for the children.

Up north, where it's mighty cold

He thought he could get me a job at the Wall Street offices but was unsuccessful because Mr. Loeb had made the firm decision not to hire anybody who had worked for Atlántica del Golfo. He was inflexible and refused to make any exceptions. Despite the distance, we always stayed in touch. The first winter Miguel Angel sent me some sweaters and got Mr. Loeb to give me a gift of $500 "just this once". Every time he traveled to New York, he would stop by to see me, always wanting to know how I was doing. "By the shirts your boss wears I can guarantee he's got class." And he would treat me to dinner. He lived in Darién for some time, where I visited with him once. He gave my children money to go to an amusement park.

Miami's warmth… and the weather, too

Yearning for the warmth of the Tropics, Miguel Angel moved to Coral Gables and continued regular correspondence with me. His letters were about personal matters, Cuba, common friends and business. Among my documents I have found only three of them: one thanking me for some petit fours I sent him for Christmas: "Even though I'm not supposed to have any sugar, I tried five of them – excellent – and Julia had… who knows how many. I hope it won't affect my diabetes." In another he comments: "I'm very happy you could take the trip to Europe with your family. When I was the right age, healthy, and had the money, I never had the time." The other, a thank you note: "Thank you all for dedicating those Masses and thank you, Rocío, for being so warm and kind to Perla." One of his last communications to us was a postcard he sent from Puerto Rico when he was there on a cruise with his brother Carlos.

It hurts not to have said good-bye

One thing that truly hurts is not having attended his funeral so my presence could bear testimony to my immense gratitude. Nobody notified me of his sudden death. Almost a week later a friend called me to give me the news; he had read about it in a back issue of the *Diario de las Américas* newspaper.

Miguel Angel was my boss, my supporter, my protector, my guardian angel, my mentor, and my friend. He was almost like a father to me. I was his employee, his private secretary, his representative, his confidant, and his front man… For my part I was loyal to him. I respected him. I defended him. I loved him; and my heart overflows with gratitude for all that he did for me. I bless his generous soul every day. His memory will remain with me for as long as I live.

My Tribute to Miguel Angel Falla:

Dr. Angel P. Naveiras

In June of 1944, I finished my high school studies in Sciences and Humanities. That was a key moment in my life. I had decided to become a professional, and my chosen path was law. I had limited means and could not afford to be a full-time university student.

At that age that straddles the line between adolescence and adulthood, everything seems possible – or at least we make it seem that way. In those days the thought farthest from our minds was that with the passing of time, only a little more than a decade later, a small cloud of very scant significance (as many people thought) would appear in our Cuba's stormy horizon. The reality was that it heralded the birth of a political/conspiratorial process that would sweep through like a dreadful gale, demolishing moral values and material assets, transforming the country into a tragic picture of death, desolation and poverty.

My first encounter with Miguel Angel Falla

But let us go back to that happy day in June, 1944. Just a few months later, in September, I received a notice for a job interview with Mr. Miguel Falla Alvarez, manager of the Adelaida Sugar Mill. The appointment was arranged through the efforts of true friends who were concerned about my future.

I have clear memories of my arrival at the Adelaida refinery; going through the turnstile, I saw a Catholic chapel on my left. On my right, across from the chapel, was a bust of Mr. Laureano Falla, founder of the company. Before me lay a broad avenue shaded by the green canopy of intertwined branches formed by the laurels planted on either side. The trees, in turn, accented the wooden houses of the employees, which gleamed in their white and green cleanness. At the end of the highway (as we learned to call it) were the main offices of the sugar mill, where I had my appointment.

Before long I was sitting in front of a tall, heavy man with tan skin and inquisitive almond-shaped eyes. He wore a long-sleeved dress shirt, khaki riding pants and brown shoes and gaiters.

Mr. Falla received me warmly. Rather than questioning me, he preferred to hear me talk about myself. I was honest. My achievements were incipient; I needed to work but had no experience; my qualifications were limited to a high school (baccalaureate) degree and my aspirations were to a PhD in Law. While I spoke his steady, watchful gaze seemed to weigh my every word. When I had finished he stood up and graciously saw me off.

I was unaware that I was entering a new phase in my life – separated from my family and facing a future I did not fear but which was unknown to me. It was a new and different environment that held the challenge of a new life and reality, which I accepted with faith in God.

I did not know it, but I had just met a person who would exert a beneficial influence on the successful progress of this new life phase – someone who would be a determining factor in my experiences as an employee and provide sustained support for my career in law.

I began to work as an office assistant for Mr. Agustín Gutiérrez, chief engineer at the mill; later I was assigned to the payroll department in the main offices.

Straight forward and humane Manager

One night after dinner I went to the offices; seeing me come in, Miguel Angel (who allowed employees to call him by his given name) introduced me to his companions. (I found out later that Miguel Angel was in the habit of sharing ideas with his trusted employees in this way.) After the introductions he made a comment I still remember clearly: "If you take after your grandfather, you will be a worthy man." Until his death a few years earlier, my grandfather had been the Spanish vice-consul in the city of Morón, near which was Central Patria, the Sugar Mill where Miguel Angel commenced his Sugar Industry Experience.

Miguel Angel was blessed with a remarkable personality. His presence inspired authority and respect, as did his psychological scrutiny of people when they spoke with him. He was sincere and direct and would not "pussyfoot" when it came to expressing his thoughts. Tough though his negative criticism may have been, he was lavish in his dispensation of sincere praise and recognition.

Miguel Angel's actions bore testimony to his kindness when a serious illness struck my only brother. He made arrangements with Mr. Raúl Román, manager of the Patria Sugar Mill, for the latter's brother, a distinguished doctor, to provide my brother with the specialized care he needed. During my stay in Havana, where my brother was transferred for treatment, I was covered by a leave of absence planned and authorized by Miguel Angel.

An ever present Manager

A tireless worker, Miguel Angel was obsessed with efficiency and responsibility, and he expected the same of his employees. Once during the midnight shift I was conducting the staff roll call for the mill, when I saw Miguel Angel at a distance, talking to the furnace chief. When I had finished my task I returned to my room. At eight o'clock sharp Miguel Angel was walking into his office. Just a few minutes later he called me in to ask me whether all the centrifuge workers were at their posts. As I handed him the notebook with the list, I answered that one person was absent. With an approving smile he said, "I knew that, but I wanted to confirm it with you."

Always offering opportunities to his staff

Rumors were growing about plans calling for changes in the management of the Patria Mill. I never imagined that the plans included me.

One morning Miguel Angel called me into his office. After greeting me and gesturing for me to take a seat, he fixed his gaze on me and said, "I know your goal is to become a lawyer, and that's fine. But there are plans to make changes in the management of the Patria Sugar Mill, and I want you to head the payroll department. I need you there."

"You, Miguel Angel, support me in my studies and therefore, gratitude would compel me to accept your appointment; but even if that were not the case, I would still accept because it is a gesture of trust on your part and a source of pride for me." The plans never materialized, but a feeling of gratitude and personal satisfaction remained etched in my heart.

Personal issues and other factors not under my control, such as the closing of the University of Havana, delayed my graduation – which I always saw as an unchanging goal. When the university reopened in 1959, I immediately decided to make up for lost time.

His foresight, an opportune advise

In 1960 I received my diploma from the School of Law. Having stopped first to register officially at the Havana Bar Association, I went to Miguel Angel's offices to show him the diploma. He took the time to look at it carefully, rolled it up and handed it back with one hand while he shook my right hand with the other and said, "Congratulations!"

When I answered "yes" to his question about my registration at the Bar, he added that he would instruct his legal office to involve me in their activities and begin my contributions for retirement. After a pause his penetrating gaze was veiled by a fleeting, somber thought shadow. In a prophetic voice with a slight trace of bitterness, he said, "Naveiras, the future, it seems, will be dark… Let's wait." I agreed with him.

His foreboding came true. Approximately one year later we would be in exile. The disaster came and with it, the terrible tragedy that had such an impact on all of us. It truncated a promising path that seemed to have opened up for me when I achieved my goal of graduating

What I learned with him – a summary

My undying gratitude goes to the man who extended to me his hand and his consistent support. In his office, there in that small gem called the Adelaida Sugar Mill, we learned the fundamentals that are indispensable for success in life with dignity: integrity, respect, discipline, orderliness, organization and a firm commitment to justice. All these served as guiding principles for me in the field of teaching, the profession I adopted in the United States of America.

My Memories of Miguel Angel Falla

José Medardo Pino

I worked in the Central "Patria", "Adelaida's" younger brother which Mr. Falla visited from time to time. I judged him, with great apprehension and respect, so as not to say fear, from the first time I saw him.

After some time had passed, I was informed that I would be transferred to "Adelaida", my first impulse was to turn down the offer, but I swallowed my tongue when they told me they would increase my salary. As an accountant, graduated from the Commerce School of Santa Clara, they hoped my services would be useful in helping to implement a more modern accounting system that they were working on.

The Office Manager in the Central "Adelaida" was an affable, friendly man who was always humming some song or another. As he was just about to retire, he was not interested in getting tangled up in the task of learning new accounting methods. As his substitute they named the Head of the Agriculture Department, much too austere and not too diplomatic. More than once he reprimanded me for small mistakes or simply for the way that I worked. He was very clear about us not getting along well.

On a certain occasion, I made a mistake on the "Forest Reports", and he pulled me aside and began to reprimand me in unbecoming ways. All that of "guajiro cerrao" [hard headed farmer], which I was holding inside, I let loose and responded very inappropriately while simultaneously turning in my resignation. Miguel Angel, sitting in his office, had heard the whole event. I returned to my office, which was right next to his, and began packing. When I looked up I saw Miguel Angel in the doorway. With a smile on his face, he put his hand on my shoulder and advised me not to take things so seriously, to continue working. If I did not want to work under the head of the department anymore, he had another position available for me. He also gave me the rest of the day off to get over the unpleasantness of the morning. This kind gesture of his revealed his humanness and abruptly changed the image I had mistakenly formed of him. Being the newest employee, (and not the best) I couldn't believe that he backed my complaint against the head of the office.

On another occasion, I was out sick for three or four days secluded in my room. On a daily basis, Miguel Angel sent me orange juice and other appropriate foods to help in my recovery from his house. I will never forget that.

If I am asked now, in the year 2002, what my impressions of Mr. Miguel Angel Falla were, from my heart, I can sincerely say that he was a true angel, not just by name.

As a Manager I would esteem that he stands tall amongst the best. That summarizes my perception.

Chapter III

The Industries Miguel Angel Commanded

The Industries Miguel Angel Commanded

Oscar A. Echevarría

In Chapter IV, we will present the overview of the Sugar Industry. Here we will limit ourselves to the data about the two sugar groups that embrace all of the working life of Miguel Angel Falla, "The Succession Falla-Gutiérrez" and "The Cuban Atlantic Sugar Company."

In the excellent testimonials presented in the preceding pages from first hand witnesses of Miguel Angel's work, and the overview prepared by Ena Curnow, historian and journalist, the reader has available an unsurpassable wealth of data to gain a meaningful insight on our subject. The purpose of this section is thus limited to provide the economic dimension of the arena where Miguel Angel learned and made his mark on the Sugar Industry.

A. The best Manager of the Falla-Gutiérrez' Sugar Interest

1. Origin and Scope of the Sucesión

Don Laureano Falla Gutiérrez, Miguel Angel's uncle, went into sugar production later in his life, at 42, after earning both fame and fortune as a merchant, cattleman, farmer and sugar cane producer in the South of the Province of Las Villas in the area of Cienfuegos.

In 1901 he joined Don Nicolás Castaño, Don Domingo Nazábal and Don Agustín Llorente in the purchase of the "Santísima Trinidad"[1] mill. In 1903 he gained hands-on experience in "Central Andreíta", which he later bought in association with Castaño and Nazábal. Later between 1903 and 1905 he co-managed with Nazábal "Central Lequeito", leaving it in exchange for Nazábal's shares in "Andreíta". He then took control of "Central San Agustín", which he managed until 1912. He moved his residence to Habana in 1915 while maintaining his offices in Cienfuegos, and in 1917, jointly with Castaño and others bought "Central Patria", situated 2 Km from Morón in Camagüey[2]. To this venture he invited his younger brother, Don Miguel, Miguel Angel's father, who joined him with a 20% interest.[3] From "Patria" he moved to build "Adelaida". Besides the sugar mills, Don Laureano had many other business interests in real state, electricity, paper making, which made him a premier captain of industry. For our purposes, we will follow the sugar angle.

Upon Don Laureano's death in 1929 his business interests were kept within his estate in what was called "La Sucesión Falla Gutiérrez", run as a privately held Corporation by a succession of his heirs. When Castro intervened in the Cuban sugar mill, Alín Suero, Don Laureano's grandson, was the Chief Executive Officer. The book "Las Empresas de Cuba 1958"[4], lists that the group controlled the following seven sugar mills: Adelaida, Andreíta, Manuelita, Fidelidad, Patria, Violeta. Other sources list the Punta Alegre, the last one managed by Miguel Angel before going to manage the Cuban Atlantic.

As the purpose of this section is not to document the important economic interest of "La Sucesión" but only what relates to Miguel Angel Falla's role in the Cuban sugar industry, we will cover only the three mills where he worked for La Sucesión: Patria, Adelaida and Punta Alegre.

2. The learning at Central Patria

As mentioned before, Central Patria, near Morón on Camagüey Province, was the first of Laureano's sugar venture to which he invited his younger brother, Miguel Falla. Patria has now gained international recognition, as it was featured on the

---

[1] Ichaso, León. Don Laureano Falla-Gutiérrez – Su vida y sus Empresas. Cultural S.A. 1930, La Habana, Cuba. Pages 9, 16.

[2] Ibid pages 17 through 21.

[3] Cervera Falla, Miguel. Recuerdos de Mi pasado. Unpublished manuscript.

[4] Jiménez, Guillermo. Las Empresas de Cuba 1958. Ediciones Universal. Miami Florida USA. 2000. Page 544.

front page of The Washington Post as the first sugar mill decommissioned by Castro in the closing of half of Cuba's mills in 2002[5]

Not withstanding being the oldest son of the Patria's General Manager, and having finished business school in the United States, his father insisted he learn the trade from the bottom up, doing all the different chores, even sweeping the office as he would later fondly recall to his youngest daughter and travel companion, Elena. Here is where Miguel Angel learned the sugar industry and worked his way up to Manager of the Office. Under his father, a tough hands-on and hard working General Manager, Miguel Angel learned from the University of life what allowed him to be the model manager of the Falla Gutiérrez group taking care of the most difficult assignments.

3. Adelaida and Punta Alegre

After Central Patria, as well documented in the Remembrances, Miguel Angel went on to manage the jewel of the family, Central Adelaida and from it to reorganize the newly acquired Central Punta Alegre. While at Punta Alegre he also supervised the Managers of the two mill he had managed before.

From the testimonials of Saturio Rocío, Juan de la Cruz, Angel Naveiras, Rita Blain and José Medardo Pino, the reader will be able to learn about Miguel Angel the man and the manager, so we will end this section with the following table which provides an insight on the economic dimension of the sugar interest which Miguel Angel handled within a sugar group that, according to the book Las Empresas Cubanas, in 1958 ranked second in number of mills and, with 33,000 MT of milling capacity was third by that yardstick[6].

So to end this section, it will suffice to present, in the table below the economic dimension of the three mills managed by Miguel Angel.

[5] Ending an Era, Cuba Closes Sugar Mills Icons of Revolution Become Museums for Tourism, the New Moneymaker By Mary Jordan, Washington Post Foreign Service, Monday, July 29, 2002; Page A01.

[6] Jiménez, op. cit. Page 545.

Table I - Mills of Sucesión Falla Gutiérrez Managed by Miguel Angel Falla					
		Central Adelaida	Central Patria	Central Punta Alegre	Total
Manager in 1959		Viriato Gutiérrez Falla	José Manuel Antuña Perales	Ricardo Díaz González	
Capacity (TM/day) - 1959		4,121.87	2,481.40	5,160.16	11,763.43
Yield (sugar % cane)		12.74	11.98	12.14	12.31
1952	Production Sugar (TM)	62,195.77	40,637.83	72,739.84	175,573.43
1958	Days of Milling	99	97	88	
	Cane Milled (TM)	377,934.81	228,888.02	450,391.59	1,057,214.43
	Sugar Production (TM)	48,850.72	29,030.58	55,246.02	133,127.32
1959	Days of Milling	106	110	96	
	Cane Milled (TM)	382,282.45	253,924.23	448,937.83	1,085,144.51
	Sugar Production (TM)	50,731.62	30,237.64	56,902.28	137,871.54

Source: Manual Azucarero de Cuba - Gilmore - 1960

B. CEO of The Cuban Atlantic Sugar Company, the World's largest

The relationship of John Loeb with Cuba began fortuitously in 1928, after he cancelled his planned vacation at the Princess Hotel in Bermuda, upon receiving a confirmation from the hotel stating that "they had [their] rooms, everything was fine and in keeping with their high standards. [You] will be glad to know that we do not cater to Jews".[7]

After his first trip to Cuba, when he met, among others, Alín Suero, Miguel Angel's cousin, he went back every winter, and even established a winter residence at Varadero. As he grew fond of Cuba he developed an interest in the sugar industry. His first attempt was to buy Central Violeta but Julio Lobo beat him to it. After that he turned his attention to the "Cuban Atlantic Sugar" that was publicly traded in New York and was at that time the largest sugar company in the World, producing 10% of Cuba's sugar.[8] The process of taking over the company makes for very interesting reading on the ways and means of business in the late fifties.

[7] Loeb, John I. All in a Life Time John L. Loeb, New York, NY, 1990, page 161.
[8] Ibid. Page 162.

In anticipation that he would soon gain control of the Company, Loeb turned to his friend Alín Suero to help him find a suitable CEO to which Alín responded, "The best Sugar Executive in Cuba is my cousin Miguel Angel Falla."[9] And thus began Miguel Angel's relationship with Loeb and the Cuban Atlantic when it was controlled by Loeb in December of 1956.

To facilitate the understanding of such a complex array of sugar installations as those of The Cuban Atlantic interests, and adapt to space limitations, we have broken the tables in four. The first one is a Summary of the Violeta, which had a milling capacity of 8,249 MT/Day and produced 113,000 MT of sugar in 1952 but only 82,300MT in 1959, as consequence of the Revolution.

Table II – Central Violeta		
Manager in 1959		Raúl Román Crespo
Capacity (TM/day) - 1959		8,249.73
Yield (sugar % cane)		12.64
1952	Sugar Production (TM)	113,000.17
1958	Days of Milling	91
	Cane Milled (TM)	616,728.18
	Sugar Production (TM)	83,182.30
1959	Days of Milling	98
	Sugar Milled (TM)	663,163.07
	Sugar Production (TM)	82,315.79

Source: Manual Azucarero de Cuba - Gilmore - 1960.

[9] This was John Loeb's statement when, at his request, I joined Elena at one of their regular lunches at The Four Seasons, after she moved back to New York. At that luncheon he also reminisced on Elena's picking him up at Havana Airport in the first days of The Revolution, and how, convinced about Castro's true color, upon his return, he urged the then Secretary of State, John Foster Dulles not to stand idle. This latter point is covered in detail in his book, under the Section The Holland Loeb Plan pages 169 and 170.

The six mills that were left in the Cuban Atlantic after Miguel Angel sold the Violeta and the Hersey Group are divided according to their location. Those in the Matanzas Province: Alava, Conchita, and Mercedes, had a capacity of 12,503 MT/Day and produced 127,000MT in 1952; those in Camagüey Province: Lugareño, Morón and Stewart, had a milling capacity of 22,000 MT/Day, producing 430,000 MT in 1952. The last, The Hersey Group, constituted by Hersey Sugar Mill and Refinery, The Rosario, and the San Antonio had a capacity of 11,200 MT/Day, producing 186,000 MT in 1952.

In total, in 1958 the Cuban Atlantic had 10 raw sugar mills with a total capacity of 52,000 MT per day, and produced 856,377 TM in 1952, which represented 12.02% of Cuba's production that year, when the production level of 5.5 million tons was lifted by Batista to gain popular support after his unjustified and illegal Coup in March 10, 1952. To attest to what this means as capacity of response in a very complex production process the reader should know that the milling season in Cuba starts in late November or early December and ends by May. So when the lifting of restrictions were announced, the balance to be produced was less than 1.6 million MT, but those fields and factories responded with an additional 3.2 million MT, double that quantity, for a total production of 7.2 million.

Table III- COMPAÑIA AZUCARERA CUBAN ATLANTIC (Matanzas)

		Central Alava	Central Conchita	Central Mercedes	Total
Manager in 1959		José Manuel Lastres García	Juan M. Campanería	Rafael Matacena y Ferrara	
Capacity (TM/day) - 1959		4,770.87	4,001.81	3,730.94	12,503.63
Yield (sugar % cane)		12	12.22	12.24	12.19
1952	Sugar Production (TM)	42,400.26	51,018.81	33,882.13	127,301.20
1958	Days of Milling	107	124	77	
	Cane Milled (TM)	358,278.15	638,811.56	254,746.46	1,251,836.17
	Sugar Production (TM)	43,944.30	43,664.72	32,651.08	120,260.10
1959	Days of Milling	87	103	88	
	Cane Milled (TM)	366,964.36	368,120.92	282,525.70	1,017,610.98
	Sugar Production (TM)	45,575.06	44,139.84	35,190.90	124,905.80

Source: Manual Azucarero de Cuba - Gilmore - 1960.

Table IV - COMPAÑIA AZUCARERA CUBAN ATLANTIC (Camagüey)		Central Lugareño	Central Morón	Central Stewart	Total
Manager in 1959		Juan de la Cruz de la Paz	Ing. Alberto Deschapelles Fesser	Leonardo Fandiño López	
Capacity (TM/day) - 1959		5,632.76	7,156.17	9,483.76	22,272.69
Yield (sugar % cane)		11.87	12.14	12.08	12.03
1952	Sugar Production (TM)	85,105.47	192,219.80	152,814.14	430,139.42
1958	Days of Milling	88	106	94	
	Cane Milled (TM)	469,699.49	1,028,841.38	806,717.83	2,305,258.70
	Sugar Production (TM)	58,854.47	132,731.97	104,510.10	296,096.54
1959	Days of Milling	118	133	123	
	Cane Milled (TM)	520,801.02	1,166,829.26	923,632.78	2,611,263.07
	Sugar Production (TM)	61,651.65	140,310.34	109,508.73	311,470.72

Source: Manual Azucarero de Cuba - Gilmore - 1960.

Table V - HERSHEY SUGAR COMPANY		Central Hershey y Refinería	Rosario Sugar Company	Central San Antionio	Total
Manager in 1959		José A. Villamil	Rafael Villasuso	Dr. Fausto Capote Calleja	
Capacity (TM/day) 1959		2,970.60	2,609.35	3,020.15	8,600.1
Yield (sugar % cane)		11.97	11.62	12.39	12.20
1952	Sugar Production (TM)	102,246.12	46,710.34	36,977.16	185,936.62
1958	Days of Milling	114	114	123	134
	Cane Milled (TM)	656,944.53	265,225.62	293,081.67	1,215,251.83
	Sugar Production (TM)	85,042.35	41,803.79	37,115.18	163,961.32
1959	Days of Milling	129	118	105	
	Cane Milled (TM)	714,674.67	269,877.23	287,043.86	1,271,595.76
	Sugar Production (TM)	90,510.43	42,699.46	37,770.93	170,980.82

Source: Manual Azucarero de Cuba - Gilmore - 1960.

From the previous data the reader can understand the dimension and complexity of The Cuban Atlantic, of which Miguel Angel was Chief Executive Officer until its confiscation in 1960. In 1956 it was the largest sugar group, a position that Julio Lobo attained as a result of the profitable sale of the Hershey's operations in December 31, 1957, orchestrated by Miguel Angel[10]. In that transaction, closed one year after Loeb took control of the Cuban Atlantic, the Hershey Operations, which represented 20% of the milling capacity of the Group, were sold to Lobo "for $25 million in cash covering [the totality of] the Loeb investment in Cuban Atlantic".[11] In 1958 Miguel Angel also sold the "Central Violeta", that represented 12% of theoretical milling capacity, to the Succession Falla Gutiérrez. If measured not in terms of design capacity but actual production, the six mills retained by Miguel Angel produced in 1958 and 1959 63% of the total production of the original ten. Both transactions allowed Loeb to recover and even make a profit on the purchase of the Cuban Atlantic, and in 1959 the Price Earning Ratio (P/E) of the Cuban Atlantic must have skyrocketed as the investment had all been recovered. This certainly mitigated the impact of confiscation by Fidel Castro. Within this economic context the transaction of selling the Hershey mill, so well covered in Rocío's and de la Cruz's testimonies, attains new meanings.

Having covered the economic aspects of Miguel Angel "field of work", I defer again to the testimonials to offering a glimpse at Miguel Angel in action.

[10] Jiménez, op. cit. Page 545.
[11] Ibid. Page 168.

Chapter IV

Cuba and the International Sugar Market

Cuba and the International Sugar Market

Oscar A. Echevarría

To place Miguel Angel Falla in the context of the Industry to which he devoted his life, a brief overview of the Cuban Sugar Industry is in order. To accomplish such purpose, this Chapter reviews, succinctly, the evolution of Cuba's sugar production from its origin to today, the organization and income distribution of the industry, as well as its relative position in the International Sugar Market[1].

While the evolution of the economic and social aspect of the industry, as well as the increases in productivity, offer very rich analytical material, worthy of a book just in itself, we have limited ourselves to few fundamental indicators: production, exports and ownership. This decision was dictated by constraints of both length and availability of reliable data on Cuban costs and production conditions after 1959. Such limitations not withstanding, it is irrefutable proof of the success of the Cuban Sugar Industry the commanding place it had achieved and retained until 1959, both in terms of market share and as a model, of course always perfectible, of economic and social organization.

[1] The sections covering the period from 1959 to 1995 draw extensively from a paper I presented at the 1995 Annual Meeting of the Association for the Study of the Cuban Economy. At that time I was able to rely on Ralph Kazi, former Statistician and Secretary of the Board of Czarnikow Rionda. Also of great help was Maria Inez Fernández, at that time a Senior Economist at EISCA. For the remainder efforts of data search and preparation of the graphs, I had the help of my very dedicated and competent Teaching Fellow, Santiago Moralejo del Arco. To all, my gratitude

A. Evolution of the Cuban Sugar Industry

1. As a Spanish Colony

a. The beginnings

Cuba's sugar Industry traces its origin to sugar cane brought from Hispaniola by Governor Diego Velásquez in the initial years of the Colony. It received a boost in 1523 when King Carlos I authorized loans to sugar developers. A second and more powerful boost came in 1595 when, at the behest of the Governor and The Council of Habana, Felipe II authorized loans from the Crown to promote sugar production. The Monarch provided other stimulus such as exempting imported tools and equipment for the industry from Custom Duties, prohibiting the repossession of capital goods in cases of unpaid debt, and reducing taxes on sugar sales by 50%. By 1602, 17 landowners had received 40,000 Gold "Ducats"[2]. By 1762, there were 70 "trapiches" as the small sugar mill propelled by mules, horses, oxen and even human's were called, producing an average of 12,400 MT per year. The following figure shows export in five-year intervals.

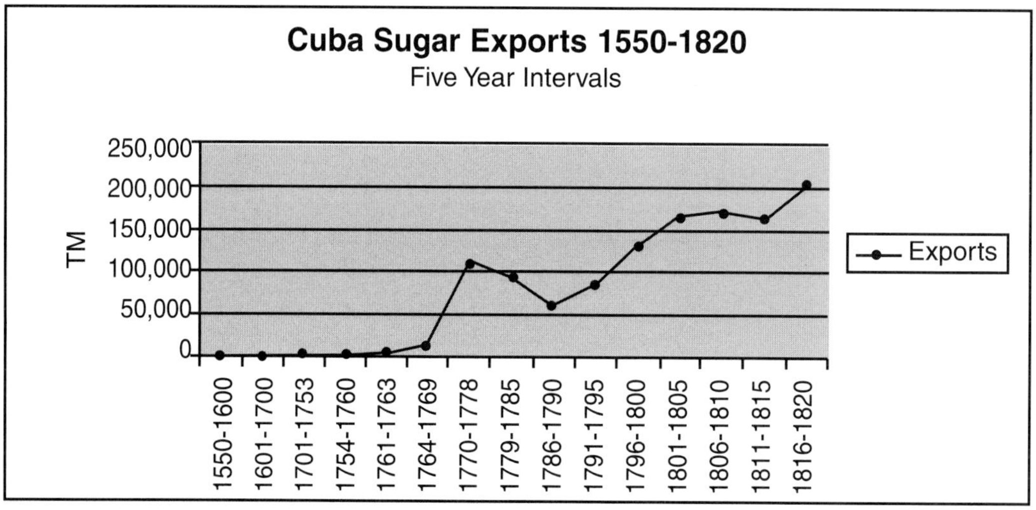

Source: Ramiro Guerra y Sánchez, Azúcar y Población en Las Antillas, Segunda Edición, Madrid, Cultura S.A., 1935. Annex II. According to him, estimates for the period 1550 - 1600 are exaggerated. He estimated 147.45 TM for that period.

[2] Grupo Cubano de Investigaciones Económicas. Un Estudio Sobre Cuba. University of Miami Press, Miami Florida, United States of America, 1963. Pag.173.

b. The XIX Century - From animal traction to steam power

As the five years interval records show, by 1818, when free trade was granted, average yearly production had increased to 41,000 MT and by 1850 had reached 226,720 MT, a compound rate of increase of 5.15% per year.[3]

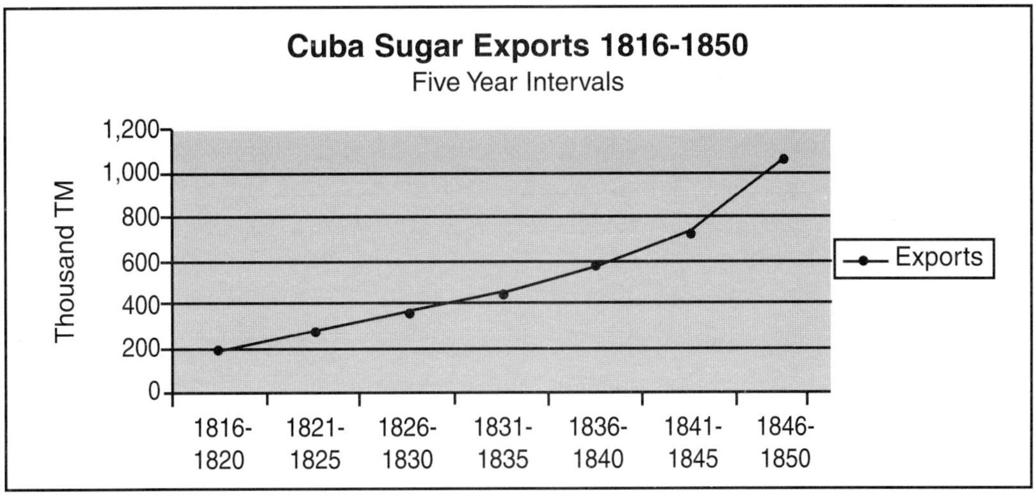

Source: Ramiro Guerra y Sánchez, Azúcar y Población en Las Antillas.

In the next decade the use of centrifuges for separating the sugar crystals from the molasses was introduced, and by 1860 the number of "trapiches" had reached 390, producing 42,400 MT. The water-propelled mills then numbered 6 with a production of 2,830 MT, an average of 472 MT, more than four times the smaller "trapiches." But 91.2% of production came from 942 steam-powered mills with an average of 500 MT, for a total production on the Island of 454,115 MT[4]. Of the steam-powered mills, 79 had modern equipment and their average production of 1,125 MT was two and a half times the average of the rest of the steam-powered mills.

[1] Ibid. Pages 176, 178.
[1] Ibid. Pages 182, 184.

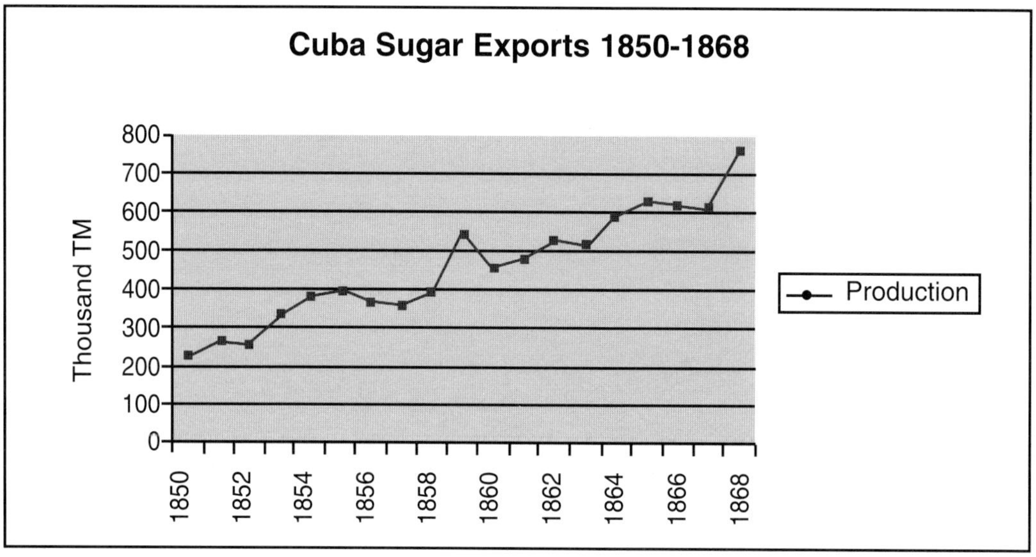

Source: Ramiro Guerra y Sánchez, Azúcar y Población en Las Antillas,
Segunda Edición, Madrid, Cultura S.A., 1935

c. The Wars for Independence 1868 to 1898

At the beginning of the 1868 War for Independence production had reached 760,980 MT, with a rate of increase of 2.2 % per year, less than half the previous period. By the end of the war in 1878 production had dwindled to 541,530, in part due to the continuous drop in prices. It took until 1891, when production was 832,830 MT, to surpass the previous peak, reaching a record of over 1 million in 1894 and 1895. The value of sugar in those three years averaged $67.30 per MT or 3.05 cents per pound. By 1894 Cuba's population was 1.7 million so, as in 1895, it exported 1,054 million MT. This represented an average of 0.62 MT per person, equivalent to $41.73 in current prices. As a result of the War of 1895, which led to the end of Spanish Sovereignty over Cuba by 1898, production dropped dramatically to some 310,430.[5]

[1] Ibid. Pages 199.

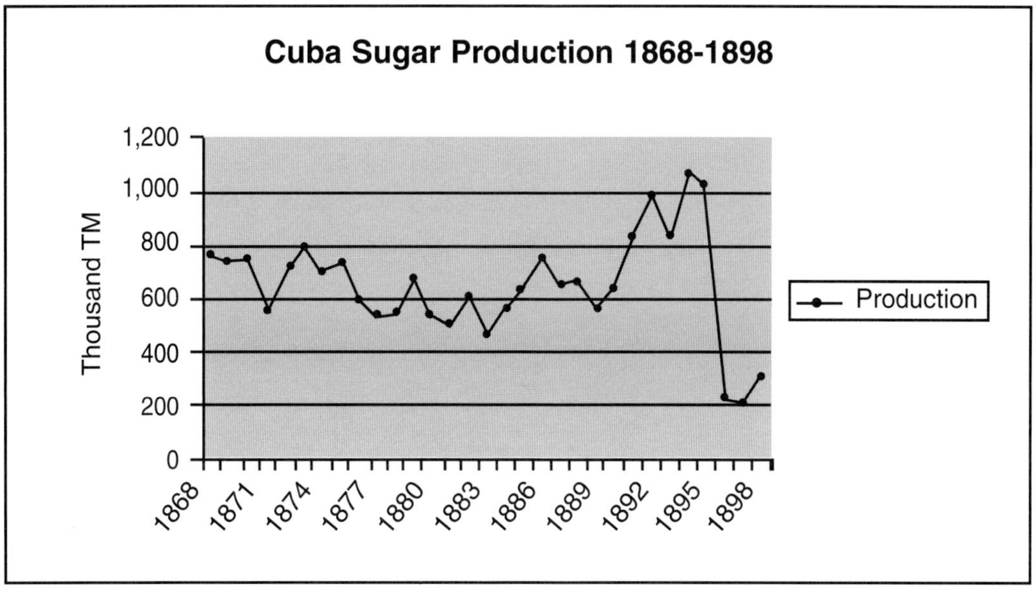

Source: Ramiro Guerra y Sánchez, Azúcar y Población en Las Antillas, Segunda Edición, Madrid, Cultura S.A., 1935

2. As a Republic from 1902 to 1959

a. Early XX Century - Becoming the World's premier Sugar Producer.

In 1900 Cuba's sugar production was 304,870 MT, representing 2.7% of the World's total. In 1902 there were 171 mills operating, and the value of 864,000MT produced was $36.8 millions. By 1918 the number of mills reached a peak of 198 with a production of 3,5 million MT. By 1925 the number of mills had consolidated at 183, and production reached 5.3 million MT. with the production value reaching $295 million, equivalent to $89.4 per person. This is more than double the average reached in 1894 but only 26% of the income per capita provided by the "zafra" of 1920. At that time 192 mills were producing a total of 3.8 million MT, which represented a 22.4% share of world production. The international sugar price of 12.13 cents per pound meant a total value of the sugar crop of $1,022 million.

In the next 5 years the boom in prices brought production to 5.2 million MT. However, Cuba's world share was reduced slightly to 21.1%, as other countries responded to the price stimulus and to better production and trade conditions after the end of World War I. But a more meaningful expression of Cuba's sugar predominance is the fact that it represented 34% of the International Sugar Market.

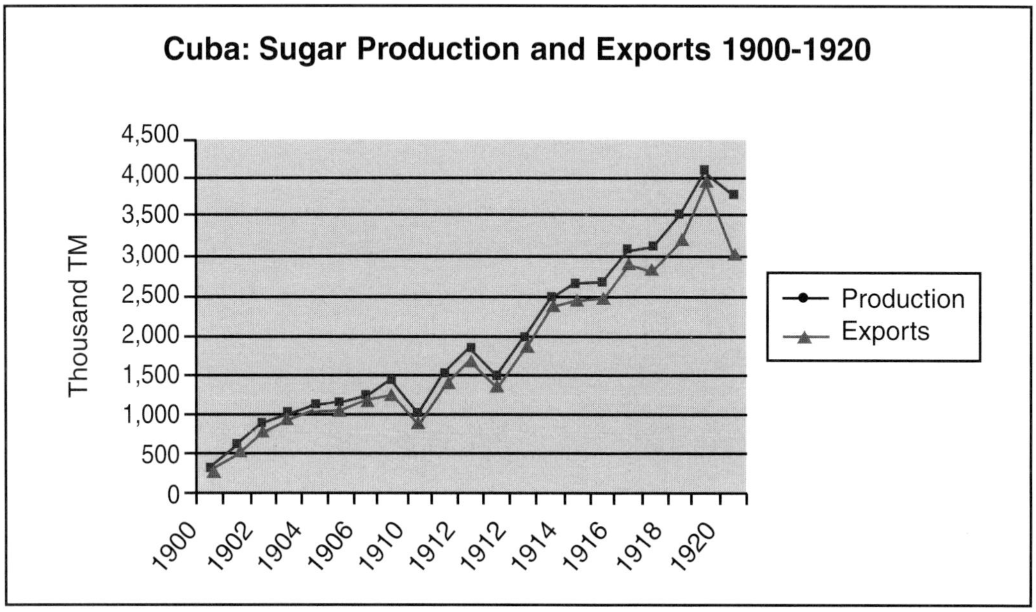

Source: Ramiro Guerra y Sánchez, Azúcar y Población en Las Antillas, Segunda Edición, Madrid, Cultura S.A., 1935 for production. Grupo Cubano de Investigaciones Económicas, Estudio sobre Cuba, University of Miami Press, Miami, 1963.

By 1927 there were 177 mills in operation, of which 63 were built between 1899 and 1927, and 32 of them in the years 1914-1920.[6] Later on, as a result of the Great Depression, the number of mills dropped to 125 by 1933 and production came down to 1.99 million MT. International prices dropped to $21.30 per MT, given a value of the production of $53.7 million, equivalent to $ 13.56 per person. It represented a drop to 32% of 1894 production value per person and a 15% of what it was in 1925.

[6] Problems of the New Cuba. Report of the Commission on Cuban Affairs. Foreign Policy Association. New York. United States of America, 1935, page 236.

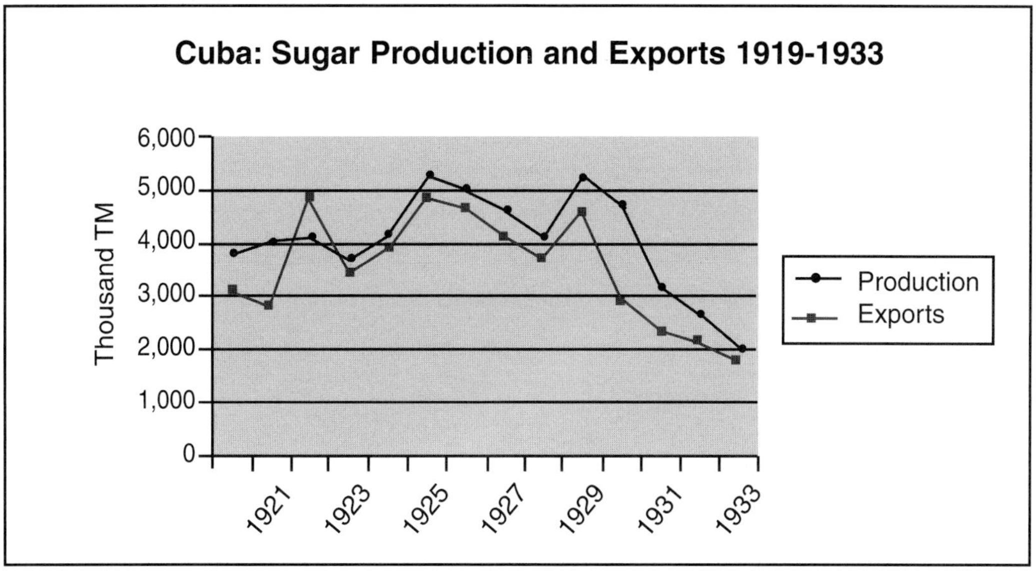

Source: Ramiro Guerra y Sánchez, Azúcar y Población en Las Antillas, Segunda Edición, Madrid, Cultura S.A., 1935 for production. Grupo Cubano de Investigaciones Económicas, Estudio sobre Cuba, University of Miami Press, Miami, 1963.

As Cuba's Gross Domestic Product was highly correlated to sugar income, few can fathom what it meant to have an 85% drop in income per capita within the short period of 8 years. As a matter of comparison the dramatic drop in income per capita in Russia, after the dismantling of the Communist Regime, was just 50%. As Keynesian economics had not become common doctrine the Cuban government missed public employee's payments and continued a series of repressive measures that led to its downfall in 1933.

Subsequent legislation, the recovery of the US economy, and the war in Europe were instrumental in changing the structure of the industry so that by 1940 157 mills were operating and producing 2.8 million MT, valued at $110.1 million.[7]

[7] Un Estudio Sobre Cuba. Op Cit. Pages 441, 443, 446.

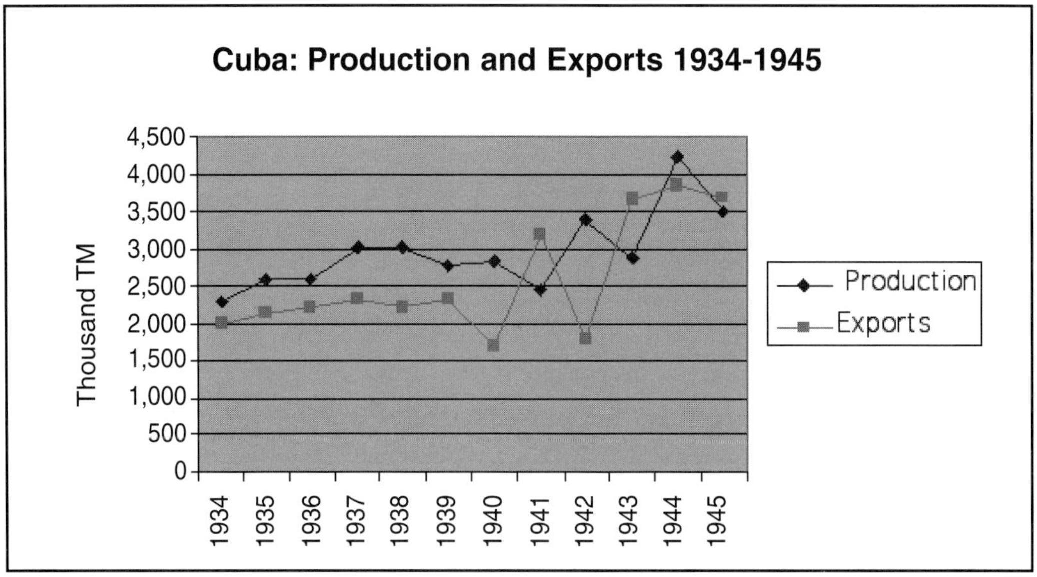

Source: Grupo Cubano de Investigaciones Económicas, Estudio sobre Cuba, University of Miami Press, Miami, 1963.

c. From World War II through 1959

After the Second World War, Cuba's competitive advantage and its privileged access to the U.S. sugar market helped Cuba to consolidate its commanding role in sugar production, and more so in the international sugar market. In 1932 Cuba represented 11.4% of the 22.3 MT of World Consumption, and while this reached 42 million MT by 1957, an increase of 88%, Cuba's production growth of 111% outpaced it claiming a 12.8% share by 1957. So Cuba retained over 35% of the International market, estimated at close to 15 million MT.

[8] Guerra, José Antonio, "La Industria Azucarera de Cuba". Published in Siglo y Cuarto. Diario de la Marina, La Habana, 15 de septiembre de 1957. Reproduced in the book of the same title by Ediciones Páginas Cubanas, Miami Florida, USA, 1987, page 98.

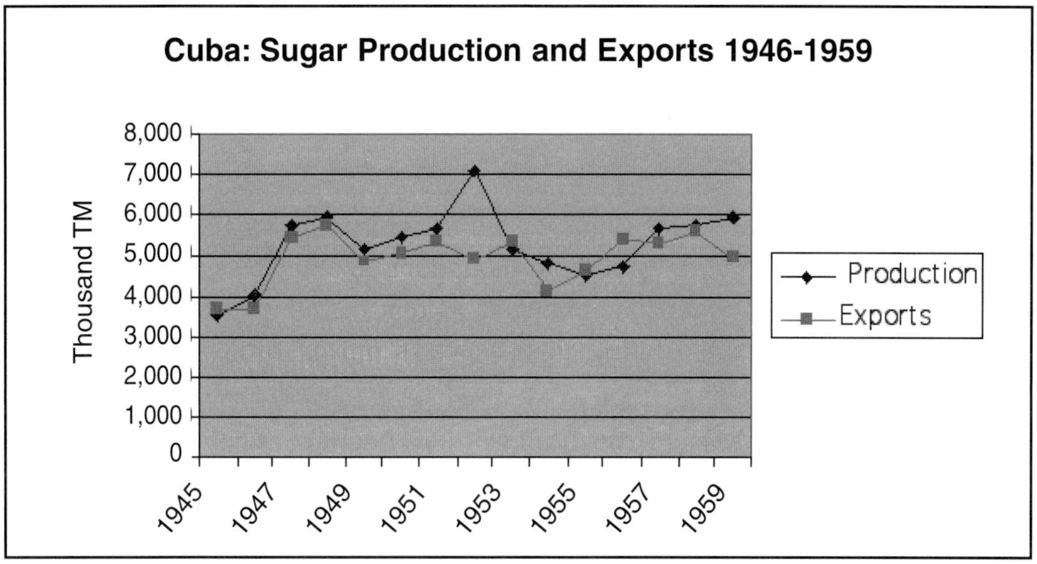

Source: Grupo Cubano de Investigaciones Económicas, Estudio sobre Cuba, University of Miami Press, Miami, 1963, and 1955-1959 F.O. Licht's International Sugar and Swetener Report, 1995.

Cuba has been either the largest or among the largest sugar producers in the world. In the 1920's, it was the world-leading producer. In the years just preceding the 1959 Revolution, Cuba's exports of around 5 million tons annually provided one-third of global sugar exports. This dominant participation in the world market, as well as its capacity to increase supply by 2 to 3 million MT in a given year, made Cuba a dominant factor in policing the International Sugar Agreement entrusted with maintaining an orderly market. During those years, Cuba was among the three largest producers and the largest exporter, surpassing in the sugar market the role of Saudi Arabia in oil exports.

3. As a vassal State the USSR

a. The first decade

Through the advent of the 1959 Revolution, the United States bought annually nearly 3 million tons, or 60% of Cuba's sugar exports[9]. This commercial relationship collapsed in 1960 when Cuba nationalized U.S. oil refineries and other businesses and, consequently, the US Congress suspended Cuba's sugar quota and

[9] Buzzanell and Alonso, Buzzanell, Peter, and José Alonso. "Cuba's Sugar Economy: Recent Performance and Challenges for the 1990s. In "USDA Sugar and Sweetener Yearbook (Washington: U.S. Government Printing Office, June 1989).

embargoed all trade[10]. Cuba was able to maintain a fairly high, but not efficient, level of sugar production due to the subsidy paid by the Soviet Union. Cuban sugar was sold to the Soviet Bloc (Soviet Union and other socialist countries in Eastern Europe) and China at prices that were far above the world market.

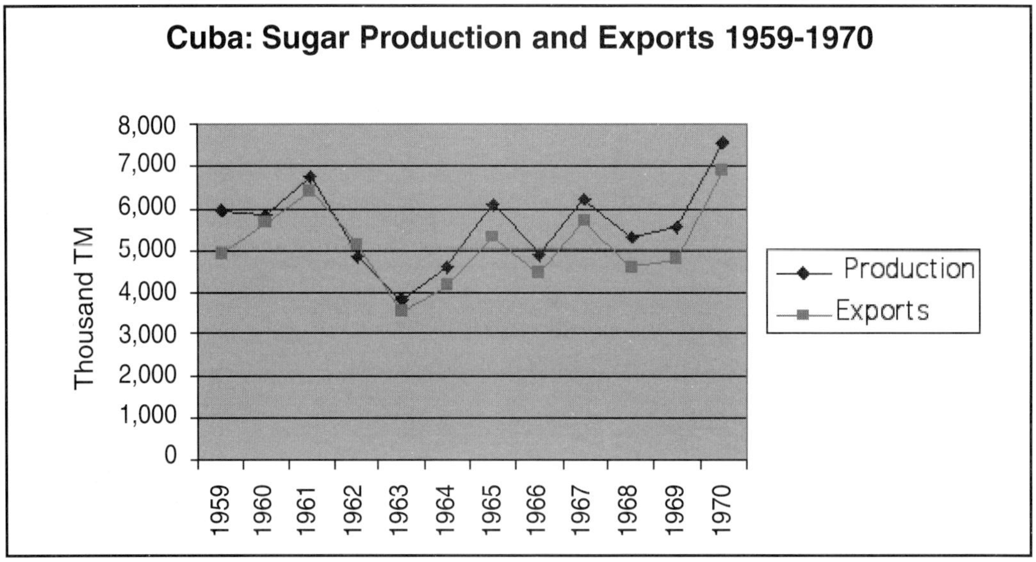

Source: 1955-1959 F.O. Licht's International Sugar and Swetener Report, 1995.

The 1960's were characterized by uneven performance in production because of the exodus of many experienced managers and skilled field and factory workers, and the transformation of production to a Socialist model. By 1965, two-thirds of Cuba's sugar exports were shipped to Socialist markets. Trade ties were solidified with these countries through a series of agreements, including access to the Socialist World's Council for Mutual Economic Assistance (COMECON).[11] Cuba sold one-third of its export to the free market to receive hard currency from non-socialist countries, such as Canada and Japan.

b. The push back to sugar

During the 1970's, Cuba's regime expanded sugar production, beginning the decade with the "long harvest" of 217 days in 1969/1970, during which the nation's

[10] The refusal of the foreign owned refineries to process heavy oil from the USSR was used by Castro to confiscate the installations. Only many years latter, while in Venezuela, I became aware of the difficulty and potential damage that will inflict in the refineries changing to heavy crude from the light oil, imported from Venezuela in 1959. No one in Cuba pointed to this fact at that time.

[11] Ibid.

physical and human resources were focused on producing a 10 million ton sugar crop. This effort, however produced a sharp fall in production the following three years, mainly because harvesting during the rainy season destroyed the fields, planting was neglected and fields were harvested prematurely. Production bounced back toward the end of the 1970's due to the expansion in area harvested and improved sugar yields.

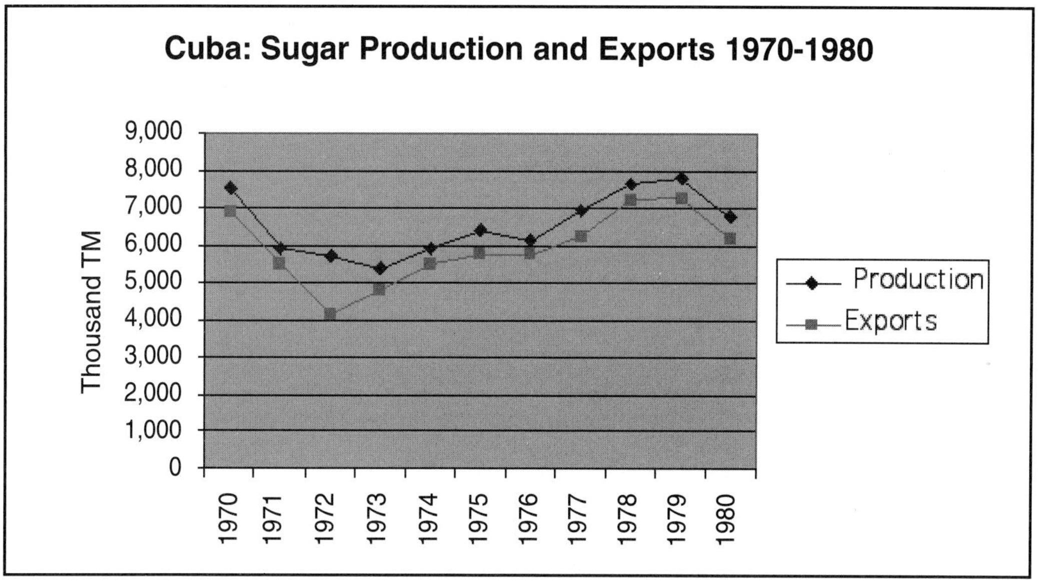

Source: 1955-1959 F.O. Licht's International Sugar and Swetener Report, 1995.

c. The final decade under the USSR

By the late 1980's, between 50% and 60% of Cuban exports went to the Soviet Union, by then the world's leading importer. During most of the 1980's, Cuba had been hard pressed to meet its commitments to COMECON countries and to produce enough sugar to sell for hard currency. In 1987 and 1988, the situation got worse, as poor crops and export over commitments led Cuba to mortgage its sugar export future: Cuba pledged part of its 1989 crop as collateral to repay over 1 million tons of sugar borrowed from a major international trade house, Sucre et Denre (Sucden), to fulfill export commitments to the Soviet Union. Many years Cuba had to go into the open market to fulfill its commitments.

Between 1970 and 1990, Cuba's sugarcane cultivation switched from manual labor to machinery. Machine combines harvested 67% of the area in 1988/1989, compared with 45% in 1980 and 25% in 1975.[12]

[12] Ibid.

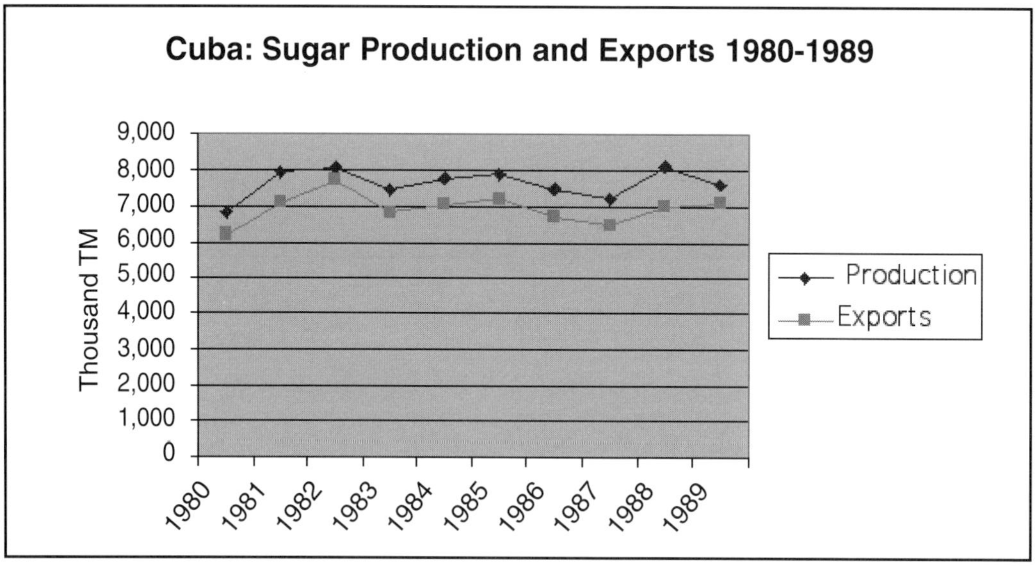

Source: 1955-1959 F.O. Licht's International Sugar and Swetener Report, 1995.

4. A drift from the former Soviet Block

After the fall of communism in the Soviet Union, Cuba's production collapsed as well. As of now, Cuba is not even among the ten largest producers of sugar and ranks only as the fourth exporter, with half the export volume of Australia. New efficient sugar exporting countries have appeared (Thailand, Brazil, Guatemala, Australia and Colombia). If Cuba were to apply appropriate cost and pricing methods, it might find that it is lagging far behind those countries in terms of profitability, due to the inefficiencies of the Communist System.

Furthermore, according toa Joint Delcarationof the Sugar Producers of Cuba, Inc. the Association of Sugarcane Growers, Inc., and the National Federation of Sugar Workers of Cuba, Inc.,[13] an equal area of land in the 1994-1999 period produced only 57.8% of the sugar produced in 1958. Where in 1958 the private sugarcane growers produced 43.30 tons/hectare, in 1994-1999 the Communist regime produced only 32.03 tons/hectare. The milling yield of sugar decreased from 12.82% to 10.03% for 1994-1999 period. Both factors meant that the sugar yield per hectare decreased from 5.55 tons/hectare in 1958 to 3.21 tons/hectare in 1994-1999.

[13] Federación Nacional de Trabajadores Azucareros de Cuba, Inc., Asociación de Colonos de Cuba, Inc., Productores de Azúcar de Cuba, Inc. "La Industria Azucarera Cubana es competitiva en el Mercado Internacional y es vital para la reconstrucción de Cuba como Nación Democrática; Ante el cierre de 85 Ingenios". El Nuevo Herald, September 23, 2002 Page 5A.

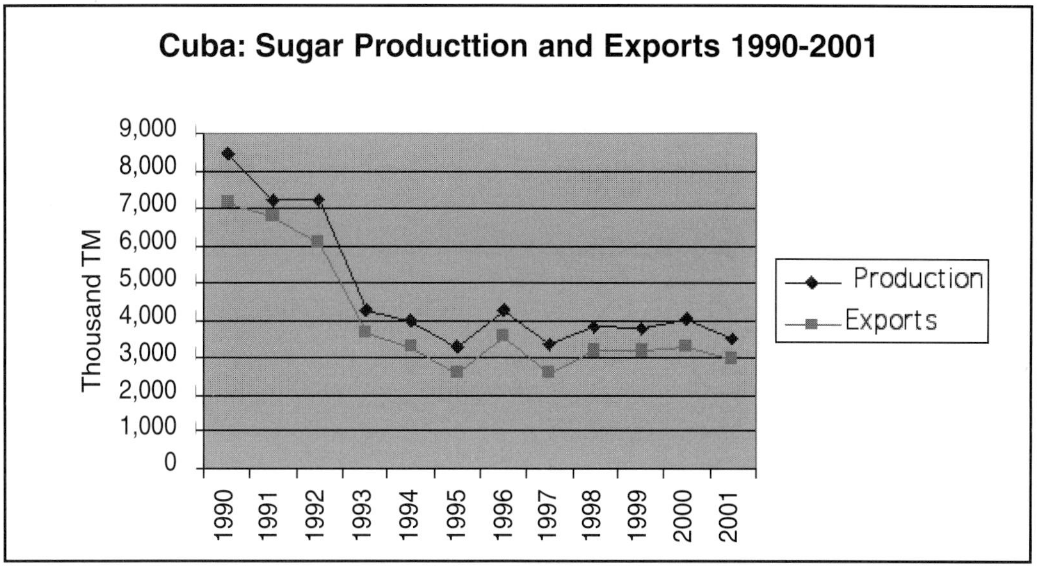

Source: 1955-1959 F.O. Licht's International Sugar and Swetener Report, 1995; 1995-2001 USDA Sugar and Sweetener Situation and Outlook Yearbook, 12.18.97 SSS-222, May 2001, SSS-231, June 2002, SSS-235.

5. 2002-Dismantling the Industry

After more than forty years of Castro's mismanagement which has depleted Cuba's sugarcane fields, ignored the maintenance of the factories, and removed the people's opportunities for advancement, thus stifling productivity, Cuba has not been able to remain competitive and keep pace with the evolution of the international sugar market. Having lost access to the US market and the production and financial capacity to police the International Sugar Agreement, Cuba's place in the international sugar market dropped significantly.

Deprived of the USSR subsidies to support his inefficiencies, Castro finally needed to face reality and announced that he will close nearly half the island's 156 sugar mills that had been operating in Cuba for most of the XX Century. This measure will deprive over half a million workers of work in an island of 11 million inhabitants. As usual the Government is hiding reality with absurd plans, promising no one will be out of work, as the mills will be converted to museums for a tourist industry that is also under pressure.

It could be ventured that with modern managers and savvy political clout, Cuba would have been able to retain the predominant role in sugar production, not allowing themselves to be outflanked by the protectionist sugar polices of the European Union and the United States. Those policies allowed the European

Union to dump 6.1 million MT into international sugar market, approximately 20% of the market volume, becoming the second largest participant, and costing the sugar exporters of developing countries more than $30 billions.[14] More over, Cuban's genius would have allowed for an orderly diversification towards other economic activities and not the abrupt process of halving the number of operating sugar mills in 2002.

B. Structure and Organization of the Cuban Sugar Industry

1. The prevailing regulatory framework and social organization

In 1926 The "Verdeja Law" gave the Government the right to establish the harvest commencement date and the amount to be produced. In 1927, a new law for the Defense on the Sugar Industry allocated quotas to the mills on the basis of previous year milling and created the Sugar Export Corporation, where all mills participated proportionally, to negotiate access to the foreign markets. In their first negotiation journey to Europe the Export Company was not as successful as they wanted. The 1928 level of production was established at 4 million MT, of which 3 million would go to the United States, evidence of the importance of this market to Cuba, and only 600,000 would be going to the International market through the Export Company.

After 1933 a series of laws were created for what was considered a model agro-industrial organization. The law of "Derecho de Permanencia" gave the cane growers the right to remain on their land and mill their assigned quota. They could not be evicted as long as they paid their rent, regulated in relation to the price of sugar, as well as their income, and provided the mill with the allocated tonnage, the price of which was also established by the Government in relation to the price at which the entire Cuban production was finally sold. The Cuban Institute for the Stabilization of Sugar, ICEA, calculated such price in accordance with the actual proceeds of the sales in the domestic, International Markets and the US Market. Under this model legislation the number of cane growers increased from 30,000 in 1932 to 62,000 in 1957.

Labor legislation advanced in parallel. The work session in the mills was limited to eight hours and paid vacations were instituted. Salaries both in the field and in the mills were regulated in relation to the price of sugar and, as the final price was not known until the end on the season, a monthly advance was provided. In addi-

---

[14] Bittersweet. The Wall Street Journal. September 16, 2002. Page A1 and A10

tion, normally at Christmas time, an advance on the "differential" (the difference between the price at which salaries were estimated and the final average price of the crop) was given, the remainder paid after the end of the "zafra". Unions were formed which, besides their role in Cuba, helped to organize labor unions among the sugar workers in developing countries to prevent that their lower pay scale gave those countries an unfair advantage. A retirement fund was created and well managed, paying monthly amounts that provided for adequate support within the Cuban social organization of extended family, where older people seldom lived alone.

Besides the Public Education System, most Mill and many large cane growers, who by enlarge were not absentee landlords, provided privately supported primary education for their worker's children. They sometimes shared the effort with the Government, which provided the teacher but, in many instances, the landlord also covered the expense of the teacher. It was not uncommon for the wives of the managers or of large cane growers to provide religious teaching in those privately supported schools.

In addition to the basic and emergency medical attention provided at the "Batey", the mill's villages, in the nearby "Pueblos" (towns) or "Ciudades" (cities) there were private clinics and hospitals operating as mutual support societies, similar to today's HMO, which provided adequate health care for a monthly fee of 3 to 5 dollars.

The next table provides evidence that, as a result of the organizational framework of the industry, the distribution of income showed a remarkably stable profile, providing the worker and cane growers a larger proportion of the value of the crop as the price and tonnage increased. In 1952 the payment to the labor factor alone was 62.8%, similar to the share of labor in the National Income in many developed countries, more so if we considered that for the 22% share of the cane growers there is a large labor payment. Rent represented that year 5% of the total and the income of the Firms, the mill's, was 10.3%. As the graph shows the mill's income appeared to have the highest volatility, being 1% in 1953, after the bumper crop of 1952 and 18.5% in 1947.

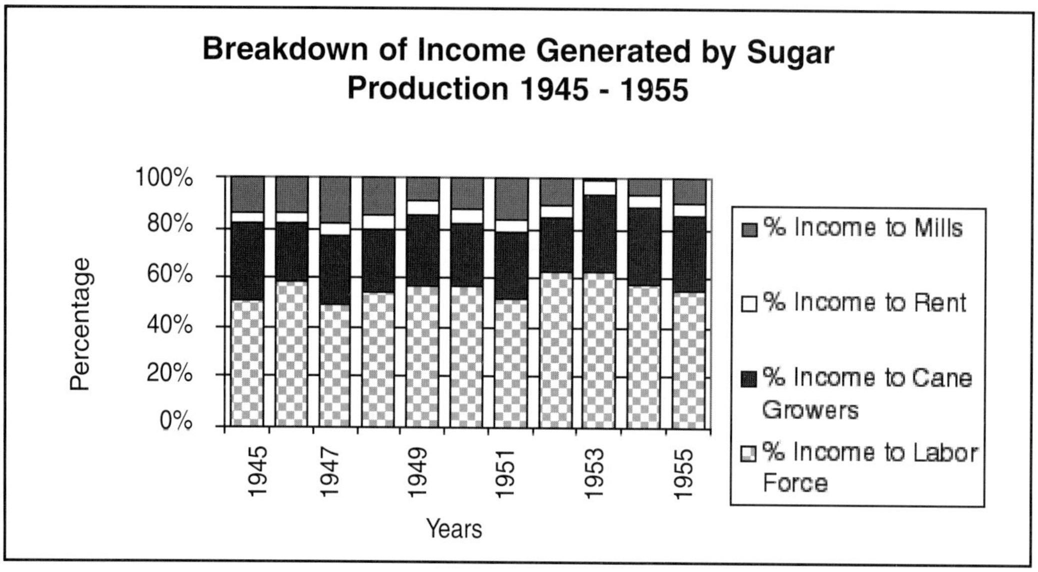

Source: National Bank of Cuba, Department of Economic Research, in José Antonio Guerra, "La Industria Azucarera de Cuba, 1932 - 1955", Diario de la Marina, Siglo y Cuarto, Ediciones Páginas Cubanas, Miami, 1987.

2. Evolution of ownership

a. From 1902 through 1939

Obviously with the end of colonialism, the period of United States intervention, and finally the Independence after 1902, the industry ownership tilted away from Spanish interests, increasing those of Cubans and Americans. In 1919 there was a total of 209 mills; 71 were classified as Cuban, 68 as American, and 41 as Spaniard, although in total production the American mills capture 51.4%, the Cubans 22.8% and the Spaniards 17.3 % .[15] Besides changes in nationality, was the tendency, at that time of "sugar merchants to sink from a prominence which they held as late as 1926" [as Sugar mills owners]. However, as we will see later in a Section devoted to them, their presence both as merchants and owners, gave Cuba, an outstanding advantage to attain and maintain its premier role in the International sugar Market.[16]

After the collapse of the sugar market most of the largest sugar companies in Cuba, both of Cuban and United States ownership were in receivership. National City Bank controlled eight mills and the Royal Bank of Canada even more, but tried to

[15] Ibid. Page 448.
[16] Problems of The New Cuba. Op. cit. page 228

preserve the title for the original owners. The Chase National Bank of New York had interests in the new Atlantic and Gulf Company and Punta Alegre and three other mills. Several others banks had also control of different mills. Even the Rionda family, long the outstanding sugar dealer in New York, had three of their sugar mills in friendly receivership. But, as we will see latter, the industry recovered and although there were some transfers of control toward Cuban interest, most of the prominent sugar names retained their significant participation in the industry.[17]

b. From 1939 through 1960

By 1939 the number of mills owned by United States interests were 66, but their 55.1 % share in total production represented an increase of only 3.7 percentage points over what their 68 mills had in 1919. By 1958 the number of US owned mills had come down to 36, 27% less mills, their share of production, at 36.7%, represented a decrease of only 33% from that of 1939. In 1939 the number of Cuban owned mills had decreased to 56 from the 71 in 1919, but the production share, at 22.4% was just slightly less than the 22.8% of 1919.

The roster of the major sugar companies in 1947, offers outstanding evidence of the resilience of many sugar firms in overcoming the financial difficulties of the late twenties and early thirties. As published in the Julian Aliene's book "Basic Characteristics of the Cuban Economy"[18] Cía Azucarera Atlántica del Golfo S.A, covered in Chapter III, was the largest with 14 mills, of which 12 were actives, producing that year 755,873 MT equivalent to 13.1% of that year's crop. Second to it, with 6 mills, all actives, was Cuban Trading Company, the Cuban trade name of Czarnikow Rionda, the Trading House based in New York, producing 367,286 MT, equivalent to 6.4 % of Cuba's production. Sucesión L. Falla Gutiérrez had also 6 mills, five actives, which gave them 6th place with 3.9% of the total. Julio Lobo, who, by 1958, had become the number one producer, followed by La Sucesión Falla Gutiérrez with 8 mills, that produced 3.1% of Cuba's output in 1947.[19]

---

[17] Ibid. Page 228

[18] I am privileged to have a copy of this book, personally dedicated by Prof. Alienes to Dr. Raul Maestri. Raul, a learned and prominent Cuban economist, who hosted the TV Program "Ante La Prensa" (Meet the Press) and had a Sunday column at "Información", prestigious Cuban daily newspaper until 1959. Raúl gave me his copy in Washington in 1961, when he realized it was printed at my father's Publishing House.

[19] Alienes Urosa, Julián, Características Fundamentales de la Economía Cubana. Banco Nacional de Cuba. La Habana, Cuba, 1948. Page 179.

By 1958 the number of mills owned by Cubans had more than double to 121and their share of production, at 62.3 was almost tripled. The 41 mills owned by Spaniards in 1919 dropped to 33 in 1939 and 3 in 1958, while their share on production was respectively 17.3%, 14.9% and 0.95% in those years. Finally there were 2 French owned sugar mills in 1939 with 0.6 % production share, down from 6 in 1919 that contributed 1.4%. By 1958 the two remaining French mills produced only 0.3% of the total.

Although there was a 37.8 % of production attributed to foreign owned mills we should stress, as Miguel Angel Falla's history proves, that Cubans managed the industry. In finishing this topic it should be pointed out that from 10 nationalities that owned the 209 sugar mills that existed in 1919, this was reduced to three for the 161 mills in 1958.

3. The Sugar Mills as development poles

By 1957 there was an increased social awareness among the sugar mill owners, and a new entrepreneurial blood in that younger generation of Cuban owners that by now controlled 77% of the mills. All the mills had good mechanical and electrical shops and trained work force, that had some idle time during before the "tiempo muerto" (the dead time). Also it became evident there were increasing demands made on capacity by the Cuban population at large. Thus, as described in the references to Miguel Angel first venture into rice planting, many mill owners and managers reached beyond sugar into rice, dairy and other compatible ventures. It will not be farfetched to propose that, taking the lead of the economic concept of "Development Poles", many sugar mills would have established light industries and other ventures that would have facilitated lessening the dependency on sugar.

C. The International Sugar Market

1. Major Producers

The top twelve producing countries, shown in the fallowing figure, accounted for 57.4 % of world production in 2001. In comparing production data for 1986 and 1959 we see countries with a very high rate of increase (such as Thailand, China, France and Pakistan, where production has increased by over 300%), while in Cuba production grew by only 23%. In fact, after 1959, Cuba had the lowest increase among major producers and was the only country among them with an increase lower than the world average. In the decade between 1990 and 2001, production increased at significant rates in countries such as India, Thailand, and Pakistan, while Communist countries such as Cuba and Ukraine had poor performances during that period.

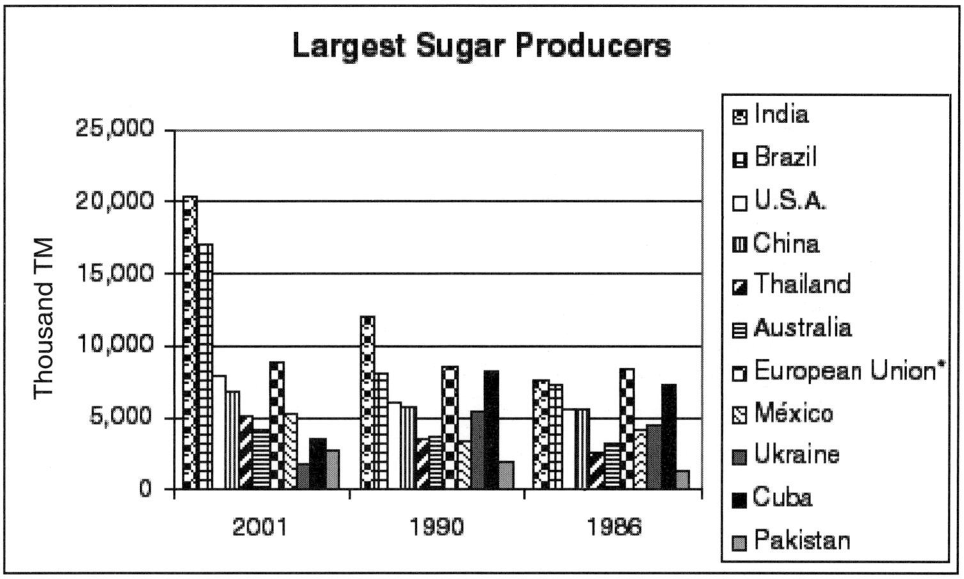

Source: 1955-1959 F.O. Licht's International Sugar and Swetener Report, 1995; 1995-2001 USDA Sugar and Sweetener Situation and Outlook Yearbook, May 2001, SSS-231, June 2002, SSS-235, and European Commission, Directorate-Generale for Agriculture.

As seen in the previous chart Cuba, which was in second place in 1990, by 2001 had had a reduction of 57%, dropping the 11th place.

2. Major Consumers

The 10 major consumers totaled 50.4% of world consumption and as the next figure shows, their differences in the benchmark years were not significant to alter their ranks. Consumption fell in Russia to its 1986 level, and grew at a slow rate in Germany, Japan and the United Kingdom but in total world consumption and production increased in parallel by 19%.

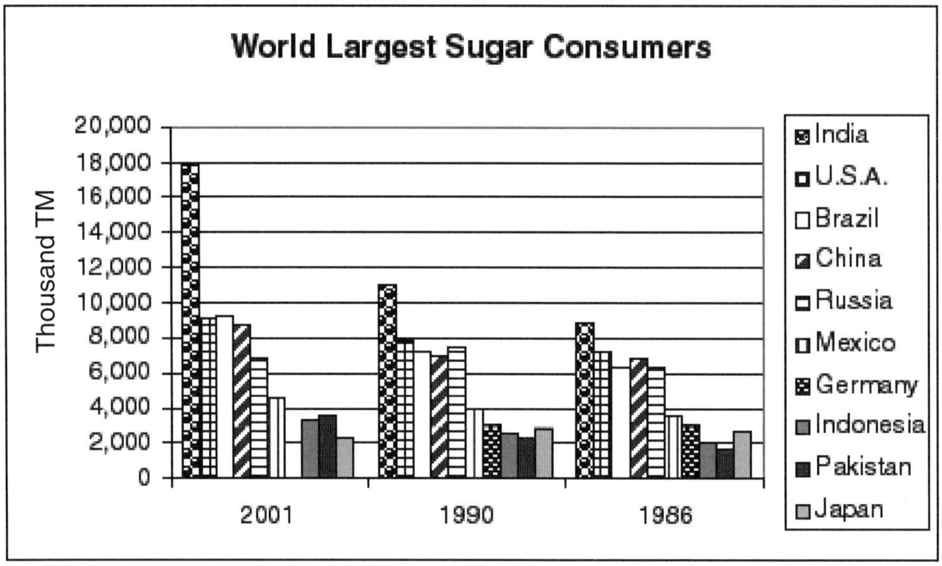

Source: 1955-1959 F.O. Licht's International Sugar and Swetener Report, 1995; 1995-2001 USDA Sugar and Sweetener Situation and Outlook Yearbook, May 2001, SSS-231, June 2002, SSS-235.

3. Major Exporters

The ten top sugar exporters are presented in the next figure. They accounted for 70% of the total export volume in 1986 but only 52.4% in 2001. In the decade between 1990 and 2001, world exports increased by 8%, while those of Cuba were reduced by 57%, in line with the decrease in production. Cuba, which had the number one rank in 1986 and 1990, dropped to 4th place in 2001

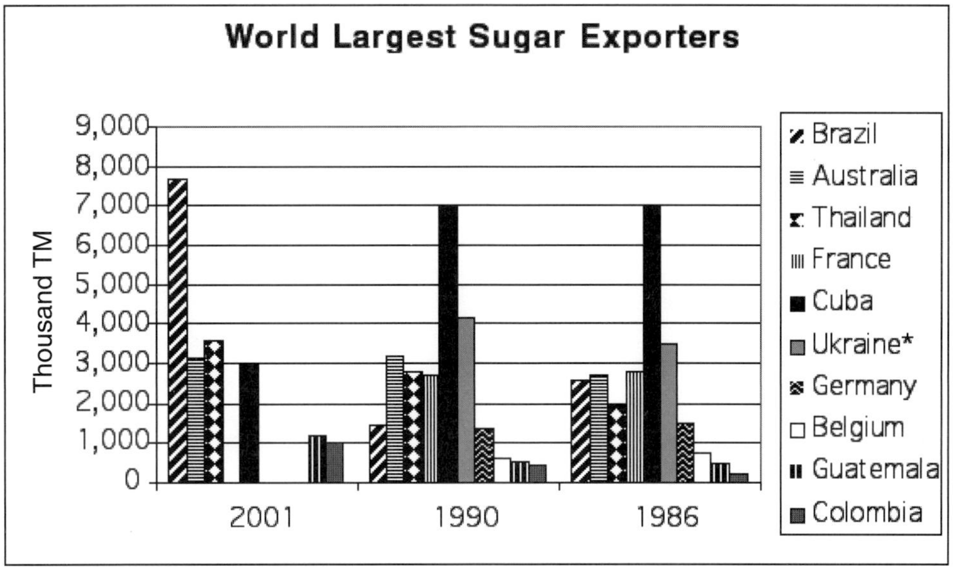

Source: F.O. Licht's International Sugar and Sweetener Report.
USDA Sugar and Sweetener Situation and Outlook Yearbook, May 2001, SSS-231.
USDA Sugar and Sweetener Situation and Outlook Yearbook, June 2002, SSS-235.
1996-1999 data for France, Germany and Belgium from Comité Européen des Fabricants de Sucre, http://www.ib.be/cefs/importexport.htm.

Ukraine has almost disappeared as exporter. South Africa has substitute Ukraine with 399 thousand metric tons in 1996, 1,056 in 97, 1,160 in 98, 1,355 in 99, 1,410 in 2000, and 1580 in 2001.

4. Major Importers

The ten major importers, shown in the next chart, represented 49% of total volume in the same year World imports increased by 1.3%, mainly due to increases in imports by China partially offset by decreases in India and the United States. Imports by Japan and Canada – Cuba's main non-Communist markets – were reduced by 2-3%.

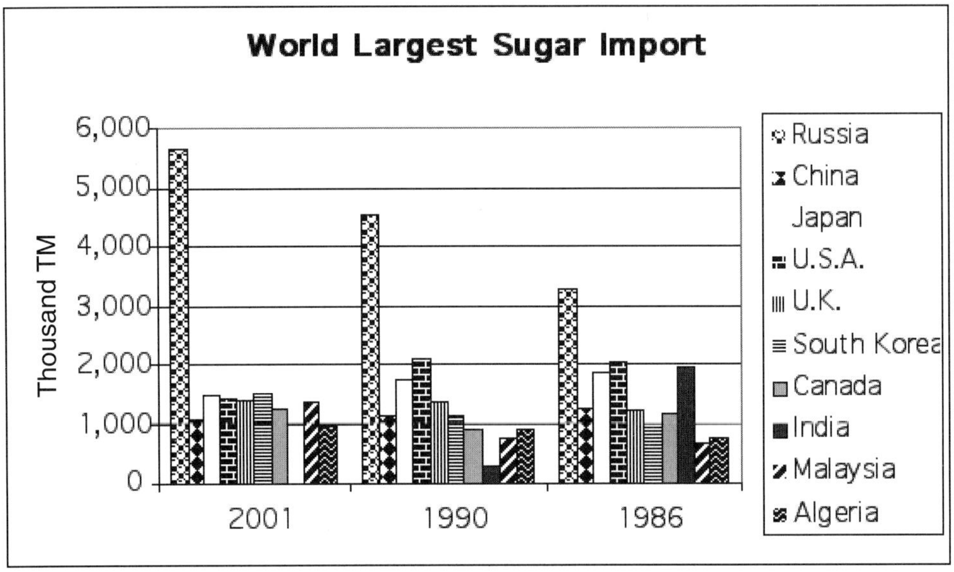

Source: 1955-1959 F.O. Licht's International Sugar and Swetener Report, 1995; 1995-2001 USDA Sugar and Sweetener Situation and Outlook Yearbook, May 2001, SSS-231, June 2002, SSS-235, and 1996-1998 data for UK from Comité Européen des Fabricants de Sucre, http://www.ib.be/cefs/importexport.htm.

D. Cuba's place in the International Sugar Market - past and future.

1. Preeminence in Sugar up to Castro's Revolution

As seen in the preceding tables in the 1920's, Cuba was the world's largest producer and, while later relinquishing that title, its exports of around 5 million tons annually provided almost one-third of global sugar exports up to 1959. Up to that time, its capacity to increase supply by 2 to 3 million MT in a given year, made Cuba a dominant factor in policing the International Sugar Agreement to maintain an orderly market. Prior to Castro's systematic vandalism process against the Cuban Economy, Cuba was among the three largest producers and the largest exporter, representing in the sugar international market a larger force than Saudi Arabia in oil exports. Cuban-owned sugar traders dominated that commodity in the New York Sugar Exchange.

2. The sources of Cuba's Preeminence

Cuba succeeded in maintaining its dominant role due to three major factors: First, its higher productivity in sugar due to its outstanding natural conditions of soil and climate; a well organized agricultural sector; and excellent and well-maintained industrial capacity, all within a very modern regulatory framework referred to in the previous epigraph. Second its special relations with the United States consecrated in treaties and in the US law by the quota system, which reinforced Cuba's position in the world market. The third factor was the role of the Sugar Trading Houses.

a. Cuba's productivity

In his book, Alienes indicated that in 1942 Louisiana's cane was 221% the cost of Cuba's and its mill were 21% more costly to run, giving Cuba an overall advantage of 44% lower total cost.[20] The following figure plots a critical production statistic, the yield per hectare. While dropping substantially after the 1960 confiscation of the mills, the yield recovered, although we don't know at what cost. This fact points to inefficiencies in the socialist process, not the land, as the cause of Cuba's sugar crisis.

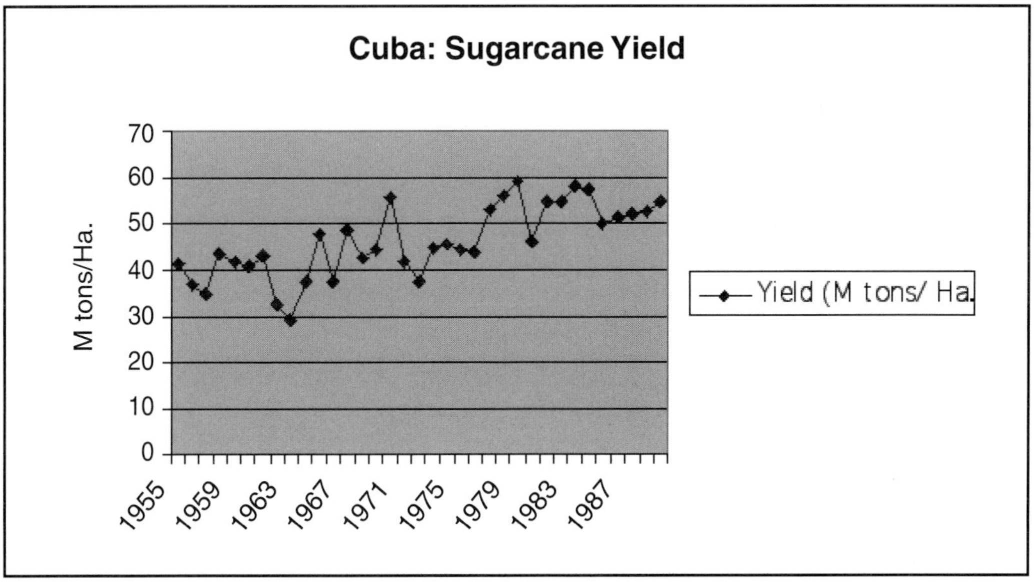

Source: Buzzanell and Alonso, June 1989.

b. Predominance in the United States market

From the beginning of the 20th Century, Cuba rapidly became the largest source of imported sugar for the United States. Cuban exports to that country increased from 17.6 % market share in 1900 to 60% by 1904.[21] Thereafter, exports to the United States remained above 50% until 1931, when they dropped to 37.2% and then to 28,2% in the following year. Exports remained at that level until 1942,

[20] Alienes Urosa, Julian. Op cit. Page 106

[21] Problems of the New Cuba. Op. cit. page 236

when they began to drop due to the recession in the United States, which was the largest consumer of Cuban sugar.[22]

The US Quota System allowed Cuba to export over 50% of its production to the United States at the highly protected prices of the U.S. market. The implicit subsidy to the Cuban economy that resulted from the U.S. quota allowed Cuba to cover profitably most, if not all, of the cost of the entire crop helping Cuba to have available a substantial stand-by reserve of almost a million tons of raw sugar and a capacity to extend the crop season and harvest for almost an additional million tons, when needed. This reserve – amounting to almost 20% of what at the time was the volume of the international sugar market – allowed Cuba to be a market leader that was very efficient and effective in controlling price and thus the cornerstone of the International Sugar Agreement.[23]

c. The Cuban Sugar Trading Houses

The Cuban owned Sugar Trading Houses, well established in the New York and London Sugar Exchanges, gave Cuba an excellent tool to prevail in the International Market. Among the most prominent were Rodríguez de Mendoza e Hijos, Galván Lobo Trading Co., and Czarnikow Rionda Company Inc. The direct ownership or control of the "physical" (actual sugar not certificates), gave the Cuban trading houses a very important competitive advantage for both Julio Lobo and Czarnikow Rionda.

Before the confiscation of their Cuban mills, the Cuban Sugar Houses had a presence in other sugar producing countries, which also provided intelligence but traded mostly Cuban sugar. By, 1959, Julio Lobo was the largest producer of Cuban sugar and even a larger trader. Czarnikow-Rionda, through its producing companies in Cuba and its trading subsidiary, Cuban Trading Co., had become the second largest exporter of Cuban sugar, with an annual volume of more than 1.5 million tons.

Upon losing his mills, Julio Lobo became very active in the Philippines, opening a larger office there. But unfortunately, burdened by the debt he had acquired to

---

[22] Estudio sobre Cuba. Pages 459 and 632.

[23] It is important to realize that while World sugar consumption and production had continued to grow, only a fraction of it is sold in the International Market. As all domestic markets have a protected price some sugar producers are able to export their surplus at their marginal cost thanks to the support of domestic sales. On the other hand Cuba's domestic market was very small so it could not provide such support, hence the importance of remaining competitive and, of course, the preferential access to the protected US market.

buy the Hershey mill and refinery in 1958, debt that was collateralized by substantial assets in the United States, and a sudden reversal of the futures market in the early seventies led to the disappearance of the Lobo name in the sugar trade.

However Lobo's impact transcended his departure from the industry, as one of his managers in the Philippines, Mr. Leandro Vázquez, was instrumental in organizing their disperse Sugar Industry after the model of Cuba's "Instituto de Estabilización del Azúcar" ICEA (Institute for the Stabilization of Sugar), becoming a key official in regulating the sugar trade of the privately owned mills of that country.

On its part, the confiscation of Czarnikow-Rionda's assets in Cuba in 1960, triggered the company's expansion of markets. The Philippines, Australia, Thailand, Brazil, the Dominican Republic, Colombia, Central America and all other major producing regions became Rionda's new clients. By 1963, the company was again a major factor in the international sugar market. Nonetheless by1968 the heirs to Manuel Rionda, who founded the Company in 1891, the Bragas, had sold 100% of the company's shares to a sugar-producing client, C. Brewer and Co., a wholly owned subsidiary of International Utilities Inc. of Canada. C. Brewer & Co. retained the management team, that by 1975, was able to fully acquire it, for $3 millions from C. Brewer & Co.

In 1982, Mr. Clark retired so the managers and – stockholders of Czarnikow-Rionda sold it for $32 million to a group from the Philippines led by Mr. Leandro Vázquez. But, with the ousting of Ferdinand Marcos, the Company leadership lost its special access to Philippine Sugar. The diminished roles of the traditional Managers, Mr. Fraites, Mr. Sterling and Mr. Kazi, and the departure of Mr. Gutman to become President of AMEROP, led to decreased activity in the 1988-1991 period.[24]

To avert the dismissal of the Company Arturo Sterling want to Arturo Mañas to propose to Gustavo Vollmer, the largest sugar producer in Venezuela and one of the wealthiest families, to re-capitalize the Company. When that deal fell through, and having done business with them in 1979-1980, both Arturo proposed the transaction to me, and on February 4, 1992 we injected fresh capital with a new group of investors from Venezuela, Peru, Panama, Nicaragua, El Salvador, England and the United States. We brought Daniel Gutman back from Amerop and named him Head Trader and President, while I retained the Chairman and CEO roles. By December of 1995, when we sold our remaining shares to the Traders, the

[24] Sterling, Arturo. "A Touch of History". Czarnikow-Rionda, 1992 Annual Report. New York, 1993. pag 5

Company had regained its leadership and become the largest Hispanic Owned business in the United States, as measured by sales.

4. Could Cuba recover its Preeminence?

Much to the sorrow of the displaced Cuban sugar workers in the island and contrary to the hopes of most of the unjustly expropriated owners of sugar mills and sugarcane plantations, whose just aspirations are to recover their properties and return to their days of glory, it is not evident that Cuba could recover its leading role in the International Sugar Market.

Under the present circumstances of Cuba's production and the new participants in production we do not foresee a return to glory even if a dramatic change were to take place in the political conditions of the island. One must recognize that a change in the political system in Cuba, and the subsequent opening of the U.S. market, will not automatically assure Cuba that it will recover its premier client, the US market. Several reasons support this statement. First the U.S. import quota has dwindled from 9.4 million tons in 1959 to the neighborhood of 1 million tons in 1995. Second the United States will not abandon its current suppliers of sugar just to accommodate a free Cuba. Finally, there is a high probability that the U.S. quota system will be abolished in light of the new attitudes towards trade in the world and the phasing in of Mexican Sugar through NAFTA by year 2008.

Thus, although the change in the political system would certainly facilitate improvements in what would remain of the sugar industry, it will not produce a miracle turn-around, whereby Cuba will again enjoy a privileged position in the U.S. sugar market, as a factor in regaining a commanding role in the World Market.

In conclusion, we hope that this Chapter has provided the reader with an adequate macro economic overview of Cuba's sugar industry, and its importance in the World until Castro destroyed it, along with the rest of Cuba's values, population and wealth.

I hope this overview will facilitate understanding, in its proper perspective, the dimension of the business interests that were under Miguel Angel's stewardship.

CAPITANES DE INDUSTRIA CREADORES DE RIQUEZA

MIGUEL ANGEL FALLA
La Industria Azucarera Cubana

Editor Oscar A. Echevarría
Prólogo Carlos Alberto Montaner

New House Publishers Inc.

Indice

A los creadores de la riqueza cubana, con gratitud y admiración

A aquellos que deben reconstruir Cuba, con ánimos y esperanza

A modo de presentación

El propósito de La Colección ***"Capitanes de Industria – Creadores de Riqueza"***, que se inicia con este libro, es evitar que queden relegados al olvido los logros y las vidas de aquellos empresarios y gerentes que situaron la economía cubana en lugar cimero para 1959.

El renovado interés por Cuba resulta evidente de la plétora de libros sobre su arquitectura, describiendo residencias que una vez fueron suntuosas, y las muchas guías de viaje recientemente publicadas. Sin embargo, el tema de la extraordinaria posición socio-económica de Cuba en 1959 ha sido relegado a artículos especializados de distribución limitada. Esta situación representa un peligroso vacío y amenaza con aniquilar nuestra inestimable herencia económica. Nosotros creemos que es necesario preservar el innovador ADN empresarial cubano. Esas características de ingeniosidad y laboriosidad han llevado a muchos cubanos en el exilio a posiciones de liderazgo en el mundo de los negocios en los Estados Unidos y en otras partes. Mantener vivo el legado empresarial cubano es el propósito de esta Colección.

Los perfiles de esos **innovadores, emprendedores y gerentes,** que situaron a Cuba en una destacada posición en 1959, ofrecen el lado humano de los hombres de negocios cubanos de esos tiempos. La descripción de los sectores económicos en que se desenvolvían estos individuos excepcionales proporcionará evidencia del éxito de la economía cubana antes que desaparezcan todos los rastros del lugar que Cuba ocupaba en la economía mundial en el año 1959.

Para facilitar la reconstrucción de Cuba sería inestimable tener los documentos originales sobre las empresas y su organización y, mucho mejor, acceso a sus creadores. Desdichadamente, la mayoría de esos pioneros cubanos ya no están con nosotros y, de igual manera, tampoco sus documentos o las empresas producto tangible de sus esfuerzos. Los recuerdos de sus descendientes sobre las dotes, esfuerzos, errores, perseverancia, y triunfos de sus antepasados son nuestro único vínculo con ese exitoso pasado económico. Facilitar esa información a las generaciones más jóvenes, quienes eventualmente reconstruirán Cuba, es la mayor contribución que la nuestra puede dar a los empresarios futuros. Esta Colección es una garantía para preservar semejante herencia.

Los próximos libros tendrán de cuatro a seis capítulos, uno por personaje, escrito, como en este caso, por un historiador o biógrafo profesional, sobre la base de testimonios, documentos y entrevistas. Economistas o analistas industriales, no necesariamente de origen cubano, escribirán una perspectiva general de la industria donde nuestros personajes se esforzaron y triunfaron. En industrias como el azúcar, cuya dimensión facilitó la existencia de muchos empresarios y gerentes excepcionales, habrá tantos volúmenes como sean necesarios.

La Colección será cuidadosa en no sucumbir a la nostalgia e idealizar el pasado de Cuba y se apegará a la verdad sobre los individuos a ser reseñados, y sobre la economía cubana en esa época. Nosotros creemos que la verdad es suficientemente poderosa y además es la única forma de merecer el respeto del Mundo Académico y de la Prensa. Pretendemos hacer la lectura atractiva para obtener un beneficio adicional o externalidad, como diríamos los economistas: el corregir la inmerecida opinión negativa que muchos americanos y europeos, aun aquellos con quienes tenemos relación, se han creado sobre la Cuba de 1959, a pesar del éxito de la comunidad de negocios cubana en todos los países en que está presente. Por consiguiente, la colección se publicará en inglés, la *lingua franca* de los negocios, para que sea accesible a una audiencia más extensa.

Este primer libro se aparta del prototipo antes descrito, ya que abarca a un solo individuo y tiene un capítulo de testimonios sobre él. Pero es una suerte que la Colección sea inaugurada con una figura gerencial clave en la Industria del Azúcar. Me explico. Primero, la producción y exportación de azúcar había sido el buque insignia de la economía cubana por más de un siglo. Segundo, el hecho de que Miguel Angel fuera un gerente sirve para resaltar que esta Colección **no es**

acerca de quienes poseían riquezas, sino de quienes la creaban, a través de innovaciones, de establecer empresas, y de su buena gerencia, todos ellos factores que contribuyen al desarrollo económico y social. Finalmente, el hecho de que "The Cuban Atlantic Sugar Company" fuera la productora de azúcar más grande del mundo en la época en la que Miguel Angel fue su presidente, nos da una perspectiva excepcional de la relación de un ejecutivo cubano con una compañía y una familia poderosa, como la de los Loeb, disipando del todo la descripción distorsionada que se ha intentado establecer sobre las relaciones cubano-americanas antes de 1959.

Así, con este libro, presentamos al lector la Colección "***Capitanes de Industria***", antes que el tiempo erosione inexorablemente los recuerdos de los testigos que aún quedan. Esperamos que muchos de los herederos de figuras semejantes nos acompañen, a Carlos Alberto y a mí, en documentar, con un toque humano, la estructura económica de Cuba antes de 1959 y, lo que es más importante, las lecciones que los "***Creadores de Riqueza***" puedan dar a generaciones futuras.

Sin más, el libro.

Oscar A. Echevarría
Washington, DC. 18 de septiembre del 2002

Prólogo

Poco antes de escribir estas líneas le puse punto final a un libro titulado *Cuba: un siglo de doloroso aprendizaje*. La obra era un recorrido por los errores y actitudes que nos condujeron a la situación actual de la Isla. Naturalmente, ese triste recuento dejaba sin respuesta una incómoda pregunta: ¿no sería acaso injusta esa visión tan negativa de nuestros yerros políticos? ¿No había nada ejemplar y salvable en la historia del país?

Por supuesto que lo había. Bastaba recorrer La Habana, aunque fuera hoy, en medio de las ruinas de esa bellísima ciudad irresponsablemente tugurizada por el castrismo, para comprobar que en ese país alguna vez hubo un grupo muy notable de creadores de riqueza. Sin duda, una de esas zonas de excelencia surgidas en el seno de la sociedad civil se encontraba en el empuje y la modernidad de cierta clase empresarial. Por eso me pareció atinadísima la propuesta de Oscar A. Echevarría – él mismo un economista y empresario de primera línea – de que editáramos una serie de monografías dedicadas a diversas personalidades quienes habían hecho posible que hasta 1959 Cuba estuviera en el pelotón de avanzada de América Latina y entre los 25 países más prósperos del planeta, de acuerdo con el Atlas económico publicado en aquellos años por Ginsberg.

También era razonable comenzar por Miguel Angel Falla, gerente de distintas empresas dedicadas a la producción de azúcar y parte de la familia Falla Gutiérrez, una de las más prominentes del país en el terreno económico. Miguel Angel, había sido, sí, el padre de Elena, la esposa de Oscar, pero lo importante no era ese entrañable lazo familiar, sino que en vida había sido un administrador muy capaz (y humano), como se ve en los Testimonios que constituyen el Capítulo II de este libro, dentro de una compleja agroindustria que constituía la espina dorsal de la economía cubana.

"Sin azúcar – decía un lema prerrevolucionario – no hay país". Afirmación totalmente exagerada que podía matizarse con otra aseveración seguramente más acertada: "sin azúcar Cuba hubiera sido totalmente diferente". Y una de las diferencias hubiera estado en el tipo de clase empresarial que se habría desarrollado en la Isla. La producción azucarera de Cuba – muy bien descrita por Echevarría en este mismo libro – tímidamente comenzada a mediados del XVI y acelerada desde fines del siglo XVIII, constituía un complcjo proccso industrial, tccnológico, laboral y económico que requería altísimos niveles de gerencia administrativa. No era sólo sembrar y cosechar. La industria azucarera debía surtirse de la caña cultivada por mas de 60.000 colonos y cortada por cientos de miles de campesinos. Y en torno a cada uno de ellos, especialmente de los mayores, surgían "bateyes" que eran, en realidad, pequeños pueblos en donde existía un cierto nivel de urbanismo y se obtenía una calidad de vida ciertamente mayor que las de los caseríos rurales que no estaban adscritos a una buena fábrica de azúcar. En general, esos bateyes solían ser limpios, pacíficos y organizados. Por otra parte, se necesitaban grandes instalaciones industriales, conocimientos técnicos, manejo inteligente del financiamiento, logística y capacidad de negociación para participar de una actividad económica basada, esencialmente, en la exportación. Dato este último – la exportación – que dictaba otro elemento fundamental: el bursátil. Sencillamente, los criollos dedicados al azúcar no podían ignorar los vaivenes de las bolsas de Londres o New York. Cuando nadie hablaba de "globalización" la clase empresarial cubana, por imperativos de la producción azucarera, estaba totalmente "globalizada", con Casas Azucareras, como las de Julio Lobo y "Czarnikow-Rionda" que, con Asientos en la Bolsa de Azúcar y Café de New York y Londres, eran señeras en el mercado.

La producción y comercialización del azúcar, pues, en la que participaban cientos de miles de personas, fueron confiriéndole al país un cierto perfil en el terreno de las transacciones económicas, elevando el nivel tecnológico general y la calidad de la gerencia administrativa, incluso en los renglones de la economía en los que aparentemente no había conexión con la industria azucarera. Cuando los cubanos, con razón, se ufanan de haber contado con el primer tren que circuló en el mundo hispánico, no suelen advertir que ese paso de avance fue dado para servir a su majestad el azúcar. Y lo mismo puede decirse de la administración de los puertos y del temprano desarrollo primero de la telegrafía y luego del teléfono.

Lo que quiero decir es que el nivel de desarrollo y de atraso de una sociedad viene dictado por la complejidad de los procesos productivos dominantes. Cuando la prensa o "cachimbo" azucarero – dos piedras que trituraban unas cañas de azúcar – proveniente de la Edad Media fue dando paso, poco a poco, al ingenio actual, en ese largo y centenario camino arrastró a toda la sociedad en la dirección de la modernidad. ¿Qué se desprende de eso? Que no es una casualidad que mediado el siglo XX surgiera un empresario como Goar Mestre – en realidad los tres hermanos – capaz de echar las bases de la televisión antes que nadie en América Latina, sino la consecuencia de un cierto nivel de excelencia que había sido establecido mucho antes por la industria dominante, que era la azucarera. Como tampoco era una casualidad que las cadenas de restaurantes de "comida rápida" y barata surgieran en Cuba (Pollos el Caporal) de la mano de Domingo Moreira al mismo tiempo que comparecían en Estados Unidos. Otros ejemplos abundan, tal es el caso de Mariano Guastela en publicidad, Crusellas y Cubas que se batieron exitosamente con Procter y Colgate, Solís, cuyos asociados después de separarse de El Encanto implantan el concepto de tiendas de Departamentos en España. La historia de estos y otros pioneros, y la de las empresas que ellos crearon o desarrollaron, será cubierta en subsecuentes volúmenes.

El azúcar había puesto el listón muy alto y la clase empresarial, seguramente sin percatarse de ello, respondía a esta secreta tradición. Y uno de los buenos ejemplos de este importante fenómeno socioeconómico, sin duda, es Miguel Angel Falla. Veámoslo de cerca.

Carlos Alberto Montaner

Introducción

En su concepción original este libro hubiese consistido en una colección de testimonios sobre Miguel Angel Falla. Era una sorpresa de cumpleaños a mi esposa Elena, que se distribuiría solamente a familiares y amigos cercanos a su padre, como tributo a él. Esta hubiese sido una tarea fácil de haberse hecho luego del fallecimiento de Miguel Angel, el 8 de febrero de 1973. No es así después de 30 años que han reducido el número de testigos directos y una diáspora que dificulta contactar aquellos que aún quedan. Es por ello que a pesar de los grandes esfuerzos de nuestra amiga Rita Moreno de Blain, a quien acudí en junio, a fines de agosto sólo teníamos 5 testimonios. Aún cuando limitados en número estos documentos me ofrecieron una nueva perspectiva de la extraordinaria capacidad gerencial y calidad humana de Miguel Angel Falla, a quien recordaba como vecino y por aquel entonces, el padre de mi "flaquita de enfrente". Su historia es digna de contar.

Ante el apremio de tener el libro para octubre opté por recurrir a Ena Curnow, elegida por Carlos Alberto Montaner para colaborar como biógrafa en una Serie que retratara a hombres de negocios cubanos de la República. El próximo paso era lógico: hacer de este primer libro sobre Miguel Angel un modelo a seguir en la Serie. Así se explica como la idea de una impresión privada de evocaciones se convirtió en un libro a disposición del público.

Esta es la biografía de un individuo extraordinario, al mismo tiempo que un recuento sucinto de la Industria Azucarera cubana, la actividad más importante del país por varios siglos. Además de datos sobre la economía cubana, se ofrece una interesante visión sobre las costumbres sociales y de negocios de la época, y permite que nos asomemos a otros influyentes personajes del momento.

El primer capítulo proporciona al lector la oportunidad de conocer no sólo detalles de la vida de Miguel Angel Falla, sino también los antecedentes de su época. Las referencias paralelas al tío de Miguel Angel, Laureano Falla Gutiérrez, el fundador del importante grupo azucarero conocido como La Sucesión Falla Gutiérrez y de otras empresas, proporciona un material excelente para aquellos interesados en las primeras etapas del mundo de negocios cubanos.

Bien significativo es el hecho de que después de la independencia cubana, por sugerencia del Gobernador de Estados Unidos, los Generales del Ejército Libertador se acercaron a los españoles adinerados para convencerlos de que no se fueran de la Isla. Como consecuencia de esos esfuerzos se forjó una amistad cercana, y posteriormente una relación de negocios, entre el General Gerardo Machado y Laureano Falla Gutiérrez, quien había sido Capitán del Cuerpo de Voluntarios del Ejecito Español. La amistad fue tan cercana y la reputación de Laureano tan honorable que, más tarde, su palabra fue el único aval que Machado necesitó para garantizar que él cumpliría un pacto político con otro líder del Partido Liberal que le disputaba su candidatura a la Presidencia.

Las anécdotas acerca del primer viaje de John Loeb a Cuba y su posterior relación con el país y la familia Falla ofrecen una visión excelente de las relaciones cubano-americanas y las costumbres sociales y de negocios después de la Gran Depresión, y hasta 1960. Como en muchas biografías, las referencias a "tiempos y lugares" rivalizan en interés con los propios personajes. Este Capítulo puede considerarse una muestra de las cuatro a seis biografías cortas que sobre cada individuo se presentarán en los libros de la Serie.

El Capítulo II, denominado *Memorias*, es privativo de este libro. En posteriores volúmenes de la Serie, los testimonios serán incorporados al texto al estilo del Capítulo I, incluyendo, si están disponibles, citas de las cartas de los personajes reseñados. Si bien creímos preferible no anticipar en la introducción el contenido de este capítulo, sí encontramos importante ofrecer nuestra apreciación sobre el mensaje implícito en estos cinco testimonios.

Antes de nada, hay que señalar que los cuatro hombres comenzaron a trabajar en posiciones administrativas de bajo nivel y sin educación superior. Sin embargo, todos ellos abandonaron la industria, después que fue confiscada, con uno o más títulos universitarios, obtenidos mientras trabajaban, en muchos casos haciendo uso del Sistema de Matricula Libre que permitía examinarse sin asistir a clase. Para ello contaron con el apoyo de la Gerencia y con el acceso gratuito a las respetadas universidades cubanas. Repitiendo la frase coloquial de Medardo, entraron los Centrales como "guajiros cerraos" y los abandonaron con títulos universitarios. Creo que esto refuta el estigma de capitalismo explotador que se quiere atribuir a la organización económica durante la Cuba Republicana.

Contribución inigualable a desmentir la falsa imagen de división y conflicto social en la Cuba anterior a 1959 son tanto que Juan de la Cruz y Saturio Rocío guardaran las cartas de Miguel Angel, como las anécdotas que de él narran. Ciertamente, no todos fueron como Miguel Angel, pendiente de que sus empleados fuesen atendidos cuando estaban enfermos, conversando y riendo con ellos en el portal de la Casa de Administración, después de la cena, tomando leche de cabra en la casa de cada agricultor cuando inspeccionaba los campos, y abriendo su casa y su corazón a sus colaboradores personales en momentos de necesidad. No obstante, la Serie "*Capitanes de Industria*" demostrará que hubo más Miguel Angeles que los "señores feudales" que se quieren presentar como el prototipo del pasado en Cuba.

Finalmente, como se evidencia de las referencias a Miguel Angel, a su padre, a su tío Laureano, y a otros miembros de la familia Falla Gutiérrez, no eran estos un grupo de propietarios absentistas. Como testificarían aquellos que conocieron la industria, la mayoría estaba en manos de gerentes-propietarios. Puede que sus familias se hubieran mudado a ciudades cercanas, o a la misma Habana, esto último tanto por ofrecer una mejor calidad de vida, como en respuesta a las necesidades de sus negocios y cuando las circunstancias lo permitían. Lógicamente, tener oficinas en la Capital era una necesidad en una industria regulada que exportaba más del 90% de su producción e importaba maquinaria y químicos industriales clave. Era en La Habana donde los dueños de los centrales podían manejar mejor sus relaciones con el Gobierno y las Casas Azucareras, y realizar sus compras en el extranjero. Sin embargo, ellos siempre estuvieron presentes en los centrales en tiempo de zafra y durante las reparaciones.

El Capítulo III sitúa a Miguel Angel en el contexto de los centrales que él dirigió. Se dan detalles de capacidad, rendimiento y producción de los tres centrales de la Sucesión Falla Gutiérrez, de los cuales Miguel Angel fue administrador, y de los 10 centrales de la compañía Cuban Atlantic, que supervisó como Presidente de la Empresa.

El Capítulo IV, "Cuba y el Mercado Internacional del Azúcar" brevemente repasa la historia de la producción de Azúcar de Cuba desde sus comienzos en 1523 hasta las guerras de Independencia. Los años de la República se dividen en períodos determinados por acontecimientos relevantes del mercado del azúcar, incluyendo la Depresión y la Segunda Guerra Mundial. Después de 1959, los períodos son determinados por las directrices políticas. Primero, el alejamiento del azúcar, por decisión del Ché Guevara. Luego se volcó el país de nuevo a la producción azucarera, formulando la meta de una zafra de 10 millones de toneladas nunca alcanzada, para lo cual se extendió la cosecha, arruinando muchos terrenos al proseguir el corte y tiro en época de lluvias y cortar campos no maduros. A continuación se cubre el período que comienza con el colapso de la Unión Soviética y la eliminación de los subsidios que ella ofrecía, y acaba con este año en que se desmantelan 70 de los 155 centrales de Cuba.

Además de revisar y analizar la información sobre la producción, el Capítulo IV cubre la estructura de la Industria, con relación a la propiedad y a la organización agropecuaria y laboral hasta 1959. Al final nos aventuramos a responder una pregunta hipotética y una prognosis. La primera es, ¿Dónde estaría la Industria hoy si el Sistema Socialista no la hubiese destruido? Hacia el futuro se ofrece un pronóstico sobre qué posición recuperaría Cuba en el Mercado Internacional del Azúcar una vez que cambie el régimen político.

Es bastante difícil hacer justicia a una industria tan compleja en tan pocas páginas. Los expertos en azúcar pueden encontrar el capítulo insuficiente, mientras que el lector no especializado posiblemente rechace tanto detalle. Ambos pueden estar en lo cierto. Igualmente importantes pueden ser las omisiones, imperfecciones y errores de interpretación en el capítulo. Esto es de esperar pues no siendo economista azucarero, como lo era mi Profesor José Antonio Guerra, ni hombre de la "Industria", carezco del dominio del tema que ellos tendrían. Mi experiencia con la industria tiene relación con la parte final del proceso, "El Comercio Internacional", lo cual es más una tarea financiera que la parte tangible y romántica de la producción, escenario en el que Miguel Angel triunfó. Cuatro años como Presidente y CEO de Czarnikov-Rionda, durante el comienzo de su segundo siglo, no me hacen un "Experto". Para compensarlo, he citado profusamente mis fuentes. Acepto cualquier comentario o crítica que venga de "azucareros históricos" y de mis compañeros economistas, lo último, por supuesto, es congénito a la profesión. Todos las observaciones serán respondidas y consideradas en ediciones futuras.

Antes de cerrar el tema azucarero quiero hacer tres afirmaciones sobre mi visión de la Industria Azucarera Cubana. La primera es que hasta 1959 Cuba fue el productor de azúcar más destacado en el mundo, por la eficiencia y organización de la industria, y el mayor exportador. El hecho de que ni mi familia ni yo fuéramos hacendados o "colonos" le da especial credibilidad a esta opinión profesional. Desafío a cualquiera a refutarla. Esto no significa que la Industria fuese perfecta, como lo demuestran los continuos esfuerzos de hacendados, colonos y sindicatos por mejorarla. Pero la industrial era la mejor en su época y en continuo perfeccionamiento. Segundo, que si después de 1960 Cuba no hubiese perdido su posición de líder en el Convenio Azucarero de Londres y el respeto de la Comunidad Internacional, no hubieran surgido nuevos productores de azúcar subsidiada en Europa y Estados Unidos, cuya sobreproducción le cuesta a los productores tradicionales de los países en desarrollo, los más necesitados, $30 mil millones al año, al deprimir los precios y negarles acceso a mercados desarrollados. Finalmente, me arriesgo a decir que, dado el ingenio de los Cubanos, quienes, sin piezas de repuesto, mantienen en funcionamiento automóviles americanos anteriores a 1959 el país hubiese evolucionado, en una forma ordenada, a otras actividades agrícolas, industriales y de servicios, incluyendo el turismo y tecnología de la información, como lo han hecho México y Brasil.

Publicar este libro ha sido muy grato, tanto por su objetivo y contenido, como porque me retrotrajo al negocio de mi padre, después de 42 años sin fungir como editor, menos aun impresor. Para mi volver al mundo editorial, que fue la vida y pasión de mi padre, tiene un gran valor sentimental. Pero como hoy no imprimimos lo que estábamos editando, como era el caso en Cuba, añoro el oler la tinta, el oír el rugir de las maquinas mientras convierten cartulinas blancas en cubiertas a todo color a 10,000 hojas por hora, y el tomar los libros, aún calientes, al salir de las encuadernadoras automáticas. Afirmo que sostener un libro siempre será una experiencia mucho más placentera que mirar la pantalla de una computadora.

Atenúa la ausencia de la experiencia inigualable de la producción en imprenta propia el que este libro se imprima en la litografía de Oscar Vidal. Durante los dieciocho años que mi padre editó en Miami, esperando siempre, al igual que Miguel Angel, el regreso, estuvo renuente a montar una Imprenta. Oscar Vidal fue su impresor desde 1965 hasta su muerte en 1979, como también lo es de este libro. Esta feliz coincidencia me inspiró a publicar, en homenaje a mi padre, bajo el nombre de su Editorial en Estados Unidos: New House Publisher, que es la traducción al inglés de nuestro apellido vasco.

Dentro de los desafíos que encontré estuvieron la limitación en el tiempo y lo secreto del proyecto. Lo primero puso una gran carga sobre Ena, las traductoras Monique Fernández e Ileana Fuentes, mi inestimable Asistenta Lara J. Evans, quien usó parte de su tiempo libre cuando estuvo en España en labores de la empresa, y Santiago Moralejo del Arco, mi Asistente en Georgetown University, para suministrar el material a tiempo. Esta carga fue aliviada por la comprensión y eficiencia de Oscar Vidal.

La fecha de entrega también chocó con el contenido de mi Capítulo sobre el azúcar, en el conflicto entre incluir muchos de los interesantes aspectos descubiertos durante el proceso y la fecha impostergable del 12 de Octubre. Espero haber incluido suficientes, pero de igual manera, más aspectos serán incorporados al editar el Capítulo actualizado en los volúmenes que incluyan otros destacados azucareros como Julio Lobo, Manuel Rionda y Francisco Blanco, entre otros.

Lo secreto del proyecto me privó del valioso apoyo de mi "Editora Principal," quien para mis documentos en inglés hace lo que Rita con los de su padre. Cuando el tiempo lo permite, Elena me proporciona excelentes contribuciones al contenido, la mayoría de las veces, y siempre al estilo. Otro precio del secreto fue la incapacidad de explicar convincentemente los motivos de estar trabajando en el "portátil" a las 5:00 a.m. Dos semanas de esta rutina provocaron una seria amenaza: "En enero vuelvo a trabajar para poder tener alguien con quien hablar, ya que mi esposo está casado con su computadora." Espero que el libro merezca que se abandone este pensamiento.

Con esta nota de buen humor, dejo los reconocimientos a los autores para otra sección e invito al lector a que se embarque en este viaje a la personalidad y vida de Miguel Angel y su mundo del azúcar, tan bien delineado por Ena Curnow y los cinco "testigos" hablando de corazón.

Oscar A. Echevarría
20 de septiembre del 2002

Capítulo I

La casa grande y la casa chica de Miguel Angel Falla

La casa grande y la casa chica de Miguel Angel Falla

Por Ena Curnow

"Vaya la guía, hombre:
y sin más ni más soltó las bridas
y dio paso franco".

(Cirilo Villaverde en "Cecilia Valdés")

Imagino a Miguel Angel Falla escuchando imperturbablemente la proposición de la oferta de que en lo adelante fuera el administrador de la joya azucarera de la familia: el central Adelaida, que su tío Laureano había fomentado con tanto esmero y cariño. No era fácil adivinar las emociones en sus ojos pequeños, – ojos pequeños para mirada grande. Como señalan los testimonios de sus colaboradores más cercanos, los fijaba directamente en su interlocutor, máxime cuando se trataba de asunto tan importante. Su apuesta y elegante presencia contribuía a impregnar el momento de mayor solemnidad. Sólo un ligero aleteo de su aristocrática nariz – respingona y altiva, el cuño de los Fallas le llama hoy su hija Elena – podría revelar, a los que lo conocieran mejor, si alguna idea preocupaba su mente.

Aun cuando pudo haber considerado un honor el nombramiento y lo apreciara, no debió sorprenderlo. De manera consistente había trabajado durante muchos años en el central Patria cuidando esa propiedad de la Sucesión Falla Gutiérrez, en que Don Miguel, su padre, tenía participación, al tiempo que iba desarrollando su actividad como colono. No era ningún improvisado ni el puesto obedecía a su jerarquía familiar. Ser descendiente directo de los Falla Gutiérrez no constituía carta blanca para escalar posiciones de liderazgo empresarial; tal era la política de la familia. Su trayectoria venía desde abajo, desde la base. Su conocimiento de la vida de los centrales se había forjado paso a paso, en el Patria, bajo la tutela de su padre, escalón por escalón, en constante desafío con la dura labor: el cultivo y molienda de la caña de azúcar. La dulce y amarga caña...

*****

Laureano Falla Gutiérrez nació en un humilde pueblo de las montañas: en Hoz de Anero, Santander, el 25 de diciembre de 1859. Años después vino al mundo su hermano Miguel. En los tiempos de la colonia, en 1874, Laureano se trasladó a Cuba llamado por el tío materno don Laureano Gutiérrez y Diego. Estudió por dos años en Cienfuegos y siguió trabajando como dependiente en la tienda de víveres del tío, situada en el caserío El Salto, término municipal de Santa Isabel de las Lajas. Como buen español inmigrante, ahorraba hasta el último centavo.[1]

Miguel ocupó el lugar de su hermano en la península, quedando al cuidado de su madre viuda, y dos hermanos menores, Juan José y María. Trabajaba duro cortando leña en el Monte de Llúa. Tan agotadoras eran las jornadas, que un mal día perdió el balance y se fracturó una pierna. Nunca olvidó el gran susto reflejado en el rostro de su madre al ver que lo traían en andas. Cuando llegó a Cuba, tenía ya 20 años de edad e inició una nueva vida trabajando en comercios de víveres, hasta tener su propio establecimiento en Lajas. También compró una colonia de caña y molía su cosecha en el ingenio San Agustín, controlado por su hermano. Laureano se convirtió en colono en 1894 adquiriendo la propiedad Villarreal, y en hacendado a partir de 1901 en el demolido ingenio Santísima Trinidad. Fue presidente de la Colonia Española de Cienfuegos - donde vivió casi siempre - y presidente del Casino Español de La Habana.

Según relata su sobrino, Miguel Cervera Falla,[2] *trabajando juntos o por separado, Laureano y Miguel formaban un dúo formidable. Los ingredientes fundamentales: el instinto del mayor para los negocios, el espíritu incansable y consistente de trabajo del otro. La primera inversión azucarera que hicieron ambos fue el central Patria, cerca de Morón, provincia de Camagüey. El ingenio era pequeño, pero dejaría suficientes dividendos para hacerse con un capital. Miguel aceptó la invitación de su hermano aportando el 20 por ciento del costo, y se quedó como administrador, mientras Laureano se ocupaba de desarrollar otros negocios desde La Habana.*

Don Laureano se mudó a la capital en 1915. Para entonces ya cada cual había formado su propia familia. Don Laureano contrajo matrimonio con Dolores Bonet y Mora y procreó a Isabel, Adelaida, María Teresa y Eutimio. Don Miguel contrajo matrimonio con Doña María de los Angeles Alvarez. Cuentan que el mismo día que se casó, se levantó a las cuatro de la mañana para inspeccionar su colonia de caña como a cuatro kilómetros de Lajas. Quería cerciorarse de que el mayoral estaba tirando caña y no aprovechaba la dispersión por los trajines

---

[1] Ichaso, León. Don Laureano Falla Gutiérrez. Cultural, La Habana, Cuba, 1930. La autora agradece a Tina Falla Trelles el facilitarle una copia de este libro del cual se han tomado extensas referencias.

[2] Falla Cervera, Miguel. Recuerdo de mi pasado. Manuscrito inédito. Circa 1979. La autora agradece a Javier Cervera Falla, hijo de Miguel, facilitar el manuscrito proporcionado valioso material para las reminiscencias sobre Miguel Angel y su padre, Don Miguel.

nupciales. La pareja tuvo cinco hijos: Miguel Angel, Laureano, Cristina, Carlos e Isabel.

Casi un adolescente, Miguel Angel comenzó como simple ayudante en el ingenio Patria – había nacido el 9 de febrero de 1903, en Santa Isabel de las Lajas. A diferencia de sus dos hermanos varones, Laureano y Carlos, graduados en Medicina y Derecho respectivamente, después de terminar sus estudios en el Colegio Montserrat de Cienfuegos, regido por los jesuitas, su padre lo envía a una Academia Comercial en Filadelfia. A los Estados Unidos iban a estudiar los jóvenes cubanos de familias con recursos, como en siglos anteriores fueron a Francia o España. "Ya estás suficientemente preparado", le dijo su padre al concluir sus estudios, considerando que el trabajo apremiaba. Era el hijo mayor.

Los hijos de Don Miguel, Carlos, Laureano, Cristina, Isabel y Miguel Angel, vestidos para una fiesta de disfraces.

En Norteamérica, adquirió una visión de la modernidad, del pujante mundo de los negocios y aprendió el idioma inglés que hablaba con fluidez y corrección, pero con acento cubano, y escribía adecuadamente. Su español era impecable. En sus cartas, que he podido leer, conservadas con gran cariño por sus colaboradores Juan Manuel de la Cruz y Saturio Rocío, se destaca su caligrafía, de trazo fuerte y alargado y con curva ascendente, reveladora de una abarcadora y decidida personalidad.

Con una inteligencia natural y sentido autodidacta, basándose en voluntad y disciplina, el joven aprendió hasta el más mínimo detalle del funcionamiento del central. Como relatan sus hijas Cristina y Elena, su padre se había encargado de rotarlo por los diferentes puestos de trabajo. Realizó todo tipo de labores, incluyendo barrer oficinas, servir de mensajero, pesar caña.

Poco tiempo después, logró su primer ascenso, pasó a ser auxiliar de oficina. Entonces aprendió a revisar facturas, organizar archivos, chequear nóminas de pago y llevar registros de producción.

Su padre, administrador del Patria desde 1917, no establecía diferencias con él. Posiblemente a veces pensaría cuál sería el propósito de semejante trato, pero luego la vida le enseñó lo importante que era doblar la frente sobre el trabajo y saber para poder mandar.

Avispado, lleno de buenas intenciones e imbuido de un espíritu de constante superación, hizo suyos los consejos de su progenitor y de los más viejos en el central, por ende más sabios. Sabía escuchar. Con una memoria privilegiada y un fino olfato para detectar los asuntos medulares, se mantuvo al tanto de la norma diaria del central, 2,500 TM, número sagrado si se quería cumplir con el plan de zafra de 225,000 arrobas.

El Patria, cerca de Morón, registrado en los libros como Azucarera Central Patria S.A, Compañía, se había convertido en escuela, fragua, para los sucesores del recio Laureano Falla, el cerebro de la fortuna de la familia. De alguna manera por allí pasaron todos: padres, hermanos, hijos, sobrinos.

Admiraba mucho a su tío. Buen observador, no se le escapaba ni el más mínimo detalle de cómo aquél actuaba. Don Laureano poseía una mente ágil y demostraba ser un estratega en las lides empresariales. Si se apelara a la Biblia, se pudiera decir que el joven Falla fue barro y aliento de su tío y de su padre. De cada uno tomó la mejor parte.

En el tiempo de zafra, su ojo se agudizaba. Veía cómo los inspectores controlaban los inventarios del almacén y el número de sacos que salían rumbo al puerto para exportarlos. Imaginativo y arriesgado, se acercaba a los técnicos y a los mayordomos y les preguntaba acerca del nivel de sacarosa del jugo, cuántas arrobas pasaban por los basculadores, o se iba a los campos para hablar con los mayorales y jornaleros.

Al hijo de don Miguel nada parecía escapársele, y ese comportamiento inspiraba admiración y simpatía. Tan alto y delgado, aprendiendo a ser hombre internándonos en el torbellino de hojas verdes. "Este muchacho. ¡Vaya muchacho!", exclamaban en voz baja, moviendo la cabeza de un lado a otro, los más curtidos por los años y la faena. El, por su parte, les correspondía con su trato afable pero cuidadoso de no traspasar los límites de la autoridad. Con su ejemplo, se impuso para que lo vieran como un trabajador más, no como un señorito acomodado. Estableció entre su personal que lo llamaran sólo por su nombre de pila: Miguel Angel.

Se ocupaba también de la colonia de caña "La Granja" que su tío Laureano financió, con un interés del 6% anual, a él y a sus primos, Ricardo, Manolo, Eutimio y Miguel Cervera, otro pilar de la familia en la administración de los ingenios. En sus memorias, Miguel Cervera relata su labor en el Andreíta, al que lo envía su tío Agustín Batista para meter en cintura el central.

Aquellas tierras, destinadas a garantizar la caña necesaria para la producción, dieron dolores de cabeza. El primer año, debieron enfrentar la enfermedad del Mosaico que atacaba con fuerza las plantas recién sembradas de la variedad Cristalina, hasta que lograron otra superior, la P.O.J. 2878, más resistente a esos embates.

*****

El 13 de agosto de 1915, don Laureano inauguró el proceso de consolidación de tierras y colonos que daría origen al central Adelaida – tal nombre en honor a su hija casada con Viriato Gutiérrez - ubicado en la antigua hacienda "Nauyú" – vocablo indígena – a unos quince kilómetros del Patria. Lo empezó a construir en abril de 1916. Alrededor del central surgió el pueblo llamado Falla. Entre 1910 y 1929, don Laureano fue fundador de varias fábricas, entre otras de papel y generadores de electricidad en Cienfuegos y Cárdenas. Y en consorcio con otras compañías, tuvo intereses y fue gerente de los centrales Andreíta, Manuelita y Cieneguita. También fue propietario de terrenos en La Habana y Cienfuegos y de numerosas fincas y plantaciones de henequén en Cárdenas. Participó como ejecutivo y accionista en empresas de seguros, de hielo (Polar); fue presidente de la Compañía Cubana de Pesca y Navegación y de la firma de seguros Unión Agrícola e Industrial, y socio, junto con H. Upmann y Armando Godoy, de José Marimón Juliach, en el Banco Español de la Isla de Cuba, quien, unido a José López Rodríguez, principal propietario del Banco Nacional, había formado una alianza del capital financiero-azucarero criollo y español contra el capital extranjero.

En junio de 1922, nombraron a Miguel Angel jefe de oficinas del Patria. La muerte sorpresiva de José Planas, administrador del ingenio Adelaida, a manos de un vengativo e inconforme colono, apresuró los cambios. Designaron a Raúl Román, anteriormente el segundo al mando, administrador del Patria y a Manolo Cervera del Adelaida. Ambas fábricas seguirían bajo la supervisión de don Miguel.

Los hermanos Falla, especialmente, sintieron la partida del amigo de tantos años. El catalán era un hombre muy querido por toda la familia. Su participación y la de su hermano mayor Manolo habían sido decisivas en adherir a los colonos que abastecerían de caña la moderna fábrica. Los convencieron para que vendieran sus tierras, quedando los mismos, y ellos también, como accionistas del nuevo central en proporción al valor de las propiedades aportadas.

En asociación con sus primos Manolo, Ricardo y Miguel Cervera, además de Eutimio, Miguel Angel adquirió otras tres colonias de caña, que unificaron y pusieron el nombre de Concha, en honor a la madre de los primeros. Miguel Cervera se esforzó bastante para sacarla adelante. Muy pronto esas tierras se convirtieron en la mejor colonia del Adelaida, ofreciéndoles grandes dividendos.

Cuando finalmente Miguel Angel tomó las riendas del Patria su padre se dispuso a descansar un poco. Ya empezaba a sentir el desgaste por la edad y el trabajo duro de los centrales. Sus visitas a las colonias, ahora no a caballo sino en el motor de línea, se volvieron esporádicas.

Siguió al pie de la letra los consejos de su padre: "No te dejes engañar. Cuando te percates de que algo no anda bien, búscale solución, empleando todo el tiempo y esfuerzo que sean necesarios". Aprendió a ver por sus propios ojos y no a esperar que le contaran. Imitó la práctica de recorrer las colonias, cabalgando hasta diez horas diarias. "Vista hace fe" fue el proverbio que guió sus pasos por el mundo agroindustrial azucarero.

En materia de oficina, sentó pautas. Implantó un sistema de contabilidad más moderno, agilizó los trámites burocráticos y perfeccionó los controles de siembra, corte, transporte, almacenaje y producción.

Administrar un central es tan complejo como la maquinaria que lo mueve. No sólo se trata de lidiar con el cultivo, cosecha y molienda sino con el difícil factor humano. Su prestancia - realzada por las altas polainas de cuero, camisa blanca de cuello y pantalones de montar - y su andar resuelto y firme, tendía a confundir, a ocultar un alma noble y grande, como refieren sus amigos y colaboradores.

Saturio Rocío, por años su secretario privado, asegura que su arrogancia era aparente y que en realidad poseía un corazón de fibra tierna y sensible. "Muchos bendecían la mano generosa de Miguel Angel". Y cita que no dudó en enviar a un hospital de La Habana a una criatura lastimada al nacer por el comadrón. Gracias a su rápida gestión, el niño pudo salvarse. A otra pequeña, hija de un trabajador de su finca "Alarcón", que perdió la vista debido a una enfermedad, le procuró atención y educación en instituciones especializadas. Y así sucesivamente expone más ejemplos que ratifican otros.

Según esos testimonios, en una ocasión, desde su casa se ocupó de enviar infusiones y comidas apropiadas a José Medardo Pino, enfermo y sin familia por esos alrededores para atenderlo. El contador nunca olvidó aquel gesto de su jefe.

El doctor Angel P. Naveiras habla de la condición humana de Miguel Angel, refiriéndose a su gestión para conseguir la asistencia de un médico eminente para tratar a su único hermano, quien tenía un padecimiento mortal. Y dice que también le concedió licencia a él mismo para ausentarse del trabajo durante aquellos tristes días.

El desarrollo de la industria azucarera cambió el paisaje rural cubano. Un central era como un poblado en menor escala donde familias enteras residían por generaciones. Y en tiempo de zafra, las filas se nutrían de trabajadores temporales, los llamados jornaleros. En los alrededores de las fábricas, los campesinos encontraban mejores condiciones de vida.

El Patria llegó a tener más de tres mil trabajadores, pero Miguel Angel los conocía y llamaba a muchos por su nombre. Convirtió en práctica mantenerse en contacto directo con sus empleados tanto del campo como del central.

En el aspecto productivo, continuó las reformas tecnológicas introducidas por su tío, ampliando la zona de cultivo y empleando abonos superiores. Era un buscador de nuevas variedades de caña, más resistentes y con mayor rendimiento. Paralelamente, se ocupaba de acometer las reparaciones necesarias en el equipamiento industrial. De esa manera pudieron mantener la norma alcanzada de ciento cincuenta mil sacos, alta para un ingenio pequeño como el Patria. Cuando don Laureano lo adquirió, en 1917, rendía sólo sesenta mil.

*****

La Sucesión L. Falla Gutiérrez, constituida el 27 de mayo de 1929, con oficinas en Oficios 110, altos, y cuenta bancaria en The Trust Company of Cuba, fue fundada para continuar los negocios del asturiano Laureano Falla Gutiérrez, fallecido el 25 de marzo de ese año. Contaba con un capital entre $65 y $75 millones. Era propietaria de siete ingenios: "Adelaida", "Andreíta", "Manuelita", "Azucarera Fidelidad", "Azucarera Buenavista", "Central Patria" y el "Violeta". Estaba clasificado como el segundo grupo más importante de los hacendados cubanos. Además poseía intereses, entre otros, en la Compañía Cubana de Refrigeración Eléctrica, un almacén para la venta de equipos electrodomésticos; Nauyú Distillering Company, la segunda mayor destilería de alcohol del país, situada en el Central Adelaida; Inmobiliaria Payret, S.A.; en Papelera Nacional, Cubana de Pesca y Navegación, Cubana de Fibra y Jarcia, Henequenera Estrella. Tenía como beneficiarios a los tres hijos de Laureano: Eutimio, Isabel y María Teresa Falla Bonet, así como a Viriato Gutiérrez, viudo de su cuarta hija Adelaida, y a Agustín Batista, presidente de Trust Company S.A. Falla Bonet. Alejandro Suero, Eutimio Falla, Agustín Batista, Carlos y Miguel Falla y Miguel Cervera eran respectivamente el presidente, tesorero y el resto consejeros.

Le dolió en lo más profundo la desaparición del tío Laureano. Toda la familia lloró su muerte. La última vez que lo vio en vida fue en las Navidades de 1927. Sintiéndose ya muy enfermo, había reunido a los suyos en la casa hacienda del central Adelaida, que en el verano anterior quedó lista para ser ocupada.

Miguel Angel decidió casarse con Julia Bulle-Merry, con quien llevaba relaciones formales desde hacía tres años. La joven era descendiente de franceses e ingleses, sumamente atractiva, de buena familia y excelentes cualidades morales. Se habían compenetrado mucho a través de una larga y sostenida correspondencia, pues Julia vivía en La Habana. Formaron una pareja envidiable. En breve y con poca diferencia entre ambas, tuvieron a sus hijas Cristina y Julia. La mayor nació en El Vedado, La Habana, y la segunda en el central Patria. Y cuando ya no pensaban encargar más, nació Elena, en la calle Almendares, del reparto Kohly, también en la capital. Cuando Elena vino al mundo todos esperaban que fuera varón y llamarle como su padre.

Don Miguel disfrutó mucho de la compañía de su nieta mayor Cristina, que como su padre creció en el central. Recuerda Cristina que, según su madre le refería, cuando su abuelo llegaba de montar, no importaba la hora, la sacaba de la cuna para jugar con ella. Ya no iba al Patria propiamente a asuntos de trabajo sino a estar con la pequeña.

Julia Bulle Merry de Falla

Al terminar la zafra 1935-36 fue cuando Miguel Angel se hizo cargo del central Adelaida, en sustitución de Miguel Cervera, a quien la junta directiva de la Sucesión determinó trasladar al Andreíta, debido a que los asuntos en ese sitio andaban mal y necesitaban de una mano firme como la suya.

Verdaderamente nada le fue ajeno a Miguel Angel en su nuevo puesto de trabajo. Conocía el funcionamiento de la empresa, no sólo porque allí estaba su colonia la Granja, la cual visitaba con frecuencia, sino porque acompañó reiteradas veces a su padre, en su época de administrador y supervisor. El, tanto o más que otro de la familia, sabía los pormenores de aquella maravilla de industria.

Confiaba en su método de apoyarse en un equipo de trabajo integrado por profesionales capaces y por empleados que mostraban interés en superarse, para vencer el nuevo reto. Con acertada visión empresarial, estimulaba y daba facilidades para continuar estudios universitarios a los que creía merecedores. Pensaba, atinadamente, que eran una reserva potencial, como ocurrió con el propio Saturio Rocío que en agradecimiento le dedicó su tesis de doctorado.

La dinámica de grupo se impuso. Esos mismos hombres recibían, a su vez, lecciones de su parte. "Como buen tutor los iba adiestrando en las maromas de la industria", recuerda Rocío. "Eso sí, cuando nombraba a una persona para una posición, exigía que diera el máximo". Y aunque al respecto señala el doctor Naveiras que "no andaba con remilgos para expresar su pensamiento", tampoco escatimaba el elogio sincero y el reconocimiento estimulante.

Juan M. de la Cruz interpretaba de manera muy ocurrente esa cualidad de su jefe. Cuando le preguntaban de qué universidad era graduado, respondía de la UCA, aclarando después: de la Universidad del Central Adelaida.

El Adelaida poseía una capacidad de producción de 330 mil arrobas, contaba con 1,063 caballerías de tierras propias (unas 21 mil hectáreas), y empleaba a 2,970 personas. Fue la empresa predilecta de don Laureano, comenzada y terminada por él mismo. A los tres años de entrar en funcionamiento, se convirtió en el ingenio que reportaba más ganancias por saco fabricado.

A partir de la zafra 1934-35 el ingenio comenzó a embarcar el azúcar por Chicola a Caibarién, en lugar de por el puerto de Tarafa. Lo que significaba un ahorro de 200 mil dólares por flete.

El ingenio estaba situado en el centro de la hacienda Nauyú que cubría unas 1,300 caballerías y el resto pertenecían al Realengo Sabana la Mar, extendido entre la hacienda y la costa. La planificación del área sentó pautas constructivas al resto de los hacendados. Poseía servicios de agua corriente, electricidad y teléfono, además de excelentes vías de comunicación, gracias a los 130 kilómetros de ferrocarril que partían en cinco ramales del mismo ingenio.

Propiamente dicho, la fábrica estaba ubicada en medio del batey y cerca, pero separados, los talleres de locomotoras, carpintería, ferrocarril y hospital de emergencia. Para acceder a sus instalaciones, debía cruzarse el torniquete. Ya en sus predios podía divisarse, a la derecha, el busto de don Laureano Falla y, a la izquierda, la capilla, donde muchas veces ofició misa Monseñor Pérez Serantes, entonces obispo de Camagüey y amigo personal de Miguel Angel. Siguiendo la tradición de

“Central Adelaida”

la familia, el hacendado ayudaba con contribuciones económicas y de servicio a las federaciones católicas. El religioso, a su vez, admiraba su desprendimiento en colaborar con las causas piadosas, el tratamiento de enfermedades contagiosas y de cáncer.

Dominaba el escenario del Adelaida una amplia avenida sombreada por laureles cuyas ramas se entrecruzaban formando una especie de bóveda verde. A ambos lados se levantaban 24 chalets, donde vivían los principales jefes; otras 20 viviendas para operarios con familia; cinco pabellones para los solteros, y dos fondas restaurantes encargadas de servir alimentos. Cerca del batey, ya fuera de sus límites, estaba la guardia rural y 30 ó 40 casas más de vivienda.

A medio kilómetro del ingenio fue surgiendo una urbanización, con calles asfaltadas y otras facilidades de la vida moderna, donde los particulares podían adquirir propiedades ya fuera para habitarlas o establecer negocios de venta de víveres a las colonias. Fue precisamente ese sitio al que se le llamó primero el reparto y luego el pueblo Falla.

La Sucesión fue originalmente administrada por el Dr. David Suero Rodríguez, esposo de Isabel Falla y padre de Alejandro Suero Falla, hasta su deceso en junio de 1938, pues ya desde 1923 había sido nombrado administrador general de los intereses de la familia. A partir de 1943, Rafael Jiménez-Rojo Saladrigas, un antiguo funcionario de Falla Gutiérrez desde 1918, fue su apoderado hasta su fallecimiento el 18 de abril de 1953. Desde 1945, Alejandro Suero Falla, hijo de Isabel, estaba al frente del consorcio azucarero y en 1958 era el presidente de todas sus empresas y Julio Prado Rodríguez – que había sustituido a Eutimio Falla Bonet – había pasado a ocupar la vicepresidencia, salvo en el Manuelita, donde estaba Urbano Monasterio Díaz. Suero también tenía intereses en "Petrolera Transcuba S.A." y en "Corporación Intercontinental de Hoteles de Cuba S.A.", de la que había sido su presidente hasta el 21 de noviembre de 1957.

En la cumbre de los Falla Gutiérrez, Miguel Angel era visto como un campeón de los centrales. Alejandro (Alín) Suero, al frente del negocio desde 1945, le profesaba especial admiración. Sin habérselo propuesto, gozaba de su afecto y simpatía, lo que no significaba que no tuvieran disparidades. Ante su primo, descubría otra faceta de su carácter: su sentido del humor. Se hacían bromas mutuamente cuando conversaban alejados del oído de los demás. A Miguel Angel también le gustaba bromear con sus sobrinas. Cristina de Cárdenas, luego, con los años, será testigo de sus ocurrencias y simpatía personal.

Juan M. de la Cruz, que trabajó a su lado por más de treinta años, relata dos anécdotas que reflejan su buen carácter. Se trata del encargo que le hace al mensajero de oficina de que le traiga una botella de agua con gas, refiriéndose a agua efervescente o de soda, pero el muchacho regresó con una de querosén, que en Cuba le dicen luz brillante. El no se molestó en lo absoluto si no que se lo tiró a jarana. El mismo joven despistado recibió en otra oportunidad la orden de ir a leer el pluviómetro y cuando le dijo la cantidad de lluvia caída, Miguel Angel supo que se había equivocado. Lo envió de nuevo, recomendándole se cerciorara primero que el medidor estuviera limpio. Efectivamente, dentro había un sapo, haciendo subir los niveles a una cantidad inverosímil. Cuando se lo dijo, Miguel Angel se estuvo riendo a carcajadas, sacándole lascas al incidente.

Acostumbraba a reírse con ganas. Cristina, su hija mayor, recuerda que por las noches se sentaba en el portal de la oficina, a más de 150 metros de la casa vivienda, y llamaba a los empleados que pasaran para conversar. Y ella sentía como su papá se reía sin parar en aquellas tertulias improvisadas.

El ingenio no era lo mismo que La Habana, sobre todo porque las niñas debían estudiar. Ya no podían permanecer todo el tiempo en el Adelaida. Aunque su madre

Julia había estudiado en las Dominicas Francesas del Vedado, la pequeña Elena iba al Sagrado Corazón. Julia, que casi siempre estaba con su esposo en el central, debía viajar frecuentemente para atender a sus hijas.

Julia Bulle de Falla con sus hijas Julia, Elena y Cristina.

En la época de vacaciones, era distinto. Toda la familia se reunía y su hija Cristina aprovechaba para acompañarlo en sus habituales recorridos por las colonias, cabalgando en su yegua Peggy. Miguel Angel, por su parte, tenía un caballo entero, que ponía a prueba sus dotes de jinete. Candela se hacía indomable cuando andaban yeguas por los alrededores. Con la excusa de saborear un vaso de leche de chiva recién ordeñada, su acostumbrada sardina y la consabida taza de café, conversaba con ellos, escuchaba sus preocupaciones, preguntaba por algún familiar enfermo y hasta si era necesario, concedía favores. Cristina, poco aficionada a la leche recién ordeñada, optaba por no bajarse.

Al igual estaban juntos en las Navidades, durante las cuales acostumbraban a ir a la misa de las 10 de la mañana en la iglesia parroquial "Nuestra Señora de la Candelaria", de Morón. Miguel Angel profesaba profunda fe cristiana. Nunca se desprendía de su rosario, que llevaba celosamente guardado en un bolsillo y lo rezaba en voz baja en situaciones de mucho dolor, como fue la muerte de su padre, ocurrida el 13 de julio de 1938.

Sintió un vacío inmenso. Lo peor fue que durante los primeros días, le parecía oír su voz, dando órdenes como siempre, aunque hiciera rato que se hubieran invertido los papeles y no fuera él sino Miguel Angel quien administraba el Adelaida. Pero su hijo nunca le dijo nada. Para él, su padre seguía siendo la primera autoridad.

El resto del año no cesaba de trabajar. Era un hombre de mucha vitalidad, no de estar sentado ocho horas en su despacho, reconocen sus colaboradores más cercanos. Hay anécdotas que los empleados del turno de la madrugada del central debían andar muy despiertos porque en cualquier momento se presentaba a pasar lista. El hecho de no dormir lo suficiente, sin embargo, no afectaba su horario rígido de trabajo. Sin fallar un día, a las ocho en punto hacía su entrada en la oficina.

Cristina Falla, hoy de Drebbin, en su yegua Peggy.

En los tiempos de la Segunda Guerra Mundial, se construyó en los terrenos del Adelaida una destilería para producir alcohol a partir de las melazas, destinado a carburante, conforme a una disposición gubernamental debido a la necesidad de economizar combustible. Aunque no muy enterado de los detalles industriales, asumió la tarea planteada por la jerarquía de los Falla Gutiérrez y sobrepasó todas las expectativas.

La Nauyú Distilling Company fue una de las mayores de Cuba con una capacidad de producción de 80 mil litros diarios de alcohol. El hecho de tomarse el tiempo necesario para construirla, con varios pisos de alto y todos los requerimientos técnicos, despertó recelo en la competencia, que se apresuró a lanzarse con el experimento etílico sin las condiciones apropiadas, con tal de no perder un minuto y ganar terreno en la obtención de ganancias.

No obstante sus previsiones, se destapó una invasión de moscas incubadas en los mostos desechados. La noticia corrió tan veloz como los vagones del ferrocarril, dentro de los cuales los pasajeros se apresuraban a cerrar las ventanillas. De todas maneras, las moscas se propagaron por otros pueblos. Pero Miguel Angel no se hizo presa del pánico, con sapiencia y constancia logró capear la crisis que alcanzó repercusión nacional a través de la prensa capitalina.

Igual ecuanimidad y aplomo demostró para resolver un desagradable incidente con un trabajador resentido que al ser despedido fraguó lentamente su venganza, como narra Rocío en su testimonio. El hombre se alistó en la guardia rural y al cabo del tiempo se apareció en la oficina del central "para arreglar cuentas", amenazando al administrador con su arma. Con sangre fría, Miguel Angel continuó trabajando con los papeles y llamó a su auxiliar pretextando revisara unos cálculos, de manera que saliera y pudiera avisar. Y así lo hizo. Al momento, el sargento se personó y apresó al intruso.

Miguel Angel era un hombre de ideas rectas y nunca permitió chantaje o extorsión alguna. En una ocasión, la prensa local publicó un artículo titulado "La verdad desnuda", el cual atacaba a la gerencia del central. Según la nota, la misma se había comprometido a facilitar los trajes a todos los niños para la toma de su primera comunión y había incumplido. Varios niños, decía, no pudieron lucirlo en la ceremonia. La información causó disgusto. A los pocos días, se apareció el periodista, autor de la nota, en el central y le propuso enmendarla, poniéndole un precio al "favor". El empresario no necesitó siquiera un minuto para reaccionar. Con ingenio, le dijo: "¿Vas ahora a vestir la verdad?"

El incidente no sería el único. La radio local, en otros momentos lo acusaría por la tala de montes para sembrar caña. Y Rocío tuvo que salir a la palestra para explicar. Así lidiaba con la prensa.

Los sindicatos también supieron de su habilidad para negociar. Mantenía relaciones cordiales con los gremios y escuchaba sus demandas, pero sólo concedía las que consideraba justas y necesarias. No avasallaba a los trabajadores pero tampoco dejaba de defender los intereses de la compañía a la cual representaba, y generalmente lograba acuerdos amistosos.

El Adelaida fue la consagración de todos sus esfuerzos. Según Rocío, aumentó el acopio de caña, mediante la tala de monte para expandir la cosecha, contando con la colaboración de los colonos; mecanizó el corte y alza e introdujo variedades de mayor rendimiento y más resistentes a las plagas. En la parte industrial, modificó todo el sistema: basculadores, cuchillas niveladoras, molinos, centrífugas, clarificadores, hornos, calderas, planta eléctrica, máquinas de coser sacos. Pronto se verían los resultados: en la zafra de 1952, la fábrica llegó a producir 421,783 sacos de azúcar de 325 libras. La molienda alcanzó los 33 mil millones de arrobas de caña.

Alín Suero, presidente de la Sucesión, le planteó a Miguel Angel un nuevo reto: cosechar arroz. Entonces tuvo que emplearse a fondo para echar adelante el proyecto, que comprendía abrir profundos pozos, debido a que este cultivo requiere mucha agua, y preparar los terrenos a la manera de terrazas bien niveladas. "Una vez más la capacidad administrativa de Miguel Angel se acrecentó y las arroceras prosperaron dando importantes ganancias", asegura Rocío.

* * * * *

Los descendientes de don Laureano acrecentaron los bienes heredados, comprando en 1946 el ingenio "San Germán" y en 1951 el "Punta Alegre". A comienzos de 1958, el Violeta y, en 1943, el banco "The Trust Company of Cuba".

Miguel Angel con su hermano Carlos.

Miguel Angel decidió tomarse un merecido descanso al lado de los suyos en su bonita casa de La Habana, situada en el Número 33 de la calle Almendares del nuevo reparto Kohly, donde viviría la familia hasta partir de Cuba. Sus hijas Cristina y Julia ya estaban en edad de casarse y de constituir su propia familia. Quiso estar pendiente de todos los detalles. Pero Alín Suero vino a plantearle que lo necesitaba. La Sucesión acababa de comprar el central Punta Alegre y quería ponerlo en sus manos. Era urgente someter el ingenio a una reestructuración total para integrarlo al sistema de operación y control de los Falla. Alín vino a tentarlo.

No podía permanecer ocioso. En cuerpo y alma siempre estaba listo para el trabajo, y en 1953, cumplidos ya los cincuenta, acepta la administración del central y vuelve al campo.

El central había sido regido anteriormente por una administración norteamericana, concediendo demasiados privilegios e "inflando" la plantilla. Todos esos niveles estaban muy por encima de los parámetros establecidos en los de la gerencia cubana. Rocío sintetiza la tarea, diciendo: "Era cuestión de reconstruir y modernizar el ingenio, organizando su manejo con vistas a suprimir gastos superfluos y ajustar la fuerza laboral".

Siguiendo su estilo, trajo consigo a su grupo de especialistas de confianza y acometió la delicada y complicada labor de evaluar cargo por cargo y su desempeño. Debía determinar cuáles eran verdaderamente necesarios.

Comenzó por la parte industrial y continuó con la agrícola. En la fábrica, se dio cuenta que sobraba personal y que se producían gastos injustificados. En el campo, detectó infinitas irregularidades. La más preocupante: la caña había sido sembrada solamente en los perímetros, lo que ponía en peligro la molienda y, por ende, la producción de azúcar. Sin pérdida de tiempo, hizo que el inspector de campo lo acompañara a ver las colonias. Demostrada su incompetencia, el hombre prefirió renunciar ahí mismo.

Muchos temieron entonces perder sus trabajos, pero el gerente les devolvió la tranquilidad. A la par que se deshizo de los irresponsables, supo estimular a los que cumplían eficientemente su trabajo, ascendiéndolos en sus cargos. Los cambios fueron radicales.

Con la casa grande en orden, ahora pudo reservarse algún espacio para romper la rutina diaria y despejarse un tanto. El central estaba ubicado en un sitio paradisíaco. La vivienda estaba al lado del mar y, recuerda Elena, contaba "con un muelle en el cual el cocinero iba con una red a pescar "majúas" y las comíamos fritas". Muy cerca estaban los cayos Media Luna y Guillermo los que podía visitar en su yate "Ailicec".

*****

La Sucesión Falla Gutiérrez continuaba con su interés en expandir su capacidad de producción. Un objetivo posible hubiera sido comprar algunos de los centrales de la "Cuban Atlantic Sugar Company, propietaria entonces de 10 centrales: el Violeta, tres de la Hershey Corporation (Hershey, Rosario y San Antonio), tres en la provincia de Matanzas (Alava, Conchita y Mercedes,) y tres en la de Camagüey (Lugareño, Morón y Stewart). La Atlántica del Golfo era además propietaria de las destilerías Morón y Violeta. Desde los años 30 la Atlántica había sido considerada el más importante consorcio azucarero del mundo. Desde antes, Alejandro Suero Falla, cabeza dirigente del consorcio azucarero de la "Sucesión", formaba parte de su Junta de Directores.

En La Habana se encontraba Miguel Angel cuando su primo Alín Suero vino a su encuentro. Alín había estado hablando con John L. Loeb, quien recientemente completara la toma de control de la Cuban Atlantic, adquiriendo en la Bolsa de New York el bloque de acciones que necesitaba para la mayoría. En su conversación, Loeb le había dicho la urgencia de reestructurar la Atlántica del Golfo y encontrar el hombre adecuado para ponerlo al frente de tal tarea.

Alín y Loeb eran amigos desde el primer viaje del segundo a Cuba en 1928. Alín, que parecía siempre tener una respuesta para todo, no dudó: "Mi primo Miguel Angel es el mejor administrador de ingenios que yo conozco".

No es fácil discernir la gama de motivaciones que dieron origen a la recomendación. Podríamos especular que, además de la convicción en la capacidad de su primo Miguel Angel y el deseo honesto de servir al amigo, podría estar el legítimo interés de la cabeza del segundo grupo azucarero más importante de Cuba. Alín no dudaría en reconocer las ventajas de tener al frente del gigante de la Atlántica a Miguel Angel, que tan bien conocía los intereses azucareros de la Sucesión, donde había administrado por tantos años los tres centrales de Camagüey. Con el nombramiento de su primo, Alín tendría la oportunidad de una primera opción en cualquier venta de intereses de la Atlantic.

La oferta no podía ser más tentadora, pensó Miguel Angel. No se trataba ahora de administrar un central y atender los asuntos de dos – en los últimos tiempos, llevaba las riendas del Punta Alegre y supervisaba el Patria y el Adelaida. Traspasaría el umbral. Daría el salto. La Atlántica tenía diez centrales. El destino ponía la oportunidad en sus manos. El destino se llamaba Alín. Podría alcanzar la cúspide de su carrera como Capitán de Empresas.

El magnate financiero de Wall Street citó a Miguel Angel al Hotel Nacional del Vedado. Con su estilo colonial y aspecto majestuoso no había en la capital mejor sitio para discutir asuntos de peso.

Aunque no hay referencias exactas de la reunión, Miguel Angel debe haber llegado puntual e impecablemente vestido, con una elegancia especial dada la ocasión.

Y cuando conversaron, demostrar saber todos los pormenores del cultivo y molienda de la caña de azúcar, haciendo gala de una mentalidad de empresario fuera de lo común. Un punto obligado que posiblemente trataron fue la necesidad de mejorar las condiciones de vida de los cortadores de caña en los centrales. Loeb sabía que los Falla, y en especial Miguel Angel por su posición, eran muy progresistas en ese sentido y quería implantar la misma política en el gigante empresarial.

La estrategia sería la siguiente: Miguel Angel asumiría en los primeros momentos el cargo de apoderado plenipotenciario. Dos o tres meses después, el de presidente de la Atlántica.

*****

La compañía Atlántica del Golfo, con una producción cercana a 900,000 TM de azúcar en 1952, era en 1956 el mayor grupo azucarero del mundo. Era dueña de 550 millas de ferrocarril y de una destilería en el central Morón iniciada el 1 de marzo de 1944. Su capital nominal, registrado en Cuba, ascendió en 1957 a más de diez millones de dólares, pero su valor en Bolsa era mucho mayor. Su control estaba en manos de Loeb & Rhoades and Co., la casa de Bolsa de John Loeb. En ella también tenían acciones los Rionda y la Sucesión Falla Gutiérrez.

John L. Loeb era el presidente de la Junta [Chairman of The Board of Directors] y Lawrence A. Crosby, presidente de la firma y de sus subsidiarias. El origen de la Atlántica data de 1915 con la Cuban Cane Sugar Corporation, constituida por Manuel Rionda Polledo, la que a partir de 1921 quebró. Luego de intentos por recuperarse, bajo el nombre de Cuban Cane Products Company Inc. demolió la mitad de sus centrales y pasó bajo la égida del grupo Rockefeller y Sullivan & Crownwel, de quienes Loeb toma el control mediante compras en la Bolsa de New York.

Félix bajó por la calle 23 y luego dobló a la derecha en la calle Infanta hasta estacionar frente al edificio de Ambar Motors. Era un chofer como pocos: de esos que conducen veloces, pero respetando las señales de tránsito – importante en La Habana para una jungla de automóviles y autobuses en esos tiempos de esperanza.

Miguel Angel descendió del vehículo e instintivamente miró hacia lo alto. En los pisos superiores estaban las oficinas de la Atlántica.

"Me propusieron que me hiciera cargo de ayudarle a familiarizarse con los distintos departamentos y con el personal. En principio iba a ser para mí sólo un período provisional mientras durara la transición a la presidencia", dice Rita Blain en sus memorias de Miguel Angel.

El encuentro de Rita y Miguel Angel fue mágico, como lo es todo lo bueno para Rita. Desde el primer momento se despertó entre ambos una corriente de simpatía y camaradería, basada en el respeto mutuo, que no variaría ni un ápice con el correr de los años; al contrario, esos vínculos se extenderían a las dos familias. Rita y Elena, la hija menor del empresario, en el futuro serían tan buenas amigas que pudiera decirse que se querían como hermanas.

Miguel Angel se movía entre bambalinas. No quería herir la susceptibilidad de Lawrence A. Crosby a quien sustituiría en breve. "Respetó su rango y se condujo con gran discreción para no hacerle sombra, si bien iba tomando el control de la compañía", asegura Rocío, a quien trajo consigo como parte de su política de apoyarse siempre en un competente y eficaz equipo de trabajo.

Tan atareado estaba estudiando cómo encaminar sus pasos, que lo sorprendió la llegada de su primer cheque. De regreso a su casa de Kohly, le dio un beso a su esposa Julia, y con una sonrisa de triunfo en los labios, le extendió su primer sueldo como regalo.

Ya en posesión plena de la presidencia, acometió todos los cambios necesarios, tanto en lo referente al personal de la empresa como en la estructura organizativa de los distintos departamentos. En la parte financiera, revisó todas las partidas, el concepto y nivel de gastos y redondeó los números para ajustar el presupuesto. Rita califica esas medidas como de gran envergadura y Rocío, por su parte, no las considera tan radicales si se les compara con las tomadas en el central Punta Alegre. Y sintetiza diciendo: "Era cuestión de reconstruir y modernizar los ingenios", refiriéndose a los sistemas de control administrativo.

De todas maneras, el plan de Loeb ya estaba en marcha. Su suprema aspiración era hacer los ingenios de la Atlántica a imagen y semejanza de los de la Sucesión, que consideraba modelo. Y para lograrlo ya tenía al hombre clave en la presidencia de la Atlántica.

Llegado el momento de decidir con cuál secretaria quedarse, Miguel Angel no quiso deshacerse de la del presidente saliente y trató de mantenerla, pero a diferencia de lo sucedido con Rita, no se sintió cómodo con ella. Entonces trató de convencer a Rita para que regresara a su lado, y finalmente lo logró cuando la propia señora fue a hablar con ella diciéndole de manera amable y cooperativa que entendía perfectamente lo sucedido.

Le gustaba mucho su despacho. Desde todos los ángulos podía verse el mar, porque el edificio hace cuchilla. El mar que le recordaba tanto el Punta Alegre. Acomodó la decoración, con la ayuda de su secretaria. "No había nada extraordinario. Su estilo era sobrio y con un toque muy varonil", describe Rita, quien cada mañana le ponía una rosa fresca en el buró.

El empresario concentró entonces toda su atención en fortalecer y renovar la estructura productiva de los centrales, en algunos casos promoviendo empleados y, en otros, dándole cabida en su empresa a varios de sus antiguos colaboradores. Eso provocó el disgusto de Alín quien pensaba que estaba perjudicando los ingenios de la Sucesión. Pero Miguel Angel le dio una explicación convincente sobre los casos de Rocío y Juan M. de la Cruz, que eran los que más le molestaban. Al último lo había trasladado del Adelaida al Lugareño, de la Atlantic, en condiciones más ventajosas: primero como jefe de oficinas y al cabo de los dos años promoviéndolo a administrador. Por su parte, Rocío había dejado el Punta Alegre por razones estrictamente personales.

Le preocupaba un asunto en particular: la empresa Hershey. Según Rocío, era muy compleja. Además de sus tres centrales, "tenía una mezcolanza de industrias paralelas: producción de azúcares crudos, refinería, producción de aceite de maní, de jarcia, de henequén, ferrocarriles eléctricos, producción de electricidad, entre otras". Y hacia allá encaminó sus esfuerzos, enviando un grupo de contadores e ingenieros, incluyendo a su propio hombre de confianza.

Estaba casi seguro de lo que resultaría de esa inspección. La idea seguía dándole vueltas en la cabeza cuando llegó a su hogar y distraídamente le preguntó a Julia: "¿Qué hiciste con el cheque?" "Bueno le di una parte a las monjitas que cuidan de los enfermos en sus casas por las noches para que se compraran una camioneta y poder transportarse del convento hacia allá". Está bien, le dijo Miguel Angel, "¿Pero qué más?". "Les pagué también las clases de conducción. Si no, ¿cómo iban a manejar?" "¿Y qué más?", siguió indagando como en un juego de niños con su esposa, porque en realidad nunca estuvo revisando sus gastos. "Pues finalmente pregunté a cada cual del servicio doméstico de la casa lo que querían, y se lo regalé". Movió la cabeza hacia los lados y reflexionando se dijo: "Esta Julia no cambia".

Su olfato de empresario no lo había traicionado: la situación en la Hershey era tan grave como había previsto. Recomendó a la junta directiva de Nueva York "que se deshicieran de aquel elefante blanco, concentrándose sólo en la producción de azúcares crudos", escribe Rocío. "Julio Lobo firmó una opción de compra", añade.

En esas gestiones, viajó reiteradamente a la ciudad de los rascacielos y llevó consigo en algunas oportunidades a su hija Elena, que no tenía mayores compromisos porque, a diferencia de sus hermanas, permanecía soltera. Elena se conducía muy bien en los círculos sociales, estableciendo relaciones con las esposas de los ejecutivos, particularmente se hizo amiga de Peter, la señora de Loeb, a quien la familia había puesto este sobrenombre por su personalidad que recordaba tanto al mítico personaje Peter Pan. Juntas iban de compras, el hobby preferido de todas las mujeres.

La hija menor del presidente de la Atlántica recuerda que, durante esos viajes, su padre acostumbraba a rezar el rosario, pero una vez no le dio tiempo a concluirlo antes de aterrizar y tuvo que atropellar los Ave María para no quedarse sólo en el avión. Le dio mucha gracia. Si no hubiera sido por lo serio del asunto, le hubiera soltado una carcajada en su misma cara.

Miguel Angel y su hermano Laureano en el compromiso de su sobrino Celso Miguel González, en casa de su madre.

Otro de esos días, le fue imposible llevarla consigo y se quedó desconsolada. Para recompensarla, le trajo el vestido más caro y lujoso que encontró. Cuando se lo dio, Elena para sus adentros pensó: "este traje costó más que el viaje y la estadía en el hotel Waldorf Astoria". Después no supo qué hacer con el regalo y lo guardó en una caja. Su padre era así, espléndido, pero hombre al fin, despistado para comprar.

*****

Quería vender el central Hershey por tres razones: primero, me preocupaban las actividades de Castro en las montañas; segundo, la Sucesión Falla [de donde venía Miguel Angel] era experta en cultivo de la caña y la producción de crudos, pero no tenía experiencia en la producción de refino ni sus ventas; tercero, en 1956 y 1957, el alzamiento en Hungría y la Crisis del Canal de Suez, junto a una pésima cosecha de remolacha en Europa y la sequía en el Caribe, coincidieron para desatar un boom especulativo en el mercado mundial que duplicó el precio del azúcar. Las condiciones no podían ser mejores para su venta y Julio [Lobo] estaba dispuesto a pagar el precio, y como [de acuerdo con el análisis de Miguel Angel] la refinería era muy costosa de operar y necesitaba de nuevos equipos, todo encajaba perfectamente.[3]

La recomendación de Miguel Angel fue escuchada. Pero, como explica el mismo Loeb, no fueron las razones de índole administrativo y las condiciones internas de la compañía las únicas que llevaron a la mesa de negociaciones. La situación de inestabilidad política en Cuba, con Fidel Castro en las montañas, y otros factores de orden internacional, a la postre, apresuraron la toma de decisiones.

Julio Lobo recibió el ultimátum: si quería comprar, el cierre debía hacerse antes de las 12 de la noche del 31 de diciembre de 1957 o expiraría la opción de compra. Y ese mismo día se apareció acompañado por sus abogados.

Miguel Angel, como presidente que era, encabezó la junta de accionistas y cuenta Rocío la versión dada por su jefe de que el acuerdo no estaba listo para cerrar antes de la hora en que vencía la opción: 12 de la noche del 31 de diciembre de 1957. Por la importancia de la transacción, sin embargo, todo el mundo concordó en hacerse el "despistado" cuando uno de los abogados, viendo que sólo faltaban unos minutos, se levantó de su asiento y detuvo el reloj que presidía el salón. Cuando ya todos se pusieron de acuerdo, se paró de nuevo y lo echó a andar. Unos minutos después sonaron las doce campanas y todos alzaron sus copas saludando, a las 4 de la mañana del día primero de enero, la llegada del nuevo año y el fin de la negociación.

[3] Loeb, John. All In a Life Time. John L. Loeb, New York, NY, 1990, p. 168.

*****

Poseía Miguel Angel un fino tacto para lidiar con sus empleados. Estaba al tanto de sus problemas personales y llegado el caso trataba de ayudarlos. Juan M. de la Cruz, por ejemplo, quedó sorprendido cuando estando en La Habana, discutiendo en el Ministerio del Trabajo un nuevo contrato con el Sindicato, el abogado comunicó que a instancias del señor Falla quedaba suspendida la sesión hasta tanto de la Cruz no regresara de Morón, adonde debía ir de inmediato porque operaban de urgencia a su madre. Cruz dice que él nunca supo cómo Miguel Angel se enteró, pues él no había comentado nada de la aflicción que lo embargaba desde que conoció la noticia.

En semejantes circunstancias emocionales se encontraba Rita cuando su padre, el doctor Eduardo Moreno, fue intervenido quirúrgicamente. Entonces fue al hospital a verlo y a ofrecerse en lo que fuera necesario. Resulta muy humana y enaltecedora la imagen que traslada de Miguel Angel en esa ocasión: "Cuando entró en el cuarto, mi padre, que todavía estaba bajo los efectos de la anestesia, lo saludó diciéndole "cómo está, doctor", evidentemente lo confundía con uno de los médicos. Y él le contestó "yo no soy doctor". A lo que mi padre le dijo: "Pues mejor, ya que cualquiera se hace doctor, pero señor se nace", lo que significaba una salida ingeniosa y un halago para el jefe de su hija.

Su secretaria, que lo conoció tanto y compartió interminables horas de trabajo con él, posee muchas anécdotas pero la que más le retrató su sentido de estimular a sus empleados y su propia humildad fue cuando una vez asignaba los asientos para una cena con el personal del Atlántica y le propuso sentar a su mesa al Tesorero y a otros jefes de departamentos. Fue en ese momento que él le sugirió distribuir los puestos más democráticamente para que se sintieran todos en un plano de igualdad: "Y, por favor, pon a Gener a mi lado", añadió. Gener era un humilde empleado del departamento de correo.

La situación interna en Cuba, efectivamente, preocupaba. En el hogar de los Falla era tema frecuente de conversación. Julia estaba apesadumbrada con los juicios sumarísimos y los fusilamientos trasmitidos por la televisión y no cesaba de preguntarle a su marido qué iba a pasar. En los círculos financieros y empresariales se hacían la misma pregunta: ¿Qué irá a pasar? Nadie sabía con certeza, pero se temía lo peor. Ante la expectativa de un futuro oscuro, los hombres de empresa, incluyendo los de la Atlántica, frenaron la ejecución de nuevos planes. Era mejor esperar.

Las experiencias de Miguel Angel con los barbudos de la Sierra fueron puramente referenciales. Rocío recuerda su reacción cuando oyó lo que le decía un amigo administrador de un ingenio en la provincia de Oriente, donde campeaban los insurrectos. "Se quedó anonadado con aquellos relatos de primera mano: las exigencias de dinero, los impuestos revolucionarios, los latrocinios, las extorsiones, los fusilamientos".

Y sucedió lo temido: el armagedón cubano. Castro se apoderó del poder el 1 de enero de 1959 y comenzó sus medidas arbitrarias, demenciales. Aparte de hundir a la isla en un mar de sangre, igualó al pueblo en la pobreza total.

Los primeros zarpazos se hicieron sentir en la Atlántica, con la ley de reforma agraria, promulgada el 17 de mayo de 1959, que ponía fin a los latifundios – en definitiva para después crear los latifundios del Estado con la invención de las cooperativas y las granjas agrícolas que demostraron ser un fracaso. Por ende, las colonias de los centrales fueron confiscadas. Se producen las primeras fricciones entre Estados Unidos y Castro. Empezaba el caos.

"Fui a entrevistarme con el recién nombrado embajador norteamericano, Philip Bonsal, y le expresé mi opinión de que Castro era un redomado comunista y que no había forma de hacer negocios con él", relata sabiamente John L. Loeb.

Al Instituto Nacional de Reforma Agraria (INRA), a cargo de todas las tierras confiscadas, dirigido directamente por Castro, debía Miguel Angel rendir informes. Rocío incursiona en las amargas experiencias durante esos primeros días del poder comunista, que su jefe calificara como "desconcertantes y deprimentes" al recibir noticias del desastre administrativo en que se hundían sus centrales asaltados por los simpatizantes del régimen.

"De los ingenios le llegaban informes que le llenaban de inquietudes", dice su colaborador y amigo. Y a continuación cuenta de un viaje que hicieron por carretera a su finca "Alarcón", en Camagüey, en que pudo comprobar por sus propios ojos la situación de anarquía absoluta y como se abría paso la política de Castro de tomar para sí todo lo que no era suyo, sino sudado por la frente de otros.

Ya no había nada que hacer y Miguel Angel decidió poner a su familia a buen recaudo, llevándola a los Estados Unidos.

******

En un día espléndido de sol del mes de julio de 1960, Miguel Angel abordó el Ferry atracado en el muelle de La Habana. Lo acompañaban su esposa Julia, su hija Elena, dos de sus pequeños nietos, hijos de Cristina; la nana y su hija; el perrito Huesito, mascota de Julia, y sus 57 canarios. El empresario quería pasar lo más inadvertido posible, por eso delegó todos los asuntos del viaje en su hija Elena. No obstante los 57 canarios, no había nada inusual, la familia podía ser una más de las tantas que iban a Miami en viaje de placer.

Apenas la hija menor de Miguel Angel, Elena, subió, se encontró casualmente con Ben, quien llevaba de regreso a la Florida a su esposa Jan para dar a luz a la más pequeña de sus hijas. Lo vio con alegría pero saludó con discreción. El sólo hecho de su presencia, sin embargo, le erizó la piel. Revivían las imágenes del pasado reciente, el cual pensaba estaba dejando atrás en aquel momento.

Benjamín C. Evans (Ben) era el joven Political Attaché de la Embajada de Estados Unidos y mantenía una buena relación con Oscar Echevarría, encaminada a realizar actividades que impidieran el control del gobierno por parte de los comunistas. En ese tipo de relación es necesario contactos que sirvan de correo y permitan coincidir sin levantar sospechas en la casa de un tercero. Entonces lo mejor es que todos sean amigos.

Elena había regresado a Cuba después de haber estado nueve años estudiando pupila y graduarse de high school en Eden Hall, la escuela de monjas del Sagrado Corazón de Jesús, cercana a Filadelfia. Al regresar al hogar, su madre, estricta en la disciplina, la obligó a matricular secretariado al tiempo que, respondiendo a un llamado del padre Spiralli, atendía como voluntaria a enfermos en el Dispensario San Lorenzo. Su devoción la hizo pensar convertirse en enfermera pero a Julia no le gustó la idea. Al llegar la Revolución, tal vez presintiendo el futuro, sus padres la instaron a adquirir experiencia en el trabajo y se emplea en la embajada de los Estados Unidos en La Habana.

Allí conoce a Ben, el recién llegado agente encubierto de la CIA en funciones de attaché político. Ben pensó que el hecho de trabajar en la sede diplomática y vivir frente a Oscar, con quien ella salía y el cual con los años sería su esposo, la convertía en un enlace de primer orden sin arriesgarla demasiado.

Recordó Elena todos esos detalles, incluyendo las veces que por emergencia, tenía que romper la forma muy recatada o "proper" como diríamos en inglés, en que se conducía con Oscar y tomar la iniciativa de llamarlo para invitarlo al Carmelo de

Elena, posando por sugerencia de su madre, cuando los tanques de Castro pasaron por Kholy en enero de 1959.

Calzada con la excusa de merendar. Su imaginación la hizo verse en peligro si establecían su conexión con Ben y Oscar en ese preciso instante de la partida.

A unos pasos, en la cubierta, su madre hablaba con uno de los tripulantes del Ferry. Elena pasó unos minutos por su camarote y después fue a ver a su madre al suyo. Sólo estuvo fracciones de segundos, demasiadas emociones en su cabeza para estar en aquel zoológico ambulante: Julia tenía allí, además de la perra, los 57 canarios, que afortunadamente estaban cubiertos y no cantaban, con lo que no podía trasmitirles su nerviosismo.

La embarcación zarpó. Apenas recorrido unos cuantos nudos, se escuchó por los altavoces que llamaban a Elena a reportarse al puente de mando. Se le doblaron las piernas, el G-2 detrás de ella, pensó, pero muy cerca estaba Ben. "Vamos y sonríe", le dijo tomándola firmemente por el codo, para infundirle fuerzas. El también estaba preocupado por Elena. Pensó en Oscar, a quien consideraba como un hermano. Y como tenía franquicia diplomática – aún no estaban rotas las relaciones entre Estados Unidos y Cuba – quiso estar al lado de la muchacha. A Ben nada lo hacía perder la sangre fría, aunque tuviera fijo en mente el papel de enlace de Elena y cómo ella había puesto su propio auto Riley a disposición de Oscar para visitar la casa de Ben algunas noches y trasladar de un lugar a otro a perseguidos por la policía secreta.

En el puente los esperaba el capitán del barco, quien simplemente se limitó a decir: "Le informo, señorita, que de los cuatro camarotes le puedo asignar uno extra para que no tengan que estar junto a los canarios. La acompaño para que lo vea".

No hubo más contratiempos en el viaje y Miguel Angel respiró aliviado: finalmente estaban en Miami. Para hospedarse escogieron el hotel University Inn, en la céntrica arteria US1 de Coral Gables. Allí, los demás se aglomeraron frente a la carpeta, mientras Elena llenaba los formularios de registro. El empleado que la atendía levantó la vista y, señalando a la nana de los pequeños hijos de Cristina y a la hija de la misma, aclaró: "La política del hotel es no recibir negros". Y cuenta Elena que su madre, con su característica mirada que fulminaba cuando estaba molesta y hablando un inglés marcadamente correcto, le respondió: "Joven, yo estoy alquilando tres habitaciones durante tres meses, y no me importa si ellas son verdes o negras. Ellas se quedan con nosotros". Y así fue como Julia - siempre Julia con sus salidas inesperadas, humana e ingeniosa – plantó la bandera del antirracismo, en el verano de 1960, en la elegante cadenas de hoteles, convirtiéndose de hecho en una precursora del derribamiento de tan absurdas barreras.

*****

Estando su familia a salvo, Miguel Angel regresa a Cuba. Como buen Capitán de Empresa tenía que defender su barco y sobre todo a su tripulación. Ya había dado los primeros pasos. En julio, antes de dejar a su familia a salvo en el exilio, había convocado a los administradores de todos los centrales a las oficinas de La Habana, para informarles de la situación y, como narra Juan de la Cruz, hacerles entrega personalmente de un cheque de cinco mil dólares, advirtiéndoles: "Consideren ese dinero como un préstamo: si nada sucediese, están obligados a devolverlo en su oportunidad". Otra demostración de su solidaridad y sentido de

Tarjeta postal que Miguel Angel envió a de la Cruz, en 1964. Es un recuerdo de la acción integracionista de Julia.

responsabilidad. No quería dejar desamparados a sus mejores hombres que se quedarían sin trabajo si Castro se apropiaba, como lo hizo, de los ingenios. El propio Juan de la Cruz da cuenta que el Lugareño, el cual administraba, lo intervinieron en agosto.

En el apogeo de la temporada ciclónica, en octubre de 1960, Castro dio el tiro de gracia a la libre empresa y a la pujante industria de la isla: fueron expropiadas casi la totalidad de las empresas nacionales y extranjeras, de éstas la gran mayoría norteamericanas.

Se cerraron todos los caminos. Sólo quedaba una salida. Esa tarde Miguel Angel le entregó un maletín ejecutivo a Rita con el encargo que lo mandara con el chofer a su casa. Por la noche, el timbre del teléfono de su secretaria sonó. Al otro extremo se oyó su voz: "Rita ese maletín era para llevármelo. Mañana temprano salgo para los Estados Unidos".

Rocío fue a su encuentro. Se quedó allí toda la noche, hasta esperar acompañarlo al aeropuerto y que saliera el avión. Esta vez, Miguel Angel viajaba sin fecha de regreso. Todavía el aparato no había remontado vuelo, cuando Julia llamó para saber de su esposo y la cocinera, muy sabiamente le informó: "El señor fue a misa y de ahí seguía". Siempre su esposo desayunaba en casa. Julia entendió el mensaje.

Terrible, desolador, infinitamente triste debe haber sido ese último viaje de Miguel Angel. Dejaba atrás años de esfuerzos y sacrificios de generaciones. Hombro con hombro habían trabajado su padre y su tío, sus hermanos, sus primos, él mismo para forjar un patrimonio que ya no existía. No podía explicarse tan cruel destino. Muchas veces seguramente rezó el rosario, como solía hacerlo, durante la travesía. Era un inmigrante diferente. No iba a los Estados Unidos en busca de fortuna, dejaba la suya atrás, pero hecha añicos y en manos de aquéllos a quienes no les pertenecía. La suerte de sus mayores fue diferente, alcanzaron un sueño atravesando los mares, pero lo hicieron a una edad en que se puede empezar, cuando todavía los huesos no duelen y las energías parece que se renuevan. Para él no habría segundas vueltas. Se cerraba su ciclo.

Las cuentas bendecidas rodando entre sus dedos en la letanía de los Padre Nuestro y las Ave María, le devolvieron un poco de paz y sosiego. Quién sabe, a lo mejor no era definitivo. Quizás todo se resolvería en cuestión de meses. Sí, así será. Dios no permitiría que ese sistema arbitrario, asesino, comunista dure toda la vida. Sacó fuerzas de su corazón y se dijo a sí mismo: "Regresaremos a Cuba".

*****

"De Cuba no sé nada y a veces es peor saber; se mortifica uno sin beneficio. Fidel se ha de caer ¡pero qué queda si han destruido todo! Tengo entendido que ahora rebajan los salarios azucareros un 40 por ciento.
El ha destruido a Cuba con azúcar a 3 centavos o menos, un surplus bárbaro en el mundo y todos los inventarios agotados y los líquidos (cash) robados. ¿Quién levanta la industria azucarera? Yo estoy muy pesimista".

(Del epistolario de Miguel Angel Falla)

Reunida toda la familia, al cabo de los meses decidieron mudarse de Miami a Darién, Connecticut, cerca de su segunda hija, Julia, y sus nietos. Elena se fue a trabajar a New York y visitaba a sus padres los fines de semana. También a Rita, que desde su llegada fue a su encuentro y después se veían con frecuencia.

A Miguel Angel le angustiaba en especial la situación de sus más cercanos colaboradores varados en Cuba. Estaba el tanto de su situación. Se cruzaban correspondencia sistemáticamente. Los testimonios de Juan M. de la Cruz y de Saturio

Rocío reflejan esa inquietud. "No quiero que corras riesgos personales bajo ninguna circunstancia. Esto ya no tiene remedio", aconsejaba al primero, mientras al segundo le daba indicaciones de cómo cuidar de los pocos bienes que aún le quedaban en Cuba. Rocío, por su parte, le rendía cuentas de sus gestiones y agradecía el automóvil Riley que le regaló Elena antes de partir – y que fue el mismo que usó Oscar – el cual le era ahora a Rocío de mucha utilidad.

A los pocos meses, Rocío se valió de una visa de turista y llegó con su esposa y sus hijos. Miguel Angel lo fue a buscar al aeropuerto y lo hospedó en su casa. Luego lo acompañó a poner en orden sus papeles para solicitar el asilo. A Rocío no le fue bien en Miami y se mudó para la Gran Manzana.

Traer a Juan M. de la Cruz y a su familia fue toda una odisea. Fue a ver a Loeb para que intercediera e involucró en las gestiones a su hija Elena, la cual conocía a personajes que podían ayudar. Al amigo también le hizo otros favores para que aprendiera inglés y encontrara un trabajo decoroso.

Pero ellos no fueron la excepción. Por sus cartas sabemos que extendió una mano a quienes se la pidieron y estimó merecedores, como solía hacer en Cuba. Al respecto dice Juan M. de la Cruz: "He conservado con mucho celo varias de sus cartas en la que puede verse como siempre se preocupó por sus amigos, entre los que yo me honro en contarme... Confío que las mismas sirvan para que sus hijas conozcan una faceta de su padre que quizás no tuvieron la oportunidad de apreciar".

Como sabía que llegaban sin un centavo, le pidió al mismo Loeb les concediera una remuneración, argumentando que habían sido ejecutivos de la Atlántica, la cual consiguió y a saber dio a Rocío y a de la Cruz.

Leer ahora las cartas de Miguel Angel permite adentrarse en ese otro mundo interior resultado de su salida al exilio. Unas veces más optimista, otras menos. Por ejemplo, en la del 27 octubre de 1960, escribe "Es que no me he sentido bien y tengo un disgusto y contrariedad que sólo hago lo que no me queda más remedio. Es desidia, es desinterés, es apatía o son tantos golpes. (sic) Los edificios se los ha cogido el gobierno. Todo lo que quedaba, las rentas... Así y todo tenemos que darle gracias a Dios de estar en este país".

Al estilo de todos los exiliados, él también seguía el conteo de los meses que le quedarían a Castro en el poder, con la esperanza de un pronto regreso.

Mientras, se mantenía activo en la lucha contra el castrismo desde esta otra orilla. Como se aprecia en su correspondencia, se involucró en las tareas del Sertoma

Cuban Club, siendo uno de sus directores. La organización, que dice hacía una gran labor, atendía a los refugiados y allí mismo Julia iba a llevar ropas cuando podía. Según su carta del 25 de diciembre de 1965, su esposa iba al lugar y facilitaba ropas, hablaba y alentaba a los recién llegados.

En el propio escrito, aprovecha para definir su posición política: "Todos tenemos que hacer un esfuerzo en alguna organización anticastrista y anticomunista".

Pero nada de aquello amargó su carácter y su eterno sentido del humor. Su sobrina Cristina de Cárdenas se ríe cada vez que se acuerda de su tío el día que fueron juntos a tomar el examen de conducción. Miguel Angel nunca condujo en La Habana, y en el ingenio no era muy diestro con el timón. La propia Elena se burlaba diciéndole: "¿Papi, fue la mata la que se corrió y se puso en el medio del camino?" Lograr obtener la cartera era una de sus metas desde que llegó a Miami. Ese día, terminando cada uno la prueba, se encontraron de nuevo y Cristina de Cárdenas se le adelantó, mostrándole la tarjeta y diciéndole, con una expresión de satisfacción: "Lo pasé". Y con semejante actitud, él la sorprendió respondiéndole: "Yo no. Pero no te preocupes que yo trato otra vez". Agrega Cristina que después siguieron conversando y él tirando a broma todos los errores cometidos. "Ese era tío Miguel", enfatiza.

Por sus cartas también sabemos acerca de sus incursiones en la bolsa de valores. "Yo creo que el mercado seguirá bajo, pero se recuperará", asegura a Juan M. de la Cruz, el 7 de junio de 1967. Pero en el fondo su propósito era mantenerse activo invirtiendo su dinero y al mismo tiempo entretenerse tentando la suerte, porque en otra misiva dice: "En fin, esto es gambling".

Ya por esa fecha, Miguel Angel, cansado de vivir en el Norte, ha regresado a Miami, quizás porque quería estar en un ambiente más cubano o empezaba a preocuparle su salud. El sábado 14 de 1970, sin aclarar el mes, señala: "Yo he mejorado el problema del corazón al suspenderseme un medicamento."

A principios de febrero Elena viajó a Miami de paso para Long Island. Trajo consigo a sus hijas Patty y Maggie. Estuvo unos días con ellos, pero antes de despedirse, Miguel Angel le regaló su reloj de bolsillo, diciéndole "sé que tú querías el de tu madre pero aquí tienes el mío". En esos días su padre había tenido un fuerte dolor de pecho y al partir Maggie le encomendó a su abuela, Julia, "cuida mucho a abuelito, no vaya a morir".

A la siguiente semana, el 8 de febrero de 1973, estaban él, su esposa y Cristina en su apartamento, ubicado en el edificio, propiedad de Miguel Angel, en la calle Valencia número 240, en Coral Gables. Allí también tenían residencia, facilitada por él, otros miembros de su familia extendida.

Mientras Julia y Cristina se preparaban para llevar a la perra Susana al veterinario, Miguel Angel, quizás posiblemente sintiendo un leve escozor en la garganta, se acordó de una venta especial en Woolworth y dijo en voz alta: "Me voy a Miracle Mille a buscar Listerine".

Entró a la tienda. Recorrió el pasillo. Al final estaban las medicinas y el Listerine. Tomó la botella más grande. Pensó en la cara que pondría Julia. Seguramente diría con sorna "compraste Listerine para todo Coral Gables". No tenía apuro. Se acercó a la caja registradora. Y en el momento que ya había pagado el producto, sintió un dolor inmenso en el pecho. Se dobló hacia delante, poniendo su mano derecha sobre el corazón, mientras instintivamente llevaba la otra al bolsillo, donde siempre guardaba el rosario. No pudo. Se desplomó en el piso. A su lado se oyeron gritos pidiendo ayuda. Pero él sólo escuchó su propia voz viniendo como de lejos, en un sostenido eco: "Juan, cuando regresemos a Cuba pienso comprar un ingenio pequeño para que tú lo administres".

*****

Nota al margen

Agradezco a Carlos Alberto Montaner y a Oscar A. Echevarría la oportunidad de escribir este perfil biográfico de Miguel Angel Falla, una figura prominente en la industria azucarera cubana. Es difícil escaparse al embrujo de lo que fuera su vida. Por eso y por factores de tiempo, como se explica anteriormente, no pude acometer un estudio más profundo del entorno que lo rodeó ni indagar, como corresponde en una obra más acabada, en otros factores políticos y sociales de la realidad cubana – incluyendo las luchas sindicales del sector azucarero – durante el espacio de tiempo que le tocó vivir a él, en particular, y a sus ancestros, hacedores en definitiva de las bases del patrimonio de la familia Falla Gutiérrez.

Tampoco ése era el propósito del libro. Esa otra cara de Cuba ha sido bastante divulgada e intencionalmente exagerada por Castro en la isla y por sus personeros en el exterior. Se ha convertido también en manía de la izquierda académica sobredimensionar tales hechos, olvidando que en aquellos tiempos los patrones se sentaban a conversar con los trabajadores y que en última instancia era posible ir a la huelga. Ventajas de la democracia y derechos negados en las autocracias totalitarias.

Ahora se trataba de hacer una historia distinta, centrada en un personaje, para resaltar los logros de esa Cuba del 59, forjada al empuje de una clase empresarial con dotes sobresalientes para competir en el mercado internacional. Cuba, que despuntaba como uno de los países del continente con más perspectivas de un futuro mejor, como bien dijera el economista norteamericano Byron White "que podía compararse con Dinamarca", y que dos años más tarde el Departamento de Comercio de los Estados Unidos señalara que no era un país subdesarrollado en el sentido habitual de la palabra.

Los ingenios de la Sucesión Falla Gutiérrez, por otra parte, no podían ser señalados como centros de trabajo donde se atropellaban a los trabajadores y empleados ni donde existían desigualdades marcadas. El propio John L. Loeb lo subraya: "Los Falla fueron progresistas y ellos apoyaron nuestros deseos de proveer mejores condiciones de vida para los trabajadores[4]". Quizás, si no es por el armagedón del 59, muchas de esas medidas se hubieran puesto en práctica, como otras en el ámbito nacional facilitadas por el ritmo de crecimiento económico sostenido en la nación y el influjo positivo llegado del Norte.

Ena Curnow
Septiembre 2002

[4] Loeb, John I. All in a Life Time. John L. Loeb, New York, N.Y., 1990, p.168

Capítulo II

Recuerdos de Miguel Angel Falla

Recuerdos de Miguel Angel Falla

De tener que ofrecer un título a estas líneas introductoria las llamaría “en sus propias palabras” pues de llamarla introducción hubiese corrido el riesgo de revelar parte del contenido del capítulo. Tal ocurrencia hubiese privado al lector de recibir, como primicia, en el estilo muy personal de cada testigo, los sentimientos que con tal vivencia exponen nuestros cinco interlocutores.

Consecuente con lo anterior, el propósito en esta presentación es sólo destacar lo que ha significado para mí, y que espero lo signifique para el lector, la simple existencia de estos testimonios, la forma en que surgieron y el mensaje que ofrecen sobre el personaje.

De la lectura de los testimonios pude deducir tres elementos importantes.

Lo primero es la espontaneidad y entusiasmo con que reaccionaron tanto Rita Moreno de Blain, mi fuente inicial, y después, sucesivamente Saturio Rocío, quien logró rápidamente la colaboración de Juan de la Cruz, a la que se sumaron de motu propio Angel Naveiras y José Medardo Pino.

El lector también coincidirá conmigo en apreciar la claridad y firmeza de estos recuerdos tras más de cuarenta años. Igualmente importante la evidencia de que para estos testigos la única motivación es la sincera devoción a Miguel Angel, pues obviamente ellos no necesitan, ni pueden esperar, beneficios materiales por el hecho de su adhesión a este homenaje.

Por último quiero resaltar la coincidencia de los cinco testigos sobre la personalidad humana y gerencial de Miguel Angel. Tal coincidencia ha permitido que la biógrafa Ena Curnow pueda entrelazar una amena semblanza de Miguel Angel. Este material fundamental pudo ser complementado con otras fuentes. Todas ellas prueba de la lealtad y devoción que inspiraba este recio colono y administrador de ingenio, respetando la denominación de hacendados para quienes ejercían el control accionario de un central azucarero.

Sin mas preámbulos, los recuerdos en sus propias palabras.

Unos recuerdos sobre Miguel Angel Falla

Rita Moreno de Blain

Cuando nuestro amigo, Oscar Echevarría, nos dijo de su proyecto de iniciar una colección sobre hombres de empresa cubanos pre-Castro, y que iba a incluir una semblanza de Miguel Angel Falla tejida con recuerdos de familiares y amigos, nos pareció una idea estupenda. El propósito de Oscar es regalarle el libro a su esposa, Elena Falla, la hija menor de Miguel Angel, con motivo de su cumpleaños.

Oscar me pidió mi colaboración ya que desde el año 1954 hasta el año 1960 yo trabajé en la Cuban Atlantic Sugar Company, primero en el departamento de ingeniería y a partir de 1957 con Miguel Angel en la presidencia. En el verano del 60 Miguel Angel y su familia se fueron de Cuba y yo y mi familia nos fuimos unos meses después.

Cómo llegué al Sr. Falla

Fue en el año 1954 cuando en la Atlántica, después de una exhaustiva búsqueda para llenar la plaza de Presidente de esa compañía, decidieron que Miguel Angel Falla reunía los requisitos necesarios para ocupar tan importante cargo.

En ese entonces ya yo llevaba 6 años en la Atlántica, y me propusieron que me hiciera cargo de ayudarle a familiarizarse con los distintos departamentos y con el personal. En principio iba a ser para mí sólo un período provisional mientras durara la transición a la Presidencia, que se estimaba serían tres o cuatro meses. Por circunstancias posteriores, esos tres meses [que era mi asignación para ayudarlo] se convirtieron en más de cinco años en los que trabajamos juntos, lo que me dio la oportunidad de conocerlo a fondo.

Yo, en principio acepté gustosamente porque me daba la oportunidad de trabajar para un hombre con la trayectoria, prestigio y experiencia de Miguel Angel Falla, del que seguramente podría aprender muchísimo. Y así fue.

Nuestro primer encuentro fue aún más significativo de lo que ambos esperábamos ya que, casi desde un principio, se creó entre los dos una colaboración laboral basada en el respeto que duró hasta el final de nuestra asociación de trabajo, y continuó después en los Estados Unidos en el plano personal.

Ya exiliados en New York seguimos en contacto y la amistad se extendió a su familia, en especial a su hija, Elena Falla - a la que considero hoy como una hermana menor y de la cual, estoy segura, Miguel Angel se sentiría muy orgulloso, como lo estamos todos los que la queremos.

Los nobles sentimientos del Sr. Falla

Recuerdo que Miguel Angel Falla contribuyó en gran escala a realizar cambios importantes, tanto en la parte administrativa como en la interacción del personal de la Atlántica. En ocasión de celebrar una cena con el personal de la Atlántica, yo ayudé a Miguel Angel a disponer las mesas y le sugerí que en la mesa de él pusiéramos al Tesorero, a los Jefes de Departamentos, etc. Pero él me dijo "No, Rita, sería mejor que distribuyéramos las mesas en una forma más democrática y así todos nos sentiríamos en un plano de igualdad. Y por favor, pon a Gener a mi lado". Gener era un empleado del Departamento de Correo. En esa ocasión y en muchas otras me demostraba lo humano que podía ser. Las fotos de ese evento aparecen a continuación.

En el comedor del Hotel Habana Hilton: 30 de junio de 1958. De izquierda a derecha: Sr. Miguel Gener, Sr. Miguel A. Falla Alvarez, Srta. Hortensia del Pino, Sr. Bienvenido Rodríguez, Dr. Pedro Pablo de la Cámara y Sr. Leonardo Fandiño.

De izquierda a derecha, Ingeniero Michelena, Sr. Campanería, Sra. Rita Moreno de Blain, Sr. Naya, Sr. Miguel Badia, Sra. Noemí Valero, Sr. Fernández, Sra. Kiki de la Vega y Sr. Charmont, sin identificar.

El concepto en que era tenido

Recuerdo otro incidente que demuestra en pocas palabras la estima en que lo tenían muchas otras personas, incluyendo a mi padre, el Dr. Eduardo Moreno[1]. Cuando mi padre tuvo que someterse a una intervención quirúrgica, Miguel Angel lo fue a ver el mismo día de la operación y a ofrecerse para lo que fuera necesario. Llegó cuando mi padre empezaba a volver de la anestesia. Cuando entró en el cuarto, mi padre, que todavía estaba bajo los efectos de la anestesia, lo saludó diciéndole "¿Cómo está doctor?" - evidentemente confundiéndolo con uno de los doctores. Miguel Angel le contestó "yo no soy doctor". A lo que mi padre le dijo: "Pues mejor, ya que cualquiera se hace Doctor, pero Señor se nace". Creo que eso lo dice todo.

---

[1] El Dr. Eduardo Moreno era Presidente de Dunn and Bradstreet en Cuba y Decano de la Escuela de Ciencias Comerciales de la Universidad Católica de Villanueva, primera Universidad Privada de Cuba fundada por el Padre Spiralli de los Agustinos.

A modo de conclusión

Definitivamente estoy de acuerdo con Oscar, entre otras cosas, en que Miguel Angel fue uno de los importantes pilares de la economía cubana. Igualmente fue un hombre que a pesar de sus profundos conocimientos de la Industria Azucarera, primero en ingenios de la familia Falla y luego como presidente de la Atlántica del Golfo, siempre mantuvo su sencillez, su caballerosidad y su señorío. Para mí fue un honor haberlo conocido.

Mi tributo a Miguel Angel

Juan M. de la Cruz

Soy una de las personas que se consideran privilegiadas de haber conocido a Miguel Angel Falla por más de treinta años. A continuación narro alguna de mis anécdotas que reflejan su fuerte pero bondadosa personalidad.

No es mi intención realzar con este escrito mi historial personal pero es inevitable traerla a colación debido a que son experiencias que compartí con él. Confío que las mismas sirvan para que sus hijas conozcan una faceta de su padre que quizás no tuvieron la oportunidad de apreciar.

He conservado con mucho celo varias de sus cartas en las que puede verse como siempre se preocupó por sus amigos, entre los que yo me honro en contarme.

El Central Adelaida, mi Universidad

Tuve el gusto de trabajar con él, primero en el Central "Adelaida" y posteriormente, en el Central "Lugareño". Mucho aprendí de él observándolo y oyendo sus consejos. En una oportunidad me preguntaron que de dónde era yo graduado y contesté: "Yo soy graduado de UCA." El semblante de quien me había hecho la pregunta expresaba claramente que no sabía lo que significaban dichas siglas y aclarando mi broma le respondí: "La Universidad del Central Adelaida."

Tanto en uno como en el otro de los ingenios referidos aprendí la importancia del campo en la industria azucarera observando como el Sr. Falla estaba haciendo mejoras no sólo en la producción de azúcares, sino en los campos, experimentando con distintas variedades de caña, abonos adecuados, etc.

El sentido del humor de Miguel Angel

Para describir al Sr. Falla en pocas palabras yo diría que era una persona de carácter fuerte y con una mente bien definida, pero también bondadosa, que disfrutaba de hacer favores y se preocupaba por el bienestar de todos los que con él trabajaban. En muchas ocasiones le vi preguntarles a humildes trabajadores del ingenio por algún familiar enfermo e innumerables veces hacer favores a familias del Central.

Recuerdo dos o tres anécdotas jocosas que ocurrieron en el Central "Adelaida" las que exponen su naturaleza afable:

¿Agua mineral con gas o aceite carbón?

Había un muchacho nuevo sustituyendo al mensajero de oficina y Miguel Angel le pidió que fuera a buscarle una botella de agua mineral con gas. Ni presto ni perezoso, el jovencito corrió al departamento comercial y regresó con una botella de gas o luz brillante, del que se usaba como combustible para las lámparas con las que se alumbra en los campos. Tan pronto como Miguel Angel tomó el cartucho, advirtió el olor peculiar y le reprochó al muchacho: ¿Qué te encargué yo, agua mineral con gas o aceite carbón?

¿Mucha lluvia o un sapo de seis pulgadas?

Ese mismo joven, como suplente que era, había olvidado tomar la lectura del pluviómetro. Al notar Miguel Angel que no le habían dado ese reporte, le pidió que fuera a medir la lluvia caída ese día. Al rato regresó con el dato: la precipitación había sido de unas ocho pulgadas. Advirtiendo el Sr. Falla que era imposible tanta lluvia, le pidió regresara a tomarla, cerciorándose de que el pluviómetro estuviera limpio. Imagínense la risa que provocó el novel oficinista cuando declaró apenado que había encontrado un sapo dentro del aparato.

El revolvito de Félix

Otra historieta: el señor que se ocupaba de cuidar los montes del área de Chicola (el puerto por donde se embarcaban los azúcares del Central "Adelaida") era un hombre muy cumplidor y como recompensa por su trabajo y lealtad Miguel Angel quiso facilitarle la forma de que se hiciera con una pequeña colonia de caña. Muy contento llegó un día a la oficina con un pequeño revólver a la cintura y al verlo Miguel Angel, en tono de burla le dijo: "Félix, siendo tú tan chiquito, si le dispararas a un hombre con ese revolvito, es posible que te mate a patadas. Si es que quieres usar un revólver cómprate uno de verdad, que si alguien te fuera a atacar, le puedas dar un tiro."

Errorcito no, metedura de pata

Recién empezaba yo a trabajar en la oficina del Central, donde había sido transferido de la oficina del departamento comercial, me llamó el Sr. Falla a su despacho para que revisara sus cálculos del costo por metro cúbico del dragado de un canal. Tenía todos los datos necesarios: ancho, profundidad media y longitud así como las horas de labor, combustible consumido, etc. Tomé toda la información compilada y me fui a mi despacho. Tan pronto comencé a chequear los primeros cálculos, advertí que había un error que afectaba los cálculos posteriores. Repetidas veces inspeccioné mis números para asegurarme que estaban correctos y no me cupo duda. Al día siguiente, tan pronto él llegó a la oficina me preguntó si eran exactos sus cálculos. Como joven inexperto y por ser esa la primera vez que trataba directamente con él, no sabía cómo comunicarle su error. Luego de ensayar varias maneras de exponerle la verdad le informé finalmente: "Creo que ha habido un pequeño error...", señalándole lo que había descubierto. Revisó cuidadosamente mis números y tras compararlos con los suyos, exclamó: "Eso no es un pequeño error... es una metedura de pata muy grande." Y me dio las gracias.

Un gerente que confiaba en su equipo y lo protegía

El cálculo de las cuotas de molienda

Cuando se creó la Ley para la Regulación de las Zafras, por cuenta propia hice un estimado de lo que sería la cuota para cada ingenio, si bien es cierto que algunos factores no se podían calcular con base a las estadísticas publicadas. Sabedor el Sr. Falla del trabajo hecho por mí, llamó por teléfono al administrador del Central "Narcisa", donde molían sus cañas las colonias "La Loma" y "Blanquizal" y le inquirió por las cuotas correspondientes a las mencionadas fincas de su propiedad. No encontró correctas las cifras que le fueron dadas y protestó de la pretendida cuota que le iban a asignar. En no muy buena forma le comunicó a su colega que iba a mandarle a una persona conocedora de ese procedimiento para que le enseñara como calcular las cuotas. Terminada la caldeada comunicación telefónica me pidió que me trasladara al Central "Narcisa" con mis cómputos y les señalara la equivocación. Nuevamente el Sr. Falla me demostraba su confianza.

Mi cambio para la Atlántica

Ya nombrado presidente de la Cuban Atlantic Sugar Company, estuvo de visita en el Central "Adelaida" y me preguntó si estaría yo dispuesto a irme a trabajar con él, de presentarse alguna vacante. Sin el menor reparo le contesté que para mí sería un gusto poder trabajar nuevamente a sus órdenes. Me comunicó que de momento existía una vacante de jefe de oficina del Central "Rosario", pero que no me proponía esa plaza porque era muy posible que el mismo fuera vendido y que entonces yo no estaría bajo su protección. Poco tiempo después, a través de su auxiliar, fui citado a La Habana para ofrecerme la posición de jefe de oficina del Central "Lugareño". Dos años más tarde me nombró administrador del ingenio.

La cirugía de mi madre

Me encontraba en La Habana, discutiendo un nuevo contrato con el sindicato en el Ministerio del Trabajo, cuando fue necesario someter a mi madre a una operación urgente. No comuniqué a nadie mi aflicción y proseguí las discusiones obrero-patronales. El abogado que me asesoraba solicitó, a instancias del Sr. Falla y para sorpresa mía, a punto de iniciarse la sesión del día, que se suspendieran los debates hasta tanto yo regresara de Morón, a donde tenía que ir debido a la quebrantada salud de mi madre. Tanto la delegación obrera del Central "Lugareño", como los oficiales provinciales y los representativos de la C.T.C. accedieron a la solicitud. Así era Miguel Angel, no le preocupó la reacción de esos organismos obreros, ni lo que costaría el dilatar el diálogo laboral. Sólo quiso que yo, como hijo, estuviera al lado de mi madre enferma. Su gesto no es fácil de olvidar.

$5,000 de anticipo para nuestra tranquilidad

Cuando se vislumbraba que las compañías azucareras americanas iban a ser intervenidas por el gobierno de Fidel Castro el Sr. Falla convocó a los administradores de todos los centrales a las oficinas de La Habana y personalmente nos hizo entrega de un cheque por $5,000 advirtiéndonos: "Consideren ese dinero como un préstamo; si nada sucediese, están obligados a devolverlo en su oportunidad." Obviamente trataba de aliviar nuestra precaria situación económica al quedarnos sin trabajo.

Expropiación y exilio, Miguel Angel siempre al tanto

"No corras riegos, esto ya no tiene remedio"

Debido a la difícil situación imperante yo fui detenido y llevado a Nuevitas. Afortunadamente pude capear el temporal sin mayores complicaciones. Al enterarse él de mi arresto, me envió un mensaje para que lo llamase tan pronto regresara al ingenio. "No quiero que corras riesgos personales bajo ninguna circunstancia", – me dijo. "Esto ya no tiene remedio..."

En New York hay más oportunidades, vente conmigo

El ingenio fue intervenido en el mes de agosto de 1960 y enseguida me dispuse a venir a los Estados Unidos. Tenía todos mis documentos en orden. El, que ya residía en Miami, me dejó un recado para que lo llamase tan pronto arribara a estas tierras. Así lo hice. Uno de sus consejos fue que no me quedara en Miami, sino que siguiera rumbo a Nueva York donde había más posibilidades de abrirme paso. Como coincidía que él viajaba por esos días a Nueva York, hicimos el viaje juntos y hasta me invitó a hospedarme en su hotel, lo cual acepté gustoso.

Señores directores, hay que ayudar a nuestros ejecutivos en el exilio

En la junta de ejecutivos convocada, el Sr. Falla solicitó del Sr. John Loeb una remuneración para los directivos de la Atlántica del Golfo que habíamos venido a los Estados Unidos. Días después me entregó un cheque que me sirvió de mucho porque sólo había logrado sacar de Cuba $150.

Con ilusión del regreso

En viajes posteriores a Nueva York el Sr. Falla bien me llamaba por teléfono o nos reuníamos, siempre deseoso de saber cómo me iba desarrollando en el trabajo. Muchos consejos me dio. La última vez que almorzamos juntos me manifestó: "Cuando regrese a Cuba pienso comprar un ingenio pequeño para que tú lo administres". Nunca aceptó la idea de que no regresaríamos.

Mis reminiscencias de Miguel Angel

Saturio Rocío Chávez

Responder con propiedad a la solicitud de contribuir a un libro en que se tejan unas semblanzas de Miguel Angel Falla constituye para mí un reto grato y a la vez difícil. Grato porque como veremos más adelante él fue parte de mi vida profesional y personal desde mi primer trabajo en el Central "Adelaida", hasta mi traslado a New York. Difícil tarea porque no sólo se entrelaza con sentimientos personales muy profundos sino que no es fácil, en pocas líneas, cubrir una persona que fue tan importante en la industria azucarera cubana, en aquellos tiempos líder mundial del producto. Intentaré, pues, presentar mis recuerdos cubriendo los diferentes matices de su personalidad, como ser humano y como gerente, mediante las anécdotas personales de que fui testigo o partícipe.

Por la puerta ancha del "Adelaida"

Mi primer encuentro con Miguel Angel Falla tuvo lugar pocos días antes de la Nochebuena de 1941. Anteriormente le había visto en algunas ocasiones cuando iba a misa de 10:00 a.m., en la iglesia parroquial de Morón, acompañado de su señora y tres hijas. Sin embargo, nunca intercambié palabras con él, ni tan siquiera miradas.

Buscaba yo empleo cuando me informaron que en la oficina del Central "Adelaida"[1] había una plaza disponible. Camino a la entrevista, coincidí en el tren con el obispo de Camagüey, quien iba a dar misiones por los campos de dicho ingenio. Había sido yo seminarista por cinco años y aunque abandoné el estudio de la carrera sacerdotal, mis relaciones eran cordiales con Monseñor Pérez Serantes.

En mi entrevista con el jefe del departamento agrícola, éste pudo apreciar mi inexperiencia como oficinista; no obstante dejó a la discreción del Sr. Falla que me empleara o no. Esa tarde, al regresar de su recorrido por las colonias, Miguel Angel me dio el empleo, sin más preámbulos. Obviamente el Sr. Obispo, que había compartido con él un motor de líneas para visitar las colonias, me había recomendado bien después de hablar conmigo.

[1] El Adelaida, construido nuevo por Laureano Falla Gutiérrez, tío de Miguel Angel, por su capacidad de molienda de más 4,200 TM era, en ese momento, el buque insignia de la Sucesión Falla Gutiérrez.

Estudiaba yo entonces bachillerato y mis intenciones eran trabajar durante esa zafra y continuar mis estudios universitarios. Comencé como auxiliar en el departamento de campos donde aprendí bastante en cuanto a las labores de oficina, si bien no lo suficiente. Al llegar el llamado tiempo muerto, mi empleo estaba destinado a desaparecer, sin embargo, para sorpresa mía, cuando el ingenio terminó la molienda él me tomó como secretario suyo.

¿Rocío, dónde está la carta?

Pese a que aún no estaba yo maduro, con él rompí mis primeras lanzas. Como una muestra de mi bisoñez contaré la siguiente anécdota: trataba él de localizar la copia de cierta carta importante y dirigiéndose a mí me preguntó si yo la había visto. Le contesté que no.

– ¿Estás seguro de que no la archivaste?
– Bueno, le puedo decir que las cartas de ayer están todas archivadas aunque no las leí.

Una sonrisa suya despejó la tensión del momento.
– Déjame ver las cartas que archivaste.

Efectivamente en el cartapacio estaba el documento en cuestión. Con paternal cariño, me amonestó:
– Tú tienes que leer toda la correspondencia, tanto la recibida como la que sale; guardando desde luego la confidencia.

Sin ser yo taquígrafo, tomaba sus dictados a la velocidad que pudiera hacerlo cualquier diplomado, utilizando un sistema de símbolos y medias palabras inventado por mí que, ayudado por mi memoria, me permitía transcribir "ad literam" sus cartas. Eso sí, tenía que pasarlas a limpio al instante. Las más de las veces sólo me indicaba la idea de lo que quería expresar. Llegó a desarrollarse tal vínculo de confianza que firmaba mis cartas sin el menor recelo. Poco a poco fuimos compenetrándonos y me fue encomendando algunos asuntos particulares, incluyendo algunas de sus cuentas bancarias personales y la contabilidad de su finca "Alarcón", a donde con frecuencia yo lo acompañaba.

No se le puede jugar cabeza a este administrador

Tras el diario contacto con él, pude apreciar su hombría de bien, su capacidad de trabajo y su completo conocimiento de todo el proceso de la industria azucarera. No era administrador de sentarse ocho horas en su despacho. Iba a los campos de caña y departía con los mayorales y colonos. Visitaba los distintos departamentos del ingenio conversando con los obreros y escuchando recomendaciones y comentarios para mejorar su funcionamiento. A veces sorprendía al turno de media noche apareciéndose de improviso a la hora que el chino, cocinero de la vivienda, vendía los pastelitos de carne horneados luego de cumplir su faena doméstica.

En el cielo Dios, en la tierra...

Era él un hombre de apuesta e imponente presencia, siempre pulcramente vestido. Caminaba con la cabeza erguida y en su cara afable brillaban unos ojos almendrados y pequeños. Con su tono de voz fuerte imponía respeto. Otro de los rasgos característicos de su semblante era su nariz ligeramente respingona. Intuitivamente solía adivinar las intenciones de su interlocutor, de ahí que a veces hiciera contacto visual directo con él, o que dirigiera vagamente la mirada por los alrededores. Consciente de su capacidad, no dudaba lograr alcanzar la meta propuesta.

Conociéndolo yo bien, puedo atestiguar que la aparente arrogancia que algunos pudieran imputarle no era más que una malla protectora de que se revestía para ocultar los verdaderos sentimientos humanos que henchían su corazón; bastaba escarbar ligeramente para que afloraran. Sabiamente deslindaba la austeridad displicente del hombre de negocios y la sensibilidad de su conciencia íntima.

Abundan casos donde se destaca la fibra tierna de su persona. Muchos bendecían la mano generosa de Miguel Angel, como respetuosamente le llamábamos en el ingenio, por su nombre de pila. Si, como reza el refrán "para muestra es suficiente un botón", yo pudiera ofrecer un nutrido ramillete de flores con ejemplos que ponen de relieve su calidad humana:

– Conmovido por el triste cuadro en que quedaba la familia de un trabajador suicida, permitió que la viuda continuara viviendo en la casa y al hijo mayor le mejoró el empleo para que pudiera echar adelante a los numerosos hermanos pequeños que quedaban desamparados.

– Tomó muy a pecho el caso del empleado cuyo hijo recién nacido fue lastimado por la impericia o descuido del médico comadrón. El rápido traslado a La Habana logró la supervivencia del neonato.

– Y cuando la hija del encargado de su finca "Alarcón" fue fulminada por una afección que la dejó sin vista, movió cuantos resortes fueron necesarios para que la pequeña fuera ingresada y debidamente atendida en instituciones consagradas a la educación y bienestar de los ciegos.

– Desde su casa se ocupó de enviarle infusiones y comidas apropiadas a uno de los empleados de oficina que estaba enfermo y que no tenía familia por esos alrededores.

– Las federaciones católicas obtuvieron siempre que lo necesitaron toda clase de ayuda, tanto pecuniaria como en cuanto a servicios.

– Le facilitó los fondos a un obrero que pretendía emigrar para los Estados Unidos con su familia, y cuyo visado le denegaban por carecer de la garantía requerida.

– Al empleado que confrontó un caso infeccioso en su familia le consiguió que admitieran al enfermo en el Hospital "Las Animas" de La Habana, y a él le concedió un extenso permiso de ausencia para que resolviera la triste situación del allegado.

– Cuando se estaba discutiendo el contrato laboral de uno de los ingenios, personalmente solicitó que los gremios obreros y la C.T.C. [Confederación de Trabajadores de Cuba] suspendieran el "toma y daca" para que el administrador pudiera acudir al lado de su madre enferma.

Un hecho poco conocido es que durante su mandato administrativo [en el Central "Punta Alegre"] se suspendió la tácita ordenanza de los entierros raciales. Hasta entonces en aquel ingenio las inhumaciones se efectuaban en lotes del cementerio asignados conforme al color de la piel del difunto.

Todo lo anterior evidencia que era un hombre bondadoso, amigo de extenderle su mano dadivosa al menesteroso que tocaba a su puerta, máxime en casos de cáncer o de enfermedades contagiosas. Siempre presto a mitigar penas.

¿Viejo, yo?

Conversando un día con un jefe de departamento, éste hirió su susceptibilidad cuando le dijo: "Yo soy más viejo que Ud. y sin embargo, no arrastro los pies". "¿Arrastro yo los pies, Rocío?", me preguntó posteriormente.

No van lejos los de "alante"...

Seguro de sí mismo no tenía complejos de que los titulados universitarios pudieran hacerle sombra. Al contrario, se rodeó de cuantos profesionales brillantes pudo necesitar, apoyando inclusive a recién graduados cuyos diplomas tenían aún fresca la tinta. Igualmente mantenía un ojo avizor sobre aquellos empleados que proseguían estudios superiores, tratando de superarse intelectualmente. Para éstos no escatimaba cuántas facilidades necesitaran a fin de que progresaran en su proyectada carrera. Los conceptuaba como un potencial en reserva.

Mi tesis de doctorado en Ciencias Comerciales se la dediqué a quien tanto me había favorecido. Cuando le llevé a él una copia, su hija Elena comentó: "Papi, ahora podrás decir que tu nombre aparece en los archivos de la Universidad".

Tampoco pasaba por alto las aptitudes de aquellos funcionarios en quienes descubría madera de ejecutivos. Más de uno fue por él ungido, tomándolo bajo su ala y aleccionándolo de manera que desarrollara sus aptitudes latentes. Como buen tutor los iba adiestrando en el aprendizaje de las maromas de la industria hasta que lograran culminar su completa educación. Eso sí, cuando nombraba a una persona para una posición, exigía que diera el máximo de sí misma, no a medias tintas.

Aprieten pero no ahoguen

Obviamente uno de los puntos claves en la administración de un ingenio son las relaciones con el sindicato. El administrador, como representante de la empresa, tiene que ser justo y tener al mismo tiempo mano izquierda para conceder o rechazar las demandas laborales. Las relaciones de Miguel Angel con los directivos sindicales fueron cordiales, sin que esto quiera decir que les otorgara todo cuanto reclamaban. Después de escuchar con atención las exigencias del gremio, las concedía o refutaba, según el caso, tomándose el tiempo necesario para esclarecer puntos y pelear honestamente por los intereses de la compañía, sin avasallar a los trabajadores. Y si en alguna cuestión se trababan de cuernos (como suele decirse de los ciervos), inflexible defendía su posición procurando llegar a un acuerdo amistoso.

Amenazas conmigo ¡no!

No vamos a afirmar que sus decisiones fueron siempre bien vistas. Se dio el caso de un trabajador que, resentido por haber sido despedido, fraguó una venganza. Se enlistó en la guardia rural y al cabo del tiempo apareció en la oficina del central "para arreglar cuentas". A título de su uniforme se coló en el despacho del administrador y allí descargó sus rencores, amenazando con usar su revólver de reglamento. Serenamente, diría yo que con sangre fría, Miguel Angel llamó a su auxiliar con el pretexto de que revisara ciertos cálculos que anotó en un papel. Al cabo del rato el sargento de la guardia se personó en la oficina y se llevó detenido a su subalterno. La supuesta cuenta no era sino un aviso para que, sin llamar la atención, el militar viniera a desarmar al posible asesino. Mi escritorio estaba situado afuera de su oficina.

Admito que no era él muy afecto a los periodistas debido a que algunos de ellos trataron de chantajearlo. En cierta ocasión un reportero publicó una versión errónea sobre un acto religioso, involucrando a la administración del ingenio. Tituló el artículo en cuestión: "La verdad desnuda". Posteriormente le propuso a él desdecir lo publicado a cambio de dinero. "¿Vas ahora a vestir a la verdad?", fue la ocurrente reacción suya. Otro reportero se desaforó por radio delatando la tala de montes y fui yo delegado para llamar a sus cabales al vociferante.

Ofrecidas estas pinceladas sobre la personalidad de Miguel Angel y mi relación inicial con él, corresponde, para mayor claridad, tomar la secuencia cronológica de su actividad como uno de los gerentes más destacados de la industria azucarera cubana.

Aprender trabajando

[Al regresar Miguel Angel de estudios de comercio en Estados Unidos, siendo el mayor de los hermanos optó por colaborar con su padre, Don Miguel, quien era el administrador del Central "Patria"[2]. Su padre, quien también era propietario de 20% del Central, no lo trató como hijo del administrador, sino que, con gran sabiduría práctica, lo inició en las tareas más básicas y humildes del Central." Esto puso a Miguel Angel en una secuencia de posiciones que le permitió aprender y madurar en todos los aspectos de campo, fábrica y administración, que constituyen el complejo proceso de la producción de azúcar. Al dejar su padre la administración del Patria, la junta directiva de la Sucesión Falla-Gutiérrez consideró que Miguel Angel estaba preparado para ser designado administrador del Central Patria, donde demostró su capacidad y disciplina.]

Miguel Angel, el innovador

[En reconocimiento a su labor y capacidad, llegada la oportunidad, la junta directiva de la Sucesión] lo trasladó al Central "Adelaida", de superior categoría. Consciente de la importancia de la materia prima en la producción del azúcar, para asegurar su mejor éxito en la empresa que iba a dirigir, llevó consigo a algunos de sus hombres de confianza, quienes estaban plenamente identificados con su política agronómica. Lleno de entusiasmo y ambicionando un acopio suficiente de

[2] El Central Patria, con capacidad de molienda de 2.500 TM por día, fue el primero adquirido por Laureano Falla Gutiérrez, operación a la que invitó a participar a su hermano, Don Miguel, con el 20 por ciento.

cañas, mecaniza los campos y ordena la tumba de montes para fomentar grandes colonias cañeras con distintas variedades de POJ, idóneas para obtener mejores rendimientos. Convoca a los colonos y les pide su colaboración en su propósito de acrecentar la molienda.

Acto seguido enfocó su atención en la parte industrial con el fin de lograr un aumento en la producción de azúcares, para lo cual fue necesario modificar todo el sistema: basculadores, cuchillas niveladoras, molinos, centrífugas, clarificadores, hornos, calderas, planta eléctrica, equipos de coser sacos, etc. La fábrica quedó en condiciones tan ideales que en la zafra de 1952 llegó a producir 421,783 sacos de azúcar de 325 libras[3], fruto de una molienda de más de 43 millones de arrobas de caña.

Producción del saco 400,000 del Central "Adelaida" en 1949. En la foto, empleados y obreros, algunos con sus esposas.

[3] Equivalente a 62.200 TM de azúcar.

La victoria de los alcoholes

Durante la II Guerra Mundial, muchos ingenios azucareros comenzaron a producir, a partir de las melazas de caña, alcohol para carburante[4], conforme a una disposición gubernamental. La jerarquía de la Sucesión Falla-Gutiérrez se aprestó también a experimentar con esta nueva industria y le confiaron el proyecto a él. Miguel Angel no puso reparos en aceptar el reto, si bien desconocía los detalles de esta industria. Era él un administrador de cuerpo entero y estaba consciente de que lograría el objetivo cuando se rodeara del personal idóneo.

Siguiendo las pautas de la oficina matriz, dedicó todo su empeño a levantar una flamante destilería de varios pisos, una de las mayores de Cuba, con capacidad para 80,000 litros diarios de alcohol. Algunos consideraron un desacierto que la Nauyú Distilling Co., como se llamó el proyecto, [por coincidir con el nombre indígena del lugar] estuviera atareada fundiendo paredes de concreto, mientras otras empresas se lanzaban al experimento etílico en toscos "cachimbos", aprovechándose de la amplia demanda del producto durante el conflicto bélico.

Había yo terminado mis estudios de Filosofía y Letras y cursaba el tercer año de Ciencias Comerciales, y él, con el fin de que practicara mis conocimientos, me confió la contabilidad de la destilería. Mi capacidad como contador había sido ya probada al fungir como jefe de nóminas y como cajero durante las vacaciones de los titulares de ambos departamentos.

La inexperiencia en la producción de alcoholes hizo que se destapara una descontrolada plaga de moscas en todo el batey[5] del ingenio y sus comarcas, la cual proliferaba en los mostos desechados. Cuando los trenes cruzaban por el poblado de Falla, los pasajeros se apresuraban a cerrar las ventanillas porque los enjambres invadían los vagones de ferrocarril y aun así los molestos insectos se propagaron por otros pueblos. Con tiento y sapiencia, Miguel Angel logró capear esta crisis que tuvo repercusión nacional a través de la prensa capitalina.

---

[4] Como forma de ahorrar gasolina, que en su mayor volumen requería ser importada, el gobierno determinó que los motores de gasolina podían funcionar adecuadamante aun si se añadía hasta 20% de alcohol a la gasolina. Esta práctica todavía está vigente en Brasil.

[5] Nombre que los indios siboneyes daban a los poblados y que los cubanos adoptaron para las viviendas cercanas al Central que se daban en usufructo al personal de fábrica y oficina.

"Edificio de la Nauyú Distilling Co." A la izquierda el hospital del Central "Adelaida".

Además de azúcar... ¡arroz!

Al dinámico presidente de la empresa, Alín Suero[6], siempre a la caza de nuevos negocios, se le ocurrió otra innovación, ajena a la producción de azúcares crudos. Era algo experimental y hasta especulativo, mas no titubeó en encomendárselo a él. Sabía que su primo (que nunca lo defraudó) echaría adelante el proyecto. Así fue, le dio el pecho al fomento de la producción de arroz, explotación agrícola cuyo cultivo difiere mucho del de la caña. Como para estas siembras se requiere mucha agua, hubo que abrir varios pozos profundos y preparar los terrenos en forma de terrazas bien niveladas de manera que las plantas pudieran crecer con el regadío. Y una vez más la capacidad administrativa de Miguel Angel se acrecentó y las arroceras prosperaron dando importantes ganancias.

El peso de la nostalgia

Por ese entonces estuvo él considerando retirarse a vivir a La Habana. Ciertamente que por aquel tiempo no se hablaba del "estrés", pero era indiscutible que las tensiones cotidianas de la administración de la empresa y la separación de la familia estaban haciendo mella en su vigoroso organismo. Pese a que transpiraba vitalidad, consideró que era hora de hacer mutis del escenario laboral. Le estaban molestando ciertos ligeros achaques de "bursitis" y de gota lo cual tomó como aviso que

[6] Alejandro Suero Falla

era el momento de jubilarse. Además, sus hijas [mayores, Cristina y Julia] habían terminado su educación colegial y eran casaderas, y en La Habana estaban sus hermanos y otros familiares. El había rendido ya una fructífera labor.

Cerrando un ciclo en el "Punta Alegre"

Poco duró su descanso en la capital. Siendo él un hombre de acción, no podía estar ocioso. El emprendedor Alín, a quien tenía entrañable afecto, logró sacarlo del retraimiento que él mismo se impusiera. Como los Falla-Gutiérrez estaban comprando el Central "Punta Alegre", lo comprometió para que tomara sobre sus hombros la reestructuración de ese ingenio. Por su parte, él me invitó a irme con él. Sin duda era un salario atractivo, un lugar más deleitable y hasta me prometía una linda casa frente al mar; pero decliné su ofrecimiento. Los motivos que le expuse eran el no alejarme de mi familia que vivía en Morón, y más que nada, porque estaba a punto de terminar mi carrera de contador público y tenía en la mira conseguir una cátedra, bien en el Instituto de Segunda Enseñanza o en la Escuela de Comercio. Además, que la carretera del Circuito Norte, que pasaba por Falla, estaba casi terminada, lo cual me permitiría movilidad. Es decir, que todo pesaba contra la invitación que me ofrecía en bandeja de plata. Dispuesto a llevarme con él, recurrió a los buenos oficios del administrador auxiliar para que me conquistara. Este me pintó un lindo cuadro, combinando mis anhelos con las ventajas económicas que suponía el puesto, el cual me daría la oportunidad de acercarme a los ejecutivos de La Habana y quizás lograr un traslado a las oficinas de la capital. Acepté el reto.

Los hombres del equipo del administrador

Junto conmigo se llevó también al jefe de campos quien se responsabilizaría con la reestructuración de la parte agrícola de la nueva empresa. La tarea de Miguel Angel era transformar al Central "Punta Alegre" al "modus operandi" de los ingenios del bloque de los Falla-Gutiérrez. La plantilla del ingenio se había aceptado tal cual era, mas enseguida se percató que había mucha tela por donde cortar y comenzó el saneamiento. Por este motivo su llegada fue vista por algunos con suspicacia. Su conducta vertical y sus sólidos valores fueron considerados como signos de rudeza y altivez cuando él, como todo un avezado jugador, se dispuso a mover algunas de las fichas del tablero tras observar detenidamente la labor y el desempeño de cada cargo.

Cuando enfocó su atención en la parte agrícola, descubrió que no todo andaba en la debida forma. Ciertos campos de caña habían sido sembrados con aviesa intención, plantando solamente los perímetros. Se hizo acompañar del desleal inspector

La Junta de Directivos del “Punta Alegre Social Club” durante el tributo de despedida a Miguel Angel Falla, en el centro, de blanco con un "Dril 100", el traje de negocios de lino habitual de los cubanos bien vestidos.

en un viaje de reconocimiento y cuando intentó adentrarse en los plantíos, éste, al ver que había sido sorprendido en flagrante delito, renunció “ipso facto”.

Encontró ciertas otras cosas no muy claras y sin embargo recompensó con magnanimidad [aun a] aquellos que no habían sido íntegros en el desempeño de sus puestos. Esto dio motivo a que se especulara que iba a desatarse una purga y que lo miraran con ojos temerosos. Nada más falso; quien estuvo exento de culpa no tenía por qué recelar. Al contrario, a quienes demostraron competencia y lealtad, aun estando relegados, les brindó la oportunidad de ascender en sus cargos.

Cuando le mostré a Miguel Angel mi título de Contador Público, me instó a solicitar de Julio Prado, vice-presidente y contralor general de la empresa, mi traslado para las oficinas centrales. Mi carta no mereció la aceptación [de Prado] "porque eso sentaría un precedente para que otros empleados de ingenios pretendieran también ubicarse en Oficios 110"[7]. Frustrado ante este rechazo, decidí quemar las naves e irme para La Habana a correr fortuna, pero Miguel Angel me refrenó: “No te precipites, que quizás yo te pueda llevar conmigo de lograrse algo que hay entre manos”.

[7]Dirección de las oficinas de la Sucesión en La Habana.

Saturio Rocío dando las gracias por el homenaje en nombre de Miguel Angel Falla.

Luego de la ardua labor de encarrilar a "Punta Alegre" conforme a los parámetros del bloque de los Falla-Gutiérrez, su vida en el Central era más apacible y placentera. Si bien la vivienda estaba junto al mar y a su disposición estaba el yate "Ailicec" para recrearse e ir hasta los cayos de Media Luna o Guillermo, resolvió retirarse de una vez y para siempre. Era el momento de hacerlo, cuando había rebasado los 50 años y estaba aún lleno de vida y de energía. En La Habana podría disfrutar a plenitud de la vida hogareña; las dos hijas mayores, ya casadas, lo habían hecho abuelo. Era hora de disfrutar de los pequeños placeres que hasta ese entonces se había privado. Bien que lo merecía.

Como era costumbre en empresas de cierto rango y más para un hombre tan querido por la comunidad, se le organizó un homenaje de despedida en el "Punta Alegre Social Club", la institución de confraternidad social característica de todas las empresas de importancia y los pueblos del campo cubano.

En el homenaje de despedida que los empleados y obreros del Central "Punta Alegre" le ofrecieron, me tocó a mí dar las gracias en su nombre.

Tan pronto coroné mis estudios decidí casarme y lo invité para que me sirviera de padrino en la Misa de Velaciones, lo cual aceptó graciosamente. Aunque vivía él en La Habana, esporádicamente visitaba los tres ingenios de Camagüey a título de supervisor.

Miguel Angel Falla, el padrino en la boda de Saturio Rocío y Gloria Molina en la Iglesia Parroquial de Morón Nuestra Señora de la Candelaria.

A la cima de la montaña: la Atlántica

Fue en el Hotel Nacional de La Habana donde Mr. John L. Loeb, el magnate financiero de Wall Street, lo citó para una entrevista y le ofreció por recomendación de su primo Alín Suero[8] la reorganización de la Cuban Atlantic Sugar Company. La Atlántica del Golfo controlaba en la provincia de Matanzas los ingenios "Alava", "Conchita" y "Mercedes", más tres colosos en Camagüey: "Lugareño", "Morón" y "Stewart". Dicha empresa controlaba, [además] los tres ingenios de la Hershey Corporation, "Hershey", "Rosario" y "San Antonio", incluyendo otros negocios colaterales. Se trataba de una labor ingente, mas no para un hombre tan dinámico y conocedor de los "intríngulis" de la producción de azúcar. Aceptó el reto seguro de sí mismo y confiado en su capacidad. Fue una galantería para su ego.

[8] John Loeb, que era el presidente de una prestigiosa casa de Bolsa de New York y un enamorado de Cuba, percibió una gran oportunidad para invertir en su industria azucarera. Conociendo a Alín Suero socialmente desde un viaje en que coincidieron, se dirigió a él para preguntarle por un administrador para su nueva empresa y Alín, sin titubear, le señaló: " Mi primo Miguel Angel es el mejor administrador de ingenios que yo conozco".

¡Sígueme!

No olvidó su promesa y me mandó a buscar. Me nombró auxiliar suyo adjunto a la plantilla de la Hershey Corporation y a la par me encargaba la supervisión del edificio de apartamentos de su propiedad, ubicado en N y 21, en El Vedado, así como el control de sus cuentas bancarias, amén de continuar yo con los asuntos de su finca "Alarcón" donde se cultivaban arroz y caña y se criaba ganado, si bien en modesta escala. Quiero destacar que mi tesis de contador público, "Establecimiento de un sistema de contabilidad en una plantación de arroz", fue basada en mi experiencia en dicha finca.

El edificio de apartamentos de alquiler que Miguel Angel Falla construyó en N y 21, en El Vedado, la mejor zona residencial de La Habana con anterioridad al final de la Segunda Guerra Mundial. El edificio estaba situado frente al Hotel Capri, el cual junto con el Riviera, eran los dos mejores hoteles de La Habana en la década de los cincuenta. Haciendo esquina, el famoso Willie's Bar.

LUIS F. CASTRO / Herald Staff

Cuba blames 'enemies' for bombs at 2 hotels

Photos by JOSE GOITIA / Canadian Press

El edificio de N y 21 al fondo de una reciente noticia cubana de primera plana.

Mi renuncia al puesto de "Punta Alegre" no fue del agrado de Alín Suero, quien recriminó a Miguel Angel por llevarse consigo personal del ingenio. Entonces salió a relucir mi solicitud a Julio Prado y su negativa a recompensarme por haberme superado. "No todos los empleados de ingenio tratan de sobresalir y como Prado desestimó las aspiraciones de Rocío y éste estaba decidido a irse, yo lo acogí". Así apaciguó al reclamante.

Meses después volvió a enojarse Alín Suero cuando un competente auxiliar de oficina de "Adelaida" aceptó el nombramiento de jefe de oficina del Central "Lugareño", plaza que yo le ofrecí por indicaciones de él. Censuró su reincidencia en llevarle personal idóneo de los ingenios de los Falla-Gutiérrez y le prohibió que continuara engatusando a más individuos. Mas con la excusa de que la oferta había sido mía, no de él, logró acallar la querella de su primo.

Caballero empresario

Por el corto tiempo que estuvo en vigor la presidencia del saliente ejecutivo [que había encontrado John Loeb en la Cuban Atlantic Sugar Co.], Miguel Angel, vicepresidente plenipotenciario, respetó su rango y se condujo con gran discreción para no hacerle sombra, si bien iba tomando el control de las compañías. Una vez en plena posesión de la presidencia, tomó como suya a la secretaria que había trabajado para el presidente saliente, a la cual no quiso despedir, aunque pronto advirtió que no era de su estilo. Tampoco quiso degradar a un secretario, reliquia de una administración anterior, quien distaba mucho de llenar los zapatos del cargo (su inglés fue clasificado de "pidgin" por un ejecutivo neoyorquino). Así fue que decidió tomar del departamento de ingeniería una secretaria competente y activa.

Puesto que la reestructuración iba a ser total, se requería un buen contador, esto es, un organizador de sistema que no sólo contara con conocimientos, sino que se arremangara y mano a mano se pusiera a reformar la parte financiera de la empresa. Desde Nueva York enviaron a un auditor de una gran firma con un buen contrato quien no resultó ser el hombre que Miguel Angel necesitaba y, muy a pesar suyo, le rescindió el compromiso.

Debe hacerse notar que los cambios en la Atlántica del Golfo fueron menos radicales que los del Central "Punta Alegre" en cuanto a la estructura económica. Este fue un ingenio regido por una administración americana, que gozaba de privilegios y plantilla de un nivel muy superior a los de la gerencia cubana, el cual querían amoldar a los patrones de los Falla. Empero, en el caso de la Atlántica era cuestión de reconstruir y modernizar los ingenios, organizando su administración con vista a suprimir gastos superfluos y desechar mediocridades.

Desenredando la madeja de la Hershey

La empresa Hershey era compleja: tres centrales azucareros y una mezcolanza de industrias paralelas adjuntas al Central "Hershey": producción de azúcares crudos, refinería, producción de aceite de maní, producción de jarcias de henequén, ferrocarriles eléctricos, producción de electricidad, club de golf y jardines. A instancias de Miguel Angel, visité cada uno de estos ingenios, así como los de Camagüey, en misiones administrativas.

En venta el "elefante blanco"

Tuvo el Sr. Falla la intuición de que algunos de los negocios del Central "Hershey" no eran productivos y, para deslindar los costos, envió un grupo de contadores e ingenieros (entre ellos a mí) para tratar de desenmarañar aquella contabilidad, tan compleja que no pudimos desenredarla con certeza. Entonces recomendó a la Junta Directiva de Nueva York que se deshiciera de aquel "elefante blanco", concentrándose solamente en la producción de azúcares crudos. Julio Lobo firmó una opción de compra.

Contaba él que como presidente tuvo que encabezar la junta de accionistas reunidos en Nueva York para ultimar los pormenores de la compra-venta antes de expirar la fecha de opción, a la medianoche del 31 de diciembre. Faltando apenas unos quince minutos para la hora cero, uno de los abogados se levantó de la mesa y paró el reloj que presidía el salón: quedaban todavía algunas menudencias por aclarar y no habría tiempo suficiente para agotarlas. Continuaron las discusiones hasta que ambas partes estuvieron acordes en todos los detalles. Entonces volvió a ponerse de pie el mismo abogado y puso en marcha el reloj. El acta levantada era más o menos del siguiente tenor: "Faltando 15 minutos para la media noche..." (Aunque en realidad era cerca de las 4:00 a.m. del primero de enero). Cuando sonaron las doce campanadas retrasadas, todos alzaron sus copas de champaña para brindar por el cierre de la negociación y para celebrar la llegada del nuevo año.

No hay agravio

Por razones de política administrativa, en el grupo Hershey habían aflorado ciertas asperezas entre el vicepresidente ejecutivo [de esa empresa] y el Sr. Falla. Sin embargo, al concluirse la referida compraventa, él mismo, consciente del talento y la capacidad de trabajo del competente abogado, solicitó que fuera incorporado a la nómina de la Atlántica del Golfo, juntamente conmigo. Decisión que resultó muy acertada puesto que entre ambos fue desarrollándose una mutua simpatía, llegando a ser un excelente colaborador y un cordial amigo. Los nuevos propietarios acataron el "status quo", con la excepción de los dos traspasos apuntados.

Al que estudia el jefe lo ayuda

Pretendía Miguel Angel hacer del Central "Alava" una "tacita de oro" que sirviera de ejemplo y estímulo a las otras administraciones, no sólo en su parte agrícola sino también en la industrial. Para lograr sus empeños comenzó por comprar a nombre mío la colonia "Pintó" puesto que en aquella zona no se cultivaban cañas por administración. Estaba convencido que para lograr su empeño no podía depender del suministro de caña de los colonos. La colonia "Pintó" llegó a ser la de mayor rendimiento y producción.

No puedo ufanarme de ser solamente yo quien mereció el amparo suyo; todos aquellos empleados que aspiraran a superarse recibían su espaldarazo. Sabiamente acostumbraba tantear los distintos puestos, fijándose si el nominado para un cargo tenía la capacidad para cubrirlo. Era su norma buscar al hombre para la plaza y no viceversa. Siendo una misma empresa, transfirió a posiciones más relevantes en otros ingenios a profesionales que trabajaban de subalternos. Desde luego, contando que aceptaran la promoción.

Regularmente, una o dos veces a la semana, después del trabajo de oficina, solía yo acompañarle hasta el "Willie's", un bar-restaurante localizado en la esquina de su edificio. Allí confraternizaba con amigos y cambiaba impresiones con ellos. De cuando en cuando, fiscalizaba sus predios. Luego me llevaba hasta mi casa o me dejaba cerca, en la calle Línea.

Los bandidos de la Sierra Maestra

La época de actividades revolucionarias fue de zozobras y muchos planes tuvieron que diferirse. Primeramente el desasosiego y la incertidumbre frenaron los ímpetus de los ejecutivos de empresas. Se especulaba sobre el matiz político de los rebeldes y la embajada americana confundió aún más la interrogante cuando irresponsablemente aseveró que "Raúl y el Che son comunistas, pero no Fidel". Sin embargo, la visita de un amigo le confirmó los desmanes que se cometían en la región de Oriente donde estaba el ingenio administrado por él y donde campeaban los insurrectos. Miguel Angel quedó anonadado con aquellos relatos de primera mano: las exigencias de dinero, los impuestos revolucionarios, los latrocinios, las extorsiones, los fusilamientos, no eran el viso romántico y democrático que se pregonaba.

Al triunfar la revolución, su fe en que las turbulentas aguas se nivelarían por cauces normales fue menguándose. La cacareada reforma agraria requería se llenasen ciertos informes que había que presentar en el INRA.[9] Él, como presidente de la Atlántica del Golfo, se personó en las oficinas gubernamentales acompañado del abogado asesor y de mí. Tras una espera de cinco horas, un miliciano de bajo rango recogió los documentos que llevábamos y que con tanto esmero y precisión habíamos preparado, y los tiró al piso, en un rincón. Pensaba él que sería recibido por algún jefe responsable y que tendría la oportunidad de discutir determinados puntos de la legislación revolucionaria. Con gran decepción comprendió que aquello no tenía remedio; que no importaba la competencia, la laboriosidad, ni la honradez de una persona o de un negocio, que todo no era más que una farsa. Se perseguía el latifundismo y ahora el latifundio era estatal. Evidentemente no había seriedad en los planes del nuevo gobierno. Ese mismo día, Monseñor Enrique Pérez Serantes hizo antesala por casi ocho horas para entrevistarse con Castro, sin que le dieran audiencia.

De los ingenios azucareros le llegaban informes que le llenaban de inquietudes. Algunos de los administradores acataban con simpatías todas las medidas del gabinete rebelde. Era aquello desmoralizante. Decidió entonces ir a su finca "Alarcón", en la provincia de Camagüey y me pidió que le acompañara. Hicimos el viaje en su automóvil privado, manejado por su chofer. Pudo palpar el sentimiento popular y el respaldo al castrismo. De tramo en tramo, nos detenían con el fin de recaudar fondos para alguna causa revolucionaria. No sé cuántas veces tuvimos que parar. Ya se iba molestando cuando tomé la iniciativa y, cada vez que nos paraban, les aseveraba, con una sonrisa a flor de labios, que ya habíamos contribuido en la cua-

[9] Instituto Nacional de Reforma Agraria

dra anterior. Al llegar a su hacienda, el encargado le informó que el INRA le había comprado un lote de ganado, pero que en lugar de efectivo o cheque, le habían extendido una nota de adeudo toscamente manuscrita). Tristemente me comentó: "No sabes cuanto me alegro de que mi madre no viviera esta situación desconcertante y tan deprimente..."

Aquí no hay nada que hacer ya

Aunque palpaba el desastre que se precipitaba sobre Cuba, en su fuero interno abrigaba una sutil esperanza de que aquella anormal situación rebasaría. Mas los proyectos que bullían latentes en su mente aguardando tiempos mejores fueron sofocados arteramente cuando nacionalizaron los ingenios norteamericanos. Fue una noche de julio (si mal no recuerdo) que una llamada telefónica me alertó de la malhadada resolución recién vociferada en la televisión por el mismo Castro. Me comuniqué con mi jefe y me fui a su casa. Allá encontré un sombrío cuadro: caras largas y ánimos agostados que reflejaban malos augurios. Estuve con él y su familia hasta temprano en la mañana que lo acompañé hasta el aeropuerto para tomar el primer avión con rumbo a Miami.

Corto tiempo más tarde, la señora y la familia toda se le unieron. Su hija Elena me obsequió su automóvil "Riley", que me fue muy útil para llevar a cabo muchas de las encomiendas de su padre. Mis hijos bautizaron el pequeño carro como "el negrito figurín" por la imagen de nácar plástica que colgaba del espejo retrovisor: un morenito de frac y chistera blancos.

Albacea de sus propiedades

Como apoderado suyo me encargué de hacerle remesas de su dinero a Miami, las más de las veces con personas totalmente extrañas. Riesgosa faena. También me ocupaba de velar por la mamá de su señora; de pagar los salarios a los criados y observar que todo estuviera en condiciones en su casa. Hasta estuve considerando mudarme para su residencia con vista a que no la intervinieran, pero a la postre desistí del proyecto pensando que posiblemente fuera contraproducente.

Vienen a quitar lo que no es suyo

Debido a la denuncia de un vecino joyero, registraron su casa. La criada de confianza me llamó a instancia de los agentes del G-2[10] porque querían que yo les abriera la caja de fuerte, bien disimulada en un gabinete de un dormitorio. Al fin

[10] Nombre por la que era conocida la policía política.

apelaron a los servicios de un cerrajero, porque no me permitieron que regresara a mi casa a buscar la combinación. Lo único que encontraron dentro de la caja fue un "bibelot" de porcelana que al agitarlo, sonaba. Sin dudas, pensaban que eran diamantes, pero se llevaron un chasco al romperlo: eran pedacitos de la misma cerámica que habían quedado desprendidos dentro de la figura.

Esa noche me llevaron al G-2 y de allí fueron a mi apartamento porque querían ver los libros de la finca "Alarcón" donde estaba registrada la "venta" de ganado al INRA por más de $30,000. Por suerte no hubo registro en casa donde yo guardaba una respetable suma de dinero que tenía preparada para una transferencia de fondos. Ni se molestaron en ver los libros. Con Miami me comunicaba frecuentemente, todo en clave. Él me llamaba por teléfono sin usar su nombre. Yo por lo regular le escribía, dirigiendo las cartas a personas ficticias, a la dirección correcta.

Al encuentro de Miguel Angel

Cuando por fin no pude aguantar más permanecer en Cuba – el poco dinero que quedaba lo repartí entre aquellos que recibían mesadas – me embarqué para Miami. Sin un centavo para avisarle por teléfono de mi inesperada llegada, alguien tuvo la amabilidad de hacer la llamada por mí. Me recogió en el aeropuerto y por tres días me alojó con mi esposa e hijos en su casa. Posteriormente me pagó la estancia por dos semanas en un motel, insistiendo en que no me preocupara, que todo se iría resolviendo.

Como yo había venido con visa de turista, él me acompañó a solicitar primeramente asilo y después a refugiarme. Traté inútilmente de encontrar trabajo en Miami y por un tiempo trabajé de voluntario en el Refugio, con la esperanza de que se presentara una plaza y me la ofrecieran en mérito a mi desinteresada ayuda. Al fin decidí irme para Nueva York a correr fortuna. Me despidió en el aeropuerto y volvió a insistirme que no me preocupara por mi familia, la que yo dejaba detrás. Al menos una vez a la semana, paternalmente él visitaba a mi esposa e hijos pendiente de si algo necesitaban. Siempre les llevaba golosinas a los niños.

En el frío del Norte

Pensó que lograría colocarme en las oficinas de Wall Street, pero no lo consiguió debido a que Mr. Loeb se había hecho el firme propósito de no emplear a ninguno que hubiera trabajado en la Atlántica del Golfo. Inflexible rehusó hacer excepciones.

Pese a la distancia, siempre nos mantuvimos en contacto. El primer invierno me despachó algunos suéteres y consiguió que Mr. Loeb me hiciera un regalo de $500 "por una sola vez". Cada vez que viajaba a Nueva York iba a verme, pendiente siempre de mi bienestar. "Por las camisas que usa tu jefe puedo garantizarte que es un hombre de clase". Y me invitaba a comer. Por un tiempo vivió en Darién, donde una vez lo visité. Les dio dinero a mis muchachos para que fueran a un parque de diversiones.

En el calor de Miami

Buscando el calor del trópico, se mudó para Coral Gables y continuó nuestra correspondencia frecuente. Sus cartas trataban asuntos personales, de Cuba, de personas amigas y de negocios. He encontrado entre mis papeles solamente tres: una agradeciéndome unos "party fours" que le mandé por Navidades: "Yo aunque no debo comer azúcar, probé 5, magníficos. Y Julia no sé cuántos. Espero que no me afecte la diabetes". En otra comentaba: "Mucho me alegró hicieras el viaje a Europa con tu familia. Yo cuando tuve edad, salud y dinero no tuve tiempo". La otra, una nota de agradecimiento: "Gracias a Uds. por las misas y a Rocío por lo amable y cariñoso que fue con Perla". Una de sus últimas comunicaciones fue una tarjeta postal que me enviara desde Puerto Rico en un crucero de placer, acompañado de su hermano Carlos.

El dolor de no decirle adiós

Una cosa que me duele de veras es no haber asistido a su funeral para que mi presencia testimoniara mi inmensa gratitud. Nadie me avisó de su muerte súbita. Casi una semana más tarde, un amigo me llamó para informármelo. Lo había leído en un número atrasado del "Diario de las Américas".

Miguel Angel fue mi jefe, mi mecenas, mi protector, mi ángel, mi tutor, mi amigo. Nuestra relación fue casi de padre a hijo. Yo fui su empleado, su secretario privado, su apoderado, su confidente, su testaferro... Por mi parte, le fui fiel, le respeté, le defendí y le quise, y mi corazón rebosa de agradecimiento por todo cuanto hizo en mi favor. Diariamente bendigo su alma generosa. Su recuerdo perdurará en mi mente mientras viva.

Mis memorias de Miguel Angel Falla, como tributo a su persona

Dr. Angel P. Naveiras

En el mes de junio de 1944 me gradué de bachiller en Ciencias y Letras. Fue un jalón esencial en mi vida. Había decidido hacerme de una profesión y ésta sería la de abogado. Mis recursos eran limitados y no me permitían dedicarme por entero a los estudios universitarios.

A la edad que separa la adolescencia de la adultez, todo nos parece posible o hacemos que lo parezca. Estábamos entonces lejos de concebir que andando el tiempo en poco más de una década, en el convulsionado horizonte de nuestra Cuba, aparecería una nubecilla de insignificante trascendencia (así se consideró por muchos), que era en realidad la gestación de un proceso político-conspirativo que, cual tromba funesta, arrasaría valores morales y materiales convirtiéndola en un trágico testimonio de muerte, desolación y miseria.

Mi primer encuentro con Miguel Angel Falla

Pero regresemos a la fecha feliz de junio de 1944. Sólo unos meses después, en septiembre, recibí una notificación para una cita de empleo con el Sr. Miguel Angel Falla, administrador del Central "Adelaida", gracias a las gestiones de verdaderos amigos, preocupados por mi futuro.

Nítido es el recuerdo de mi llegada al batey del Central "Adelaida"; al cruzar el torniquete vi a la izquierda una capilla católica y a la derecha, enfrente, un busto del Sr. Laureano Falla, fundador de la empresa. Ante mí se extendía una amplia avenida sombreada por la verde bóveda que formaban las entrecruzadas ramas de los laureles sembrados a cada lado, los que a su vez realzaban las casas de madera de los empleados, que resplandecían su limpieza pintadas de blanco y verde. Al final de la carretera (así aprenderíamos a llamarla), estaban situadas las oficinas principales del ingenio, lugar de nuestra cita.

No tardaría en estar sentado frente a un señor alto, grueso, de piel morena, ojos inquisidores y achinados. Vestía camisa de cuello y manga larga; pantalones de montar caqui y zapatos y polainas[11] carmelitas.

La acogida del Sr. Falla fue cortés; más que interrogarme prefirió oírme hablar sobre mi persona. Fui sincero, mi historial era incipiente, necesitaba trabajar pero no tenía experiencia alguna; mis calificaciones se limitaban a un título de bachiller con aspiraciones a un doctorado en Leyes. Mientras hablaba su mirada fija, observadora, parecía aquilatar cada una de mis palabras. Cuando terminé se levantó y me despidió cortésmente.

Sin saberlo se iniciaba un nuevo ciclo de mi vida, lejos del seno familiar; frente a un futuro que no temía pero que desconocía. Era un ambiente distinto y un desafío a la realidad de una nueva vida que acepté con fe en Dios.

Sin saberlo, acababa de conocer a una persona que tendría una influencia beneficiosa en el desarrollo exitoso de mi nuevo ciclo y que sería un factor determinante con respecto a mis experiencias como empleado y al apoyo sostenido para la realización de mis estudios de abogacía.

Comencé a trabajar como auxiliar de oficina del Sr. Agustín Gutiérrez, jefe de maquinarias del ingenio; posteriormente fui asignado al departamento de nóminas en las oficinas principales.

Un estilo gerencial directo y humano

Una noche, después de comer, me dirigí a las oficinas. Al verme entrar, Miguel Angel (aceptaba que sus empleados le llamaran por su nombre de pila), me presentó a las personas que le acompañaban (supe después que era habitual que Miguel Angel sostuviera este cambio de impresiones con sus empleados de confianza); al terminar la presentación dijo esta frase que recuerdo claramente: "Si sales a tu abuelo valdrás mucho". Aclaro que mi abuelo había sido hasta su muerte, unos años atrás, vicecónsul de España en la ciudad de Morón.

[11] La forma que se designaba en Cuba una cubierta de cuero que montando sobre el zapato facilitaba ir a caballo sin necesidad de botas inglesas

Miguel Angel gozaba de una impresionante personalidad, su presencia inspiraba autoridad y respeto, unida a la apreciación psicológica que solía hacer de su interlocutor. Franco y directo, "no andaba con remilgos" para expresar su pensamiento. Si duro en la crítica negativa, no escatimaba el elogio sincero y el reconocimiento estimulante.

De la condición humana de Miguel Angel da fe su comportamiento en ocasión del grave padecimiento que abatió a mi único hermano. Su gestión con el Sr. Raúl Román, administrador del Central Patria, hizo posible que un hermano de éste, médico eminente, tuviera a su cargo la necesaria y especializada asistencia. Durante mi estancia en La Habana, donde fue trasladado mi hermano, hicc uso de la licencia dispuesta y autorizada por Miguel Angel, para ausentarme de mi trabajo.

Un gerente siempre presente

Trabajador incansable, le obsesionaba la eficiencia y responsabilidad y la exigía de sus empleados. En un turno de madrugada pasaba lista al personal del ingenio cuando vi a distancia a Miguel Angel conversando con el jefe de hornos. Terminada mi labor, regresé a mi habitación. A las ocho en punto, Miguel Angel entraba en su despacho. Apenas transcurridos unos minutos me llamó para preguntarme si todos los trabajadores de las centrífugas estaban en sus puestos. Le respondí, al tiempo que le extendía el cuaderno de la lista, que faltaba uno. Con una sonrisa aprobatoria expresó: "Lo sabía, pero quería confirmarlo contigo".

Siempre ofreciendo oportunidades

Crecían los rumores acerca de planes que contemplaban cambios en la administración del Central "Patria". ¡Cuán lejos estaba de imaginar que yo figuraba en ellos!

Una mañana Miguel Angel me llama a su despacho. Tras saludar y señalar que tomara asiento, mirándome fijamente me dice: "Sé que en tus propósitos está el de hacerte abogado y eso está bien. Pero hay planes para un cambio en la administración del Central "Patria" y quiero que seas el jefe del departamento de nóminas. Me haces falta allí".

"Usted, Miguel Angel, respalda mis estudios y, por tanto, la gratitud me obliga a aceptar su designación; pero aunque así no fuera la aceptaría, porque es un gesto suyo de confianza que me enaltece".

Los planes no se llevaron a efecto, pero dejaron impresos en mí una huella de gratitud y personal satisfacción.

Razones personales y otras circunstancias ajenas a mi voluntad, como el cierre de la Universidad de La Habana, retardaron mi graduación que siempre consideré un objetivo invariable. Al reabrir la Universidad de La Habana en 1959, me dispuse sin tardanza a recuperar el tiempo perdido.

Su visión, el consejo oportuno

En 1960, en ocasión de recoger mi título en la Facultad de Derecho y no sin antes pasar por el Colegio de Abogados de La Habana para formalizar mi inscripción, fui a las oficinas de Miguel Angel con el propósito de mostrárselo; lo observó con profunda atención, lo enrolló y devolviéndomelo con una mano estrechó con la otra mi diestra diciendo: "¡Te felicito!"

Al responderle afirmativamente a su pregunta sobre mi inscripción en el Colegio de Abogados de La Habana añadió que cursaría instrucciones a su bufete para que me dieran participación en las actividades legales y comenzara mis contribuciones al retiro.

Tras una pausa, su penetrante mirada aparece de pronto velada por una fugaz y sombría alteración; con voz profética, ligeramente acentuada de amargura, dice: "Navieras, el futuro, al parecer, es negro... esperemos". Estuve de acuerdo con él.

Su presentimiento se cumplió. En el aproximado período de un año estaríamos en el exilio. El desastre llegó y, con él, la terrible tragedia que a todos nos afectó. En lo personal truncó el camino que se me ofrecía promisorio, que parecía abrirse para mi bien a partir de la meta cumplida de mi graduación.

Lo que aprendí de él

Mi gratitud imperecedera a quien me extendió una mano de sostenido apoyo. En su taller, allá en la pequeña joya que fuera el Central "Adelaida", aprendimos fundamentos de la vida que son indispensables para triunfar en ella con dignidad: la honradez, el respeto, la disciplina, el orden, la organización y la firme actitud en defensa de la justicia. Todos ellos nos sirvieron de pauta en el campo de la enseñanza, profesión que ejercimos en los Estados Unidos de América.

Mis impresiones y recuerdos de Miguel Angel Falla

José Medardo Pino

El Patria, mi primer vistazo a Miguel Angel

Yo trabajaba en el Central "Patria", hermano menor de "Adelaida", al cual Miguel Angel visitó alguna que otra vez. Lo juzgué, cuando lo vi, con mucha aprehensión y respeto, por no decir miedo.

Mi traslado al "Adelaida"

Cuando transcurrido algún tiempo me informaron que yo iba a ser trasladado para "Adelaida", mi primer impulso fue rechazar la propuesta, mas me tragué la lengua cuando me notificaron que me mejorarían el sueldo. Como contador graduado de la Escuela de Comercio de Santa Clara, la Administración estimaba que mis servicios serían útiles en la implantación de un sistema de contabilidad más moderno que había en proyecto.

Me cambiaron el jefe

El jefe de oficina del Central "Adelaida" era un hombre de carácter afable, muy amigable, siempre tarareando bajito alguna canción. Próximo a retirarse, no quería enredarse en la tarea de un nuevo método. Como sustituto nombraron al jefe del departamento agrícola, demasiado austero y de poca mano izquierda.

Más de una vez mi nuevo jefe me reconvino por pequeños errores o por mi forma de trabajar. Estaba claro que no hacíamos "migas". En cierta ocasión cometí un error en las guías forestales (yo llenaba la primera parte y Saturio [Rocío] completaba la información), y me llamó aparte y comenzó a reprenderme en no muy buenos modos. Todo lo que de "guajiro cerrao" llevaba por dentro se agolpó en mi cabeza y le di una respuesta impropia a la vez que le presenté mi renuncia.

El incidente anterior no ocurrió en el vacío. Miguel Angel, sentado en su despacho, había escuchado todo el sermón. Llegué a mi cuarto (que, estaba al lado de la oficina) y comencé a empacar. Cuando alcé la cabeza, vi a Miguel Angel en la puerta. Con una sonrisa en los labios me puso la mano en el hombro y me aconsejó que no tomara tan a pecho las cosas, que siguiera trabajando, que si no quería continuar bajo las órdenes del jefe de oficina, que él tenía otro puesto para mí. Y para que pasara el mal rato, me dio libre el resto del día. Este amable gesto suyo me reveló su hombría de bien y cambió bruscamente la imagen que de él me había formado. Siendo yo el más nuevo de los empleados (y no el mejor) no podía imaginar que me respaldara en mi querella con el jefe de oficina.

Una de sus virtudes, cuidar de su gente sin distinción de rango

En otra ocasión en que pase tres o cuatro días enfermo recluido en mi cuarto, diariamente me mandaba desde su casa jugos de naranjas y alimentos propios para convalecientes. Esto nunca lo olvidaré.

Si me preguntan ahora, en el año 2002, que cual fue mi impresión del Sr. Miguel Angel Falla, de corazón puedo decir que fue un ángel de verdad y no de nombre solamente.

Como director de empresas estimo que fue grande entre los grandes. Esa es mi percepción.